Foucault's Nietzschean
Genealogy

D1521894

SUNY Series in
Contemporary Continental Philosophy

Dennis J. Schmidt, Editor

Foucault's Nietzschean Genealogy

Truth, Power, and the Subject

Michael Mahon
Boston University

STATE UNIVERSITY OF NEW YORK PRESS

Published by
State University of New York Press, Albany

© 1992   State University of New York

All rights reserved

Printed in the United States of America

No part of this book may be used or reproduced
in any manner whatsoever without written permission
except in the case of brief quotations embodied in
critical articles and reviews.

For information, address State University of New York
Press, State University Plaza, Albany, NY 12246

Production by Ruth Fisher
Marketing by Theresa A. Swierzowski

Library of Congress Cataloging-in-Publication Data

Mahon, Michael, 1951–
    Foucault's Nietzschean genealogy : truth, power, and the subject /
Michael Mahon.
        p.   cm. — (SUNY series in contemporary continental
philosophy)
    Includes bibliographical references and index.
    ISBN 0–7914–1149–4 (alk. paper) . — ISBN 0–7914–1150–8 (pbk. :
alk. paper)
    1. Foucault, Michel. 2. Nietzsche, Friedrich Wilhelm, 1844–1900-
-Influence. I. Title. II. Series.
    B2430.F724M334—1992   91–35092
                                                                                        CIP

10 9 8 7 6 5 4 3 2

For Mary

Contents

Preface   ix

1:    Foucault, Nietzsche, Genealogy: An Introduction   1
      A. An Overview   3
      B. The Nietzschean Face of Foucault Scholarship   9

2:    Foucault's History of Madness:
      An Invitation to a Nietzschean Genealogy of Morals   19
      A. The Moral Problematization of Madness   21
      B. The Emergence of the Three Genealogical Axes   26
          1. The Birth of the Asylum   29
             a. The Power Axis: The Space of Confinement   29
             b. The Subject Axis:
                One Becomes Mad Because One Wants to Be   36
             c. The Truth Axis:
                The Critical Experience of Madness   40
          2. The Birth of the Clinic   44
             a. The Power Axis: The Spatialization of Disease   45
             b. The Truth Axis: The Verbalization of Disease   49
             c. The Subject Axis: Death and the Individual   52

3:    Language, Time, and the Death of Man   57
      A. Language and Knowledge   58
          1. The Linguistic Paralysis of Thought   59
          2. Language in the Space of Death: Transgression   61
      B. Time: From Classical Order to Modern History   66
          1. From Natural History to Biology   66
          2. From the Analysis of Wealth to Political Economy 68
          3. From General Grammar to Philology   71
      C. The Birth and Death of Man   73
          1. The Birth of Man in the Age of Critique:
             Kant and the Analytic of Finitude   73

2. The Death of Man and the Realization of Critique:
   Nietzschean Genealogy and the Counter-Sciences   76

4:   The Notion of Genealogy   81
     Part I: Friedrich Nietzsche's Notion of Genealogy   82
        A. On the Prejudices of Philosophers   83
        B. Nietzsche's Genealogy of Morals   89
           1. Genealogy is Critique   89
           2. Critique is Genealogical:
              Genealogy as History Oriented toward the Future 95
     Part II: Michel Foucault's Notion of Genealogy   101
        A. On the Prejudices of Philosophers   106
        B. Foucault's Notion of Genealogy   107
           1. Genealogy as Critique I:
              Toward the Realization of the Critique of Reason 107
           2. Genealogy as Critique II: The Historical A Priori 114
           3. Critique as Genealogical:
              Critique as History of the Present   120
        C. Conclusion   122

5:   The Practice of Genealogy: The Genealogy of the Soul   129
     Part I: Nietzsche's Genealogy of the Soul   133
     Part II: Foucault's Genealogy of the Modern Soul as
               Individuality   140
        A. The Emergence of Humanity as Legal Limit:
           From Monarchical to Reform Penal Practices   142
        B. The Solidification of Individuality   146
           1. Surveillance and the Transformation of Space   148
           2. Discipline and the Transformation of Time   151
           3. Writing and Confession   152

6:   The Genealogy of the Modern Subject   157
        A. Nietzsche's Genealogy of the Ascetic Ideal   161
        B. Foucault's Genealogy of the Desiring Subject:
           The Premodern Experience   164
           1. The Ethical Substance: Ontology   165
           2. The Mode of Subjection: Deontology   168
           3. The Form of Relationship with the Self: Ascetics 170
           4. Teleology   173
        C. The Genealogy of the Subject: The Modern Experience 175
        D. Genealogy as Self-Critical Enlightenment   179

Abbreviations   185
Notes   187
Bibliography   233
Index   251

Preface

There are a number of ways to categorize serious readers of Michel Foucault. Literary theorists appreciate his work and are repelled by any attempt to read him from the perspective of a particular discipline. Others see Foucault as making primarily a methodological contribution to the social sciences. Another camp views Foucault as radically transforming some very traditional philosophical questions—of truth, power, and subjectivity. The present study has been most influenced by this third group. It is decidedly a philosophical study of the writings of Michel Foucault. There has long been a need to overcome the view that Foucault is a philosophical eccentric who can be readily dismissed by the philosophical community. This overcoming will be accomplished, it seems to me, by studies which link him to the philosophical and cultural tradition. By exploring Foucault's pivotal relationship with Friedrich Nietzsche I hope to help with the spadework of rooting Foucault. To root him in a tradition is certainly not to domesticate him—his works themselves defy domestication—but rather to deflate the caricature of a rootless voice crying in the wilderness, a disgruntled Jeremiah, a neo-nihilist "ninny" (Camille Paglia) spouting "anarchist claptrap" (Richard Rorty). Foucault saw himself in the tradition that extends from Hegel through Nietzsche and Max Weber to the Frankfurt School and more generally in the tradition of anti-Platonism.

The following study has its roots in a few concrete, youthful experiences. Twenty years ago while I was a part-time undergraduate and budding psychology major, Robert Costello, a professor of psychology, arranged for me to work as an aide in a small psychiatric facility. A useless appendage to the psychiatric process and more often than not just in the way, I obtained a mouse's eye view of the most fascinating set of practices I had ever encountered. Much of each day was spent playing pool and chatting with patients, and in my enthusiasm I tried to romanticize the experience. I participated in group therapy, observed the eucharist of morning medication, forcibly restrained the unruly, assisted at electroshock therapy by gently but firmly pinning patients' hands to their bellies to minimize the effects of the spasms, and all romance died. Father Costello, in his capacity as a prison counselor, also took me to tour the U.S. Military Disciplinary Barracks and the Federal Penitentiary, both in Leavenworth, Kansas. At the barracks I conversed at length with prisoners my own age, boys not as fortunate as I to have received a student's draft deferment. At the penitentiary security was much too tight, so I remained at a distance and watched the watched being watched, and stood in awe of the first "panopticon" I had ever seen, before I had found a name for it. I needed names, a language, a way to render experience into discourse—perhaps to tame the images etched in my memory. Chronology escapes me, but over the next decade I devoured what I could, from Ken Kesey to R. D. Laing, Rusche and Kirchheimer, from the cheapest prisonhouse movie to the films of Frederick Wiseman. Somewhere I encountered Foucault. His works were *not* what I was looking for. Truth, power, and subjectivity concern him, and it would be difficult to find more traditional philosophical issues, but thinking after Foucault we can no longer think these issues naively. Foucault questioned the relationship between power and knowledge, I believe, more profoundly than anyone. His questioning of our modern subjectivity, our modern relationship to the self, is, if taken seriously, gutwrenching.

I am grateful to many who contributed to this project and am happy to have this opportunity to mention a few. Rev. Robert T. Costello, S. J., of course, supported me and this project in many more ways than those recounted above. James W. Bernauer, friend and collaborator, shared his wealth of insight and information and pushed me to become serious about Foucault. Richard Cobb-Stevens and John Kavanaugh read the entire manuscript and offered valuable suggestions. Jacques Taminiaux, William Richardson, Michael Zilles, Jürgen Habermas, Maxim Pensky, David Rasmussen and Glenn Hughes helped more than they know. Parts of Chapters 4 and 6 originally appeared in *Human Studies*. Mary Lynn Czymbor read the entire manuscript, discussed it with me at length, and married me. I wish to dedicate this work to her.

1

FOUCAULT, NIETZSCHE, GENEALOGY:
AN INTRODUCTION

This is a study of the Nietzschean genealogical problematic as it informed the writings of Michel Foucault. From the time of Foucault's earliest historical study his genealogical problematic gradually emerged, "albeit in a somewhat confused fashion," in terms of the interplay of three genealogical axes—truth, power, the subject—which he makes explicit in his last writings. As he put it in a 1983 interview,

> Three domains of genealogy are possible. First, an historical ontology of ourselves in relation to truth through which we constitute ourselves as subjects of knowledge; second, an historical ontology of ourselves in relation to a field of power through which we constitute ourselves as subjects acting on others; third, an historical ontology in relation to ethics through which we constitute ourselves as moral agents.[1]

My analysis of Foucault's genealogy, then, is not an exploration of his attempts to develop a new method for studying human beings, the goal of Dreyfus and Rabinow's influential work.[2] Instead, my analysis focuses on Foucault's genealogy as the problematic which emerged for him in the course of his historical researches. My concern is the complex of axes into which Foucault was drawn, especially as a result of his early history of madness, which called forth his explicit adoption of a Nietzschean approach to his future work.

1

Under Louis Althusser and Jean Hyppolite, Foucault studied the main currents in French thought at the time—phenomenology, Hegelianism, and Marxism—but, as he reminisced in a 1982 interview, it was his reading of Nietzsche that first stimulated him to embark on his own intellectual journey.[3] Reminiscing again a year later, Foucault recalled that the influence of Maurice Blanchot's and Georges Bataille's works led him to read Nietzsche. While other French thinkers associated with Nietzsche confronted him around 1972 as a means to escape Marxism, Foucault tells us, he himself studied Nietzsche as early as 1953 in order to displace the constitutive subject of phenomenology.[4] That comment, however, seems to oversimplify. The Foucault of the early 1950s was obviously quite influenced by *both* phenomenology *and* Marxism, and the emergence of his genealogical problematic and his reading of Nietzsche led him out of that *dual* impasse.[5]

There are many Nietzsches. When the Italian philosopher, Giulio Preti, directly confronted Foucault with the question, "Which Nietzsche do you like?" Foucault replied, "Obviously, not the one of *Zarathustra*, but the one of *The Birth of Tragedy*, of the *Genealogy of Morals*."[6] Foucault is not, contra Deleuze, a devotee of Nietzsche, herald of the Overman and Eternal Return; rather, as he agrees when pursued by Preti, the Nietzsche of the "geneses" most appeals to Foucault. The Nietzsche who is so important to Foucault, first, is Nietzsche the genealogist, the one who problematized truth as intimately entwined with relations of power, who sought a multiplicity of relations of forces at the origin of our taken-for-granted values and concepts and even the things we experience. Foucault's Nietzsche, secondly, is the one who saw our prized and apparently given individuality as a historical construct, profoundly influenced by the falsifying grammatical structure of our language.

As he continued in his discussion with Preti, an even more important aspect of Nietzsche's thought is his "requestioning of the primacy, or if you prefer of the privilege of the subject in Descartes' and Kant's sense, of the subject as consciousness."[7] Foucault's Nietzsche is the one who disassociated who we are and must become from our inherited concepts of who we are, from the truth about ourselves, our nature, our essence. Foucault's Nietzsche is the one engaged in genealogical critique, the attempt to reveal the contingent, practical, and historical conditions of our existence.

This is not to suggest an identity of the two thinkers nor a reduction of Foucault's work to its Nietzschean elements. This is especially evident in terms of the three genealogical axes—truth, power, and the subject. While Nietzsche-inspired, Foucault's analysis of the relationship between language and truth in *L'archéologie du savoir* is more sophisticated and detailed than anything found in the corpus of Nietzsche. Foucault's understanding of power, secondly, is quite compatible with Deleuze's interpretation of Nietzschean power as relations of forces, but it carries none of the metaphysical baggage that Heidegger saw in Nietzsche's will to power, nor can it be interpreted psychologically as Walter Kaufmann does. Finally, Foucault's appreciation of power in terms of our fluctuating discursive and nondiscursive practices enables him to provide an account of the constitution of modern individuality without taking recourse, as Nietzsche did, to any quasi-transcendentals such as human instincts or human nature. Moreover, Foucault's construction of a counter-memory stands in stark opposition to Nietzsche's recommendation that we actively forget for the enhancement of life. In brief, Foucault is the better genealogist.

A. An Overview

Maladie mentale et personnalité of 1954 manifested Foucault's commitment to transform psychology into a rigorous, Marxist science. Reflection upon man himself[8] must stand at the center of any such science; it must focus upon the psychosomatic totality of human beings. But by 1966 he declares man "an invention of recent date" due to be "erased, like a face drawn in sand at the edge of the sea."[9] By 1976 he objects to Marxism because it manifests even the possibility of becoming a science, and he commits himself to revealing "the effects of the centralising powers which are linked to the institution and functioning of an organised scientific discourse within a society such as ours."[10] He throws into question the desire for power of anyone who wants to establish a rigorous science. He judges the attempt to think in terms of a totality a hindrance to research and dedicates his own work to local critique. Whatever happened to his pursuit of a rigorous, Marxist science of man in his psychosomatic totality? *Histoire de la folie* happened, spurred on by the logic of *Maladie mentale et personnalité*.

In *Maladie mentale et personnalité* Foucault attacks the abstract metapathologies which dominated psychological theory at the time, and he calls psychology to attend to the concrete context in which individuals find themselves in the world. Foucault's path to this desired concreteness takes him *through* three psychological dimensions of mental illness—evolution, individual history, and intersubjectivity; i.e., he makes the existentialist move to individual history and intersubjectivity. He shows each of these three to be inadequate by itself to account for mental pathology, and he makes a further Nietzschean move and shows the union of the three, rather than constituting a closed psychological system, opens the question of psychopathology to the insertion of mental illness into culture and history.

Having analyzed the three interior dimensions of mental illness, his investigation is drawn to its exterior and objective, cultural and historical conditions. *Maladie mentale et personnalité*, thus, led Foucault to raise two questions that would overturn his original project and call forth his genealogical approach: "How did our culture come to give mental illness the meaning of deviancy and to the patient a status that excludes him? And how, despite that fact, does our society express itself in those morbid forms in which it refuses to recognize itself?"[11] I want to emphasize the Nietzschean character of these two questions—the notion that a culture practically confers meaning and that a culture unconsciously expresses itself in what it refuses to recognize about itself. *Histoire de la folie* is the result of his attempt to answer these questions.

Foucault characterizes *Histoire de la folie* as a study composed "under the sun of the great Nietzschean inquiry."[12] Specifically, it is to be read under the sun of Nietzsche's inquiry into the birth and death of tragedy.[13] Reading *Histoire de la folie* through the interpretative optic of Nietzsche's *The Birth of Tragedy* allows the moral problematization of madness to emerge as the central theme of *Histoire de la folie*. According to Foucault, Nietzsche revealed the tragedy of the Western world to be the refusal of the tragic, and, therefore, the refusal of the sacred. My reading of *Histoire de la folie* shows how the moral problematization of the sacred for Foucault corresponds with Nietzsche's notion of rendering the tragic intelligible. Just as Euripidean dialectics silenced tragedy, the moralization of madness secularized the sacred.

The problematic of the three genealogical axes—truth, power, and subjectivity—arises from this central theme. By revealing the moral problematization of madness, Nietzsche's main concerns become Foucault's own. Power, manifest in the practices of interning the mad, functions positively by constituting mental illness as a phenomenon available to perception. Foucault's mature understanding of power arises from his attempt to rethink the issues of Kant's transcendental aesthetic—space and time—in a Nietzschean, radically historical fashion. The truth axis, secondly, emerges from the moral problematization of madness; in the soil of the moralization of madness, mental illness can be problematized in terms of truth, giving birth to the science of psychology. Finally, the moral problematization of madness constitutes the modern individual. On the basis of the moralization of madness modern man finds himself categorized, located in space, constrained by time, disciplined, normalized, and individualized.

Although Foucault later criticizes *Histoire de la folie* for its dependence upon a traditional, negative conception of power,[14] the major elements of his later, more developed understanding of power are operative in *Histoire de la folie.* Power in this early work is a police affair concerned with the ordering of individuals in space and time. Although he emphasizes the negative character of power (it excludes, it represses, it confines), he also shows power functioning in a positive manner, practically productive of the entities and events we encounter. Even at this early stage his appreciation of power's functioning is much closer to Nietzsche's notion of relations of forces than it is to a Leviathan or commodity model of power which he later explicitly rejects. *Histoire de la folie* reveals power in terms of relations of forces functioning at the level of our cultural practices, rather than as something possessed and exercised from the top of a hierarchy.

The subject axis begins to emerge in *Histoire de la folie.*[15] Nietzschean genealogy focuses upon those things that are assumed to have no history—reason, truth, the soul, the subject—and *Histoire de la folie* includes an account of the historical constitution of the modern individual by means of confinement practices and the general treatment of the insane; Foucault attempts to answer the question, how was psychological interiority fabricated by means of these practices? The moral problematization of madness provides the context for appreciating the role of the subject axis. The moral problematization of madness in history contributes to the constitution of the modern normalized individual.

According to *Histoire de la folie,* based upon the prior constitution of madness as a moral experience, modern man has been authorized to found our science of man, psychology; i.e., the moral problematization of madness allowed us to problematize madness in terms of truth. The negative moral judgment against madness, paradoxically, lends positive content to madness, enabling its problematization in terms of truth by medical rationality.

This medical rationality provides the focus for Foucault's next major work, *Naissance de la clinique. Histoire de la folie* revealed that, rather than turning attention to preexisting objects, the Enlightenment constituted objects to be known by means of transformations in its practical treatment of the insane. *Naissance de la clinique* puts forth the same thesis, expressed more concisely and confidently. In *Naissance de la clinique* Foucault undermines the Enlightenment's story of its progressive transformation of its mode of knowledge by showing its historical and practical constitution of a world of objects to be known.

The power axis emerges in *Naissance de la clinique* in the spatial transformations of medical institutions and medical practices. Foucault does not use the term "power" at this point, but what he later refers to as the power axis is clearly operative in his analysis of the insertion of disease into social, political, and economic space. An analysis of the role of language in *Naissance de la clinique* provides us with access to the truth axis. Foucault argues in *Naissance de la clinique* that Western man constituted himself as a positive object for a true science of medicine by grasping himself within his own language and by giving himself a discursive existence. With the introduction of autopsy into medical practice, death made possible the constitution of the individual as the object of science. Death is the concrete a priori of medical experience in which modern man constitutes himself as both subject and object of his own knowledge.

Although the power and subject axes play a significant role in Foucault's *Les mots et les choses* of 1966, the truth axis dominates. In the spirit of Nietzsche's appreciation of "the prisonhouse of language," Foucault mounts an analysis of the relationship between language and knowledge. While Nietzsche's prisonhouse of language referred especially to the words and concepts we have inherited and the grammatical structure of our language, Foucault focuses upon the prisonhouse constituted at the "archaeological" level of discourse, what he refers to as the "episteme." Foucault argues in *Les mots et les choses* that language has such sovereignty over our thought that to question language amounts to questioning thought itself; language constitutes our categories of thought and the perceptions these categories order. Mining the epistemic domain of discourse amounts to a critique of thought; i.e., it amounts to an analysis of the conditions of the existence of our thought. Foucault's concern with the episteme is focused upon the internal conditions of our discourse, as opposed to the transcendental conditions which interested Kant. With Nietzsche, Foucault maintains that the a priori rules of formation of discourse are internal to discourse, rather than in the transcendental structures of the mind, and are, therefore, historical, rooted in the tumultuous history of what has been said.

The spirit of Nietzsche's *The Birth of Tragedy* continues to influence Foucault during the early 1960s. The rules of formation internal to discourse domesticate our thought and experience much like Socratic dialectics rendered tragedy intelligible and murdered it. In response Foucault sought out the writings of his own time which maintained a sacred, tragic stance devoted to transgressing the limits imposed upon language. Foucault's notion of "language in the space of death" is at the heart of these writings. Access to the tragic and sacred, according to Foucault, is available in our time only in a "literature" which transgresses the order imposed by rational discourse.

In *Histoire de la folie* and *Naissance de la clinique* power operated to constitute mental illness and the individual body as objects of the medical gaze primarily by means of transformations in the employment of space. In *Les mots et les choses* Foucault continues his post-Nietzschean version of the transcendental aesthetic by examining time as the locale of the power axis. The condition of the possibility of modern thought is not time as an unchanging, transcendental structure of human consciousness, but time as a quite recent, historically and discursively constituted, quasi-transcendental a priori.

Kantian critique opened the space for a general critique of reason and, thereby, made Nietzsche possible, and Nietzsche is important because he "burned for us, even before we were born, the intermingled promises of the dialectic and anthropology."[16] Nietzsche connected our philosophical task with a radical reflection on language which removed man from the center of thought. Finally, Foucault places the new counter-sciences of psychoanalysis, ethnology, and linguistics in counterpoint with the human sciences and shows how these counter-sciences work in the space opened by Nietzsche and continue the project of undermining anthropology.

The most significant element of Nietzschean genealogy is the fact that it is based upon his having undermined the notion of the substratum in all the forms it has taken in the history of philosophy—substance, subject, thing-in-itself. By throwing into question the subject-object grammatical structure of our language, Nietzsche removed human consciousness from its exalted place at the source of our activity and dismantled the doer-deed model for understanding any event in the universe. By decentering man, Nietzsche shattered the unity which had previously been posited at the source of the entities, values, and events we encounter. This allowed the manifestation of a multiplicity at the origin; rather than seeking a substance in its pristine purity at the origin, Nietzsche looked for a multiplicity, complex relations of forces, which provide the conditions for the existence of the entities, values, and events of our experience. Nietzsche's genealogies are meant to trace this multiplicity at the origin, to reveal the complex relations of forces. This is the first moment of genealogy, understood as critique; it is an attempt to reveal concrete, practical, and historical conditions of existence.

Critique, secondly, is genealogical. Genealogy itself is value-laden; it is intended for the enhancement of life. Critique, the attempt to reveal concrete, practical, and historical conditions of existence, is preparatory for the critical second moment: to question the value of the entities, values, and events of our experience, whose precarious origins have been revealed, for the enhancement of life. Genealogy is history, then, the search for origins, a searching of the past, that is oriented toward the service of life and creative activity.

Foucault refines Nietzsche's notion of genealogy as a quest for origins. If by the origin (*Ursprung*) one means the locale of something's primordial truth, essence, or original identity, nothing could be further from what genealogy seeks. The genealogist foregoes any search for such metaphysical fictions and, instead, cultivates the disparate details, events, and accidents found at any beginning. This desire to avoid metaphysical fictions makes genealogy the Nietzschean heir of the critique of reason inaugurated by Kant. Genealogy is critique of reason because of its commitment to overturn reason's prejudices in favor of "unity, identity, duration, substance, cause, materiality, and being." The critique of reason is not a matter of seeking the limits of reason in order to "provide a positive foundation for the possibility of knowing";[17] instead critique is a historical investigation which unveils reason's falsifications and reveals the moral will that undergirds it. Genealogy is "effective history" because it avoids the traditional historian's metaphysical prejudices and relocates everything traditionally considered eternal into a process of becoming.

Like Nietzsche's genealogies, Foucault's too are oriented to the future. They are meant to undermine the self-evidences of our age in order to open possibilities for the enhancement of life. In sharp contrast to Nietzsche, however, there is no sense of forgetting, either active or passive, in Foucault's genealogies. Too much forgetting has already gone on, too much discourse has been systematically excluded. The task of the Foucauldian genealogist is to provide a counter-memory. The task is to dredge up forgotten documents, minor statements, apparently insignificant details, in order to recreate the forgotten historical and practical conditions of our present existence.

In 1975 Foucault's *Surveiller et punir* appeared, "my first book,"[18] followed a year later by the first of his proposed multi-volume exploration of the history of sexuality, establishing him as a mature, self-aware, Nietzschean genealogist. The history of sexuality project was radically transformed after the appearance of Volume I, then cut short by Foucault's death in 1984. These writings of 1975–84, nonetheless, stunningly reveal Foucault's mature practice of genealogy.

B. The Nietzschean Face of Foucault Scholarship

This is not the first study to proclaim Foucault a Nietzschean. Many have taken note of Foucault's Nietzscheanism, including Foucault himself,[19] and several commentators have provided developed analyses of Nietzsche's impact on Foucault.

Alan Sheridan, for example, maintains that "the 'reactivation' of Nietzsche in contemporary French thought owes much to the active role Nietzsche has played in the formation of Foucault's thinking," and he emphasizes the foundational position of a Nietzschean will to knowledge in Foucault's work.[20] Sheridan correctly maintains that there is a deep congruity between Foucault's reading of Nietzschean genealogy and Foucault's description of his own archaeology.[21] Sheridan draws our attention to the crucial role played by the body in the genealogies of both Foucault and Nietzsche. "Genealogy adopts the point of view of the body," in François Ewald's words, "that of the tortured, trained, branded, mutilated, decomposed, constrained, subjected body, that of the body which is divided, organized, separated, and reunited."[22] By revealing the "power-body conjunction," according to Sheridan, Nietzsche and Foucault provide the basis for a post-Marxist "true materialism."[23]

J. G. Merquior points out that Foucault's Nietzscheanism explains his ardent attempt to separate himself from structuralism; his Nietzscheanism accounts for "his cold-shouldering of any structuralist search for invariant universals."[24] Merquior enters the debate about the relationship between Foucault's archaeology and his genealogy by declaring, like Sheridan, that there is no chasm between them "if one bears in mind the Nietzschean temper of Foucauldian thought."[25] While claiming that Foucault's work is "arguably the prime instance of neo-Nietzscheanism in contemporary Western thought," Merquior tends to reduce Foucault's Nietzscheanism to irrationalism.[26] He describes Foucault's genealogy as "a Nietzschean reduction of forms of action or knowledge to will-to-power configurations," and, with Sheridan, he emphasizes that genealogy's focus of concern is the body, and not as Marcuse or Nietzsche himself would have it, natural instincts.[27]

The most focused analysis of the body in Foucault's and Nietzsche's genealogies comes from Scott Lash. Drawing our attention especially to *Surveiller et punir*'s dependence upon Nietzsche's *On the Genealogy of Morals*, Lash reveals how Foucault utilizes Nietzsche's notion of a memory inscribed directly on bodies. In the seventeenth and eighteenth centuries, ritual cruelty reproduced absolutist government by creating a memory directly in the offender's body and in the social body in general through the spectacle of torture. In our own time power has relinquished its transcendence, nonetheless, it continues to inscribe a memory directly on bodies; "it individuates, normalises and mobilises human bodies."[28] Although Lash objects to the passivity of the body in Foucault's writings and thinks it should be complemented with a Deleuzean theory of desire, he praises Foucault for avoiding "the aristocratic ethos of Nietzsche's genealogy" by substituting his notion of power for Nietzsche's slave class.[29]

Foucault's Nietzscheanism, according to Richard Rorty, accounts for the uniqueness, as well as the problematic nature, of his stance with regard to theory of knowledge. Rorty delineates three possible attitudes toward theory of knowledge: Cartesian, Hegelian, and Nietzschean. The Cartesian holds that in order to be genuine knowledge must correspond to a fixed reality. In contrast, the Hegelian views rationality sociologically and historically—and to this extent Foucault looks Hegelian—but progress in thought and its convergence toward the true and the real replace correspondence as the criterion of truth. From the Nietzschean point of view, the Cartesians and Hegelians are bound together by "the conviction that there is a way of rising above the present and viewing it in relation to inquiry in general."[30] Both positions are mired in metaphysics, "the desire to rise above human activities and to see them as instances of a type, or as approximations to an ideal."[31] The key to understanding Foucault correctly, according to Rorty, is to view him as "a Nietzschean enemy" of Hegelian historicism, rejecting the notion of historical progress, "rather than as one more enemy of Cartesianism."[32]

But, for Rorty, Foucault's Nietzscheanism confronts him with his biggest problem. If Foucault offers a "theory of discursive practices," or any other kind of theory to challenge more traditional theories of knowledge, does he not contradict his own Nietzschean point of view—for "a Nietzschean must not want *any* substitute for theories"? For Nietzsche, the notion itself of a theory is "tainted with the notion that there is something there to be contemplated, to be accurately represented in thought," and is therefore inevitably rooted in metaphysics.[33]

Thomas Wartenberg analyzes Rorty's contentions and responds that, "as a Nietzschean, all that Foucault must avoid, at the pain of self-contradiction, is claiming to attain the sort of nonperspectival standpoint that is the common link between the Cartesian and Hegelian positions."[34] But Foucault's perspective has always been clear—it is that of the prisoners, as Ewald claims, or, as Merquior says, that of the victims, "a most un-Nietzschean position."[35] Wartenberg suggests that Rorty assumes knowledge to be an autonomous realm, a "non-perspectival standpoint," and therefore assumes a Cartesian or Hegelian meta-epistemology. A key Nietzschean insight undergirding all of Foucault's work is that the truth cannot be separated from the procedures of its production, and, as François Ewald puts it, "these procedures are as much procedures of knowledge as procedures of power."[36] By dismissing Foucault's notion of power/knowledge as "self-indulgent radical chic," "anarchist claptrap," and "Nietzschean bravura,"[37] Rorty not only dismisses "a central feature of Foucault's view of knowledge,"[38] he undercuts the Nietzscheanism that he simultaneously attributes to Foucault. As Pamela Major-Poetzl points out, it was Nietzsche who specified philosophy's limits for Foucault. Nietzsche made it clear to Foucault that philosophy could no longer be synthesis, and he revealed the impossibility of neutral knowledge by showing thought and values to be expressions of power. Because of his Nietzscheanism it is clear to Foucault that philosophy's "proper function is criticism, diagnosis, demythologizing."[39]

The remarkable study of Michel Foucault's work by his friend Gilles Deleuze is so innovative that it ought to be appreciated as much as an advance in Deleuze's thought as an original commentary on Foucault. Although not focused upon the notion of genealogy, the second half of Deleuze's work, like the present study, found inspiration in Foucault's claim that genealogy centers on three domains or axes: truth/knowledge, power, and the subject. Like the present study, moreover, Deleuze's work draws attention to the Nietzschean character of Foucault's writings. Foucault's work, according to Deleuze's reading, is a neo-Kantianism with a differ-ence. Like Kant, Foucault is concerned with revealing a priori con-ditions. But there the similarity with neo-Kantianism ends, unless one wants to call Nietzsche a neo-Kantian.[40] The a priori conditions that concern Foucault, as Deleuze points out, are those of real experience, rather than those of any possible experience. These conditions, moreover, he seeks on the side of the object rather than in a universal, transcendental subject; i.e., the a priori conditions of existence are located in space and time and are, therefore, radically historical.[41] These conditions are constituted by the very concrete discursive and nondiscursive practices of a culture, and thus they fluctuate with cultural transformations in history.

In his very last writings published shortly before his death, Deleuze points out, Foucault drew the conclusion of all his preced-ing books by showing that "the true is only given to knowledge through 'problematizations', and that the problematizations are made only from 'practices', practices of seeing and practices of say-ing."[42] Everything is practical, according to Deleuze's Foucault, and irreducible to practices of knowledge. Accordingly, Deleuze refers to Foucault's work as a "pragmatism."[43]

This realm of concrete practices, the historical a priori condi-tions of existence, is what Foucault will later call "power," and Deleuze argues that Foucault's understanding of power is very near to that of Nietzsche—it represents, in fact, a "profound niet-zscheanism."[44] Two dimensions of Deleuze's reading of Foucault deserve special attention. First, Deleuze interprets Foucault's notion of power in terms of "relations of forces," terminology which characterized Deleuze's study of Nietzsche.[45] A power relation is not modeled on sovereignty, possessed then exercised from top down; power entails a concrete, practical interplay of forces at the level of life itself and with life as its object.[46] Power, moreover, is not a matter of repression and ideology; while Foucault is not inat-tentive to repression and ideology, he recognizes, "as Nietzsche had already seen," repression and ideology "do not constitute the combat of forces, they are only the dust raised by the combat."[47] Secondly, Deleuze draws attention to the significant role played by space and time in Foucault's understanding of power. The most effective examples of what Foucault means by power appear in his discussions of spatial and temporal transformations. To exercise power, as Deleuze indicates, is "to distribute in space...to order in time...to arrange in space-time...."[48] It is as if Foucault rethought the concepts of Kant's transcendental aesthetic in the context of his Nietzschean, concrete, and historical understanding of power.[49]

Deleuze sees in Foucault's work a contrast or opposition between life and man. In our own time, Deleuze maintains, life is suppressed by the images of man in accordance with which we interpret and govern ourselves. Nietzsche's overman for Deleuze is nothing more than the result of liberating our own potentialities for life from the concepts of man or the human essence which hinder us. The overman results from our resistance to the limitations imposed on us by the concept man. "What resistance extracts from the old man is the forces, as Nietzsche said, of a larger, more active, more affirmative life, a life that is richer in possibilities. The overman has never wanted to say anything else: it is *in man himself* that it is necessary to liberate life, because man himself is a way of imprisoning it. Life becomes resistance to power when power takes life for its object."[50]

While forgoing any reference to the overman, John Rajchman proposes an interpretation of Foucault quite in line with that of Deleuze. In Rajchman's interpretation, Foucault primarily objects to any preconceived notion of the human essence, of who we are, which would provide a basis for determining how we ought to be and behave. He calls Foucault's project a "modern practical philosophy" by which he means a philosophy which,

> instead of attempting to determine what we should do on the basis of what we essentially are, attempts, by analyzing who we have been constituted to be, to ask what we might become. It is the philosophy for a practice in which what one is capable of being is not rooted in a prior knowledge of who one is. Its principle is freedom, but a freedom which does not follow from any postulation of our nature or essence.[51]

It is precisely the task of the genealogist to manifest our taken-for-granted self-understandings, notions of the human essence or our nature, as having emerged from quite pedestrian, concrete, practical, and historical conditions, and to ask whether these self-understandings promote or detract from the enhancement of life.

Rajchman and Charles Taylor link Foucauldian genealogy with the Nietzschean interpretation of the relationship between freedom and the truth about ourselves, but they offer strongly opposed evaluations of this interpretation. Because of Nietzsche's influence, according to Taylor's critical but respectful essay, Foucault repudiates the traditionally upheld relationship between freedom and truth and, thereby, relinquishes any basis (a notion of liberating truth) for criticizing any exercise of power.[52] Because the notions of power/domination and disguise/illusion play such an important role in his studies, one would think, according to Taylor, Foucault would be inclined to affirm the two corresponding notions of freedom and truth. By asserting that "there is no order of human life, or way we are, or human nature, that one can appeal to in order to judge or evaluate between ways of life,"[53] Foucault, says Taylor, sacrifices genealogy's critical power.

Rajchman, in contrast, maintains that Foucault's greatest contribution to contemporary thought is this Nietzschean rethinking of the relationship between freedom and truth:

> Nietzsche is the philosopher who separates the problem of freedom from the problem of acquiring the truth about ourselves, who would free us from the tyrannies of such truths through an analysis of their histories. He separates our freedom from the knowledge of our nature. Foucault's genealogy is a continuation of that philosophy.[54]

Among Foucault's commentators, Rajchman shows the most sensitivity to genealogy's power as critique. Genealogy is a unique form of critique which recognizes that the things, values, and events of our present experience have been constituted historically, discursively, and practically. Genealogy is an attempt to "lay bare that constitution and its consequences;"[55] it reveals the historical, discursive, and practical conditions of existence of these things, values, and events. "If 'critique' names the exposure of unrecognized operations of power in people's lives," as Rajchman puts it, "then Foucault was certainly engaged in critique, or was a critical theorist."[56]

In an excellent comparison of Foucault's and Habermas's notions of critique, Rajchman claims, "Habermas starts with the assumption that philosophy has articulated the ideals critical theory must make practical. Foucault starts with the assumption that ideals and norms are always already 'practical'; the point of critique is to analyze the practices in which those norms actually figure, and which determine particular kinds of experience."[57] Foucault's genealogy is, thus, a Nietzschean form of critique. Because of Nietzsche's influence Foucault's critique is decidedly un-Kantian and un-Hegelian, nonanthropological and nondialectical; i.e., "he denies any foundational assumptions about our nature, and rejects the speculative theme of history as the self-realization of humanity."[58] Genealogy as critique reveals the contingency, even arbitrariness, of what appears natural and necessary, and thereby it serves to open possibilities.[59]

Barry Smart and Mark Poster similarly draw attention to genealogy's critical power, but their commitment to the redemption of Marxist social theory allows them to miss the specifically Nietzschean and historical character of Foucault's genealogical critique. For both Smart and Poster Foucauldian critique is essentially reducible to "oppositional thinking."[60] That Nietzschean sense of power's positive productivity, so central to Foucault's genealogy, emerges as secondary to opposition to exploitation and oppression. Gisela Hinkle likewise emphasizes that genealogy is critique, but critique means, primarily, opposition to unitary science.[61]

One extended study of Foucault's relation to Nietzsche also places him in the company of Heidegger and Derrida.[62] Allan Megill, in his *Prophets of Extremity*, links these four thinkers under the rubric of their "aestheticism" by which he means "a tendency to see 'art' or 'language' or 'discourse' or 'text' as constituting the primary realm of human experience."[63] Modern thought's basic categories, according to Megill, arose from the dilemma resulting from the Enlightenment's project of creating a science of society modeled on natural science while simultaneously affirming the freedom of human beings as moral agents. Kant saw the problem clearly: he was preoccupied by "the question of how a free, moral subject can exist within the deterministic world of science."[64] This Enlightenment dilemma, Megill maintains, gave rise to the familiar dichotomies of modern thought—subject/object, fact/value, mind/body, theory/practice, etc.—and to the attempt to circumvent these dichotomies, suggested by Kant in his *Critique of Judgment*, by affirming art as an autonomous realm, separate from the terms of these dichotomies yet able to mediate between them. When Nietzsche claims in *The Birth of Tragedy* that "the existence of the world is justified only as an aesthetic phenomenon,"[65] he shows himself to be the paradigmatic aestheticist, and Foucault is his faithful son. Foucault's aestheticism manifests itself in his concern for language, that is, "language insofar as it has an autonomous and self-referring, yet expansive and world-creating existence—in short, language as the ontogenetic work of art."[66] This focus upon aestheticism, as might be expected, draws Megill to emphasize the affinities between Foucault and Nietzsche on language and discourse.

What Megill finds valuable in the works of Nietzsche, Heidegger, Foucault, and Derrida is that they speak an "edifying discourse," a discourse designed to "take us out of our old selves by the power of strangeness, to aid us in becoming new beings."[67] In this regard Megill shows some affinities with those authors, such as Edward Said and David Carroll, who emphasize Nietzsche's role in Foucault's work, less as genealogist, than as an excessive, transgressive literary figure, as the mad literary genius. For David Carroll, Foucault values Nietzsche's texts, with those of Sade, Artaud, Bataille, et al., because they "resist the obscuring clarity of rational philosophical discourse."[68] "One reason therefore that Foucault seems to give artists, visionaries, madmen, and deviants (Hölderlin, Sade, Nietzsche, Beckett) so important a place in his historical and theoretical studies," in Edward Said's words, "is that they, more than the average user of discourse, exaggerate and make plain in their solitude and alienation the exteriority of discursive practice by outdoing discourse."[69] Foucault reserves the term "literature" for such transgressive expression.[70]

The best and most extensive attempt to trace Foucault's relationship to Nietzsche is Angèle Kremer-Marietti's *Michel Foucault: Archéologie et généalogie.* Kremer-Marietti gives priority among Foucault's writings to *L'archéologie du savoir* and reads it as a Nietzsche-inspired text. She claims that Nietzsche's attack on the Cartesian cogito undergirds Foucault's attack on the preeminence of the philosophical subject, the role of the author or speaker, and shows the originating subject to be, for Foucault, a function of discursive rules. Kremer-Marietti correctly interprets Foucault's archaeology as proceeding "from the same originating interrogation as that which directs Nietzsche in *On the Genealogy of Morals,* the work in which Nietzsche poses the problem of the *value* of conventional values, that of the social conditions and of the cultural milieux which have allowed their formation."[71] Reading *L'archéologie du savoir* as a Nietzschean text allows me to establish the congruity of Foucault's archaeology and genealogy.

It is generally agreed among Foucault's commentators that a major shift took place in the orientation of his work, and that the influence of Nietzsche accounts for the shift. Axel Honneth, for example, maintains that after *L'archéologie du savoir* Foucault turned to his Nietzsche-inspired analysis of power.[72] A similar position is claimed by Guy Laforest: Foucault is indebted to Nietzsche for drawing him beyond the impasse of archaeology.[73] Allan Megill emphasizes a methodological break in Foucault's work from his earlier archaeological "depth interpretation" to his later "genealogy of exteriority"; the increasing importance of Nietzsche for Foucault caused the transformation.[74] Richard Rorty concurs; Foucault's corpus ought to be divided between early and late, pre-Nietzsche and post-Nietzsche, and the break occurs after *Les mots et les choses,* apparently coinciding with "the events of May" 1968 in Paris.[75] Although they want to avoid classifying Foucault's work in terms of early and late, Dreyfus and Rabinow indicate a major transformation in his work just after 1968.[76] The most unusual classification of Foucault's work into early and late comes from Gisela Hinkle: *L'archéologie du savoir* (1969) and *Les mots et les choses* (1966) are the early writings, *Surveiller et punir* (1975), *Histoire de la folie* (1961), and *Histoire de la sexualité I* (1976) are the later.[77]

Pierre Macherey, too, suggests that the reading of Nietzsche (and Heidegger) effected the major break in Foucault's work, but he locates the break much earlier in Foucault's career, after his first book of 1954.[78] Macherey compares Foucault's *Maladie mentale et personnalité* (1954) with his revision of this work, *Maladie mentale et psychologie* (1962), and finds the revision so radical that it should be considered a new work. Macherey maintains that implicit references to Nietzsche and Heidegger in the 1962 work replace allusions to the young Marx which haunted the pages of the 1954 book. This is the appropriate place to mark the rupture in Foucault's work. The key to properly locating the break is a Nietzschean reading of *Histoire de la folie* of 1961. Jean-Paul Margot saw it clearly: if Nietzsche is a "primordial figure" in Foucault's later writings, it is because "he is omnipresent in *Histoire de la folie* and because *Histoire de la folie* orients all Foucault's later reflections."[79]

The task of the present study is to reveal what Foucault means by genealogical critique. From 1961 on, Foucault's work centers on the gradual emergence and refinement of three genealogical axes which he explicitly identifies in 1983. His first book, *Maladie mentale et personnalité* of 1954, directed his attention to the history of madness which resulted in his *Histoire de la folie à l'âge classique*. This historical study overturned the problematic of *Maladie mentale et personnalité* and gave rise to the Nietzschean genealogical problematic that he would finally formulate explicitly in 1971.

2

FOUCAULT'S HISTORY OF MADNESS:
AN INVITATION TO A NIETZSCHEAN
GENEALOGY OF MORALS

In 1954 Foucault found himself in the precarious position of having achieved certification in an allegedly scientific discipline that he viewed as not yet having attained the status of a science. A matured psychologist, having earned his *Licence de Psychologie* and *Diplome de Psycho-Pathologie* by 1952, he judged the field itself as yet immature.[1] With his first major work he tried to make psychology "rigorously scientific" by transforming it into a Marxist science of man.[2]

It would be a short-lived but important project. This initial enterprise, sketched in *Maladie mentale et personnalité*, motivated Foucault's turn to history—what he will later call genealogy—which would undermine his projected rigorous science of psychology. Foucault rewrote the second half of his *Maladie mentale et personnalité* in 1962 and retitled it *Maladie mentale et psychologie*. In the transition from the former to the latter his interest moved away from psychology as the study of personality to the study of the historical constitution of *homo psychologicus*.[3] His *Histoire de la folie à l'âge classique* lies in the interstice.

In *Maladie mentale et personnalité*, by means of an analysis of the contributions and inadequacies of evolutionary psychology, psychology of individual history, and phenomenological psychology,[4] Foucault arrives at a conjunction of mental pathology and sociology: "illness has its reality and its value as illness only at the

19

interior of a culture which recognizes it as such."[5] Two assumptions govern this 1954 enterprise: that mental illness, first, is a cultural phenomenon, and secondly, that a society positively expresses itself in the morbid forms it recognizes. Two questions follow: "How did our culture come to give mental illness the meaning of deviancy and to the patient a status that excludes him? And how, despite that fact, does our society express itself in those morbid forms in which it refuses to recognize itself?"[6] Foucault's early response to these two Nietzschean questions led him to turn his attention for several years to a study of the history of madness,[7] flowering in his 1961 *Histoire de la folie* and the overturning of his psychology project.

Foucault presents *Histoire de la folie à l'âge classique* as an investigation "under the sun of the great Nietzschean inquiry,"[8] specifically under the sun of Nietzsche's inquiry into the birth and death of tragedy. There Nietzsche revealed that, by affirming "aesthetic Socratism's" equation of moral virtue, knowledge, and happiness, and thereby equating morality, intelligibility, and beauty,[9] Euripides destroyed Greek tragedy. He reduced the tragic character of human existence to its intelligible components by moralizing it. According to Foucault's reading, Nietzsche revealed the tragic structure which constitutes the history of the Western world; this tragic structure is, paradoxically, nothing other than the refusal, the forgetting, the silencing of tragedy. The task of *Histoire de la folie*, then, is "to confront the dialectics of history with the immobile structures of the tragic."[10]

Foucault's key insight from *Histoire de la folie* is that mental illness can be examined only on the horizon of moralization. Having discovered a morally engineered madness, Foucault was drawn to examine his three genealogical axes, the three domains in which this moralization of life is constructed. Tracing the history of the moral problematization of madness reveals the power axis, manifest in the practices of confining the mad. Power functions positively in constituting mental illness as a phenomenon available to perception. The truth axis emerges from this study of the moral problematization of madness; psychology, the science of man, is founded upon the moralization of madness. In the soil of this moral problematic, madness can be problematized in terms of its truth.[11] The subject axis likewise emerges from this historical study; the moral problematization of madness constitutes the modern individual. That psychological interiority where modern man pursues his meaning, his depth, his truth, results from those practices which constituted madness as a moral problematic.

A. The Moral Problematization of Madness

Histoire de la folie provides a historical ontology of mental illness, a genealogy of psychology's object.[12] It reveals that madness has only recently attained its status as mental illness and shows that the historical conditions of psychology's existence are relatively recent.

"Generally speaking," throughout the Renaissance up to about 1650, "madness was allowed free reign; it circulated throughout society, it formed part of the background and language of everyday life, it was for everyone an everyday experience that one sought neither to exalt nor to control."[13] Madmen were rarely confined during this period although many were driven outside the city walls and left to wander the countryside.

One Renaissance practice in particular draws Foucault's attention: once expelled from the city, often the mad were handed over to merchants and pilgrims who would sail them far enough away to prevent their easy return to the city. The "stultifera navis," the Ship of Fools, did actually exist, Foucault claims, but more importantly, it haunted the literary and artistic imagination of the early Renaissance. We cannot account for the entire meaning of these ships, he insists, simply in terms of security or social utility; "Other meanings much closer to rite are certainly present, and we can still discern some traces of them."[14] Foucault's attention is regularly drawn to the spatial locale, and the water provides a symbolically rich location:

> water adds to this the dark mass of its own values; it carries off, but it does more: it purifies. Navigation delivers man to the uncertainty of fate; on water, each of us is in the hands of his own destiny; every embarkation is, potentially, the last. It is for the other world that the madman sets sail in his fools' boat; it is from the other world that he comes when he disembarks.[15]

Here we encounter a trace of the theme which Foucault will seize upon throughout *Histoire de la folie*. The symbolically rich, the sacred, is problematized morally and thereby diminished. The moralization of the sacred mirrors the silencing of tragedy by dialectics as revealed by Nietzsche.

Confinement succeeds embarkation. The hospital succeeds the ship, and the classical experience of madness is born. The key to Foucault's analysis of classical age confinement resides in the insight that confinement is a moral space. The landmark is 1656, the date of the decree establishing the Hôpital Général for the sake of the poor. Although those considered insane were confined in this space, Foucault insists that it was not a medical establishment. Rather, it was a "semijudicial structure," an "administrative entity," "a strange power that the King establishes between the police and the courts, at the limits of the law: a third order of repression."[16] The hospital had nothing to do with medicine, he insists; it is an instance of moral order.

A social sensibility, essentially a moral sensibility, must have operated in the classical age, according to Foucault, which legitimated the practice of confinement. In the Renaissance the mad were rendered a certain hospitality; confinement was rare. At the end of the eighteenth century shock was expressed at finding criminals, the unemployed, and the insane locked up together. But during the classical age this amalgam of personages in confinement was not only tolerated but required. The, for us, heterogeneous elements (criminals, unemployed poor, the insane) must have manifested a homogeneity to classical age social sensibility; "there must have been a principle of cohesion," according to Foucault, a "form of sensibility to madness" specific to this epoch which "we are accustomed to define by the privileges of Reason."[17] The practice of confinement is a new reaction indicating a new relation between man and the inhumane in his existence.

This new moral problematization manifests itself theologically, politically, and economically. In the theological milieu associated with the names Luther and Calvin, the theological understanding of both poverty and charity undergoes a radical transformation. Poverty, once indicative of a postponed, but assured, glory, gains appreciation in terms of predestination. Poverty no longer indicates spiritual glorification but moral chastisement. Poverty slips "from a religious experience which sanctifies it to a moral conception which condemns it."[18] What had been sacred is diminished to the status of a moral problematic. Charity is secularized; faith, not works, justifies.

Politically, a new sensibility to poverty emerges which corresponds to the theological transformation. A new consciousness of one's duties to society arises, and the poor and the mad appear as effects of disorder. While, theologically, poverty is removed from the "dialectic of humiliation and glory," it is in the political realm caught up in a relation of disorder to order. "What, since Luther and Calvin, manifests the marks of an intemporal chastisement, will become in the world of state charity, complaisance with oneself and fault against the grand march of the State."[19] Madness, by its association with poverty in the houses of confinement, is being formed and constituted as a moral problematic. "A new sensibility is born in its regard: no longer religious, but social."[20]

Economically, confinement entailed the imperative of labor and a condemnation of idleness. From our contemporary medical point of view we impose a benign interpretation upon seventeenth-century confinement as indicating a new benevolence toward illness. From its inception, however, the Hôpital Général had the task "of preventing 'mendicancy and idleness as the source of all disorders.'"[21] Confinement functioned in the seventeenth century as a response to economic crisis. A new mode of treating the unemployed arises; no longer ostracized to the fringes of society, he is taken in and confined. Depending upon the economic state of affairs, it could be a matter of confining the unemployed or of giving work to them and forcing them to contribute to general prosperity. "The alternation is clear," Foucault maintains: "cheap manpower in periods of full employment and high salaries; and in periods of unemployment, reabsorption of the idle and social protection against agitation and uprisings."[22]

Foucault insists, however, that this is to be understood as essentially a moral issue rather than one of mere economics. "What appears to us today as a clumsy dialectic of production and prices," according to Foucault, "then possessed its real meaning as a certain ethical consciousness of labor, in which the difficulties of the economic mechanisms lost their urgency in favor of an affirmation of value."[23] If looked at functionally, the houses of confinement were miserable failures, and they soon disappeared early in the nineteenth century. In the classical age, it was not labor's productive power, but rather its "force of moral enchantment" that enabled it to combat poverty.

The forced labor in the houses of confinement found its justification in labor's capacity to reform the inmate morally. Unlike the Middle Ages in which the great sin was pride, and unlike the Renaissance in which it was avarice, in the seventeenth century sloth was the great sin. Foucault's summary statement is worth quoting at some length; it clearly expresses the classical age moralization of what the Renaissance had perceived as sacred:

> Until the Renaissance, the sensibility to madness was linked to the presence of imaginary transcendences. In the classical age, for the first time, madness was perceived through an ethical condemnation of idleness and in a social immanence

guaranteed by the community of labor. This community acquired an ethical power of segregation, which permitted it to reject, as into another world, all forms of social useless-ness. It was in this *other world*, encircled by the sacred pow-ers of labor, that madness would assume the status we now attribute to it. If there is, in classical madness, something which speaks of elsewhere, and of *other things*, it is no longer because the madman comes from another heaven, that of the insane and bears its signs; it is because he crosses the fron-tiers of bourgeois order of his own accord, and alienates him-self outside the sacred limits of its ethic.[24]

The sacred is diminished to the moral. Poverty results from lack of discipline and moral relaxation. Forced labor reforms morally. Labor lends order to life. The houses of confinement equate order and virtue.

The poor and the mad are not alone in confinement, and the other characters in these institutions contributed their share to the constitution of madness as a moral problematic. Classical age con-finement practices drew into unity personages and values among which previous generations had never recognized any resemblance, thereby constituting a uniform realm of Unreason. Confinement linked madness with alchemy, venereal disease, profane practices, certain forms of sexuality, and thus constituted "significative uni-ties" in madness's relation with the domain of moral experience.

The classical age, according to Foucault, contributed to the constitution of madness as a moral problematic by associating it in confinement with three domains of experience: with sexuality inso-far as it deviates from the organization of the bourgeois family, with profanation in its relations with new conceptions of the sacred, and with libertinage, in new relations between free thought and the system of passions.[25] By so relating apparently disparate experiences the classical age was constituting a homoge-neous moral world from which our present experience of mental alienation emerged:

> In inventing, in the imaginary geometry of its morality, the space of confinement, the classical epoch came to find at the same time a common native land and common place of redemption for sins against the flesh and for faults against reason. Madness comes to be adjacent sin, and this is perhaps what will establish, through the centuries, the relation between unreason and culpability....[26]

Moralization as desacralization, the diminution of the sacred, is revealed by Foucault in the context of two exemplary classical age phenomena. First, he presents the 1726 writ of execution for a sodomite and claims that this was one of the last executions to take place for this activity. From then on, confinement in the Hôpi-tal or in a house of detention would be the typical sanction. This new indulgence toward sodomy, according to Foucault, results from the moral condemnation and sanction of scandal which come to be directed toward homosexuality in the classical age. Sodomites, formerly condemned to burning at the stake along with magicians and heretics, formerly condemned for sacrilege and reli-gious profanation, are condemned in the classical age only for moral reasons. Homosexuality, to which the Renaissance had allowed a certain freedom, now moves into silence, confronted by the moral condemnation of the scandalized consciousness. This, according to Foucault, results from the desacralization of sodomy.

Secondly, Foucault argues that the bourgeois family came, through a long process rather than by debate or decision, to be identified as one of the essential criteria of a reasonable and moral existence. The sexual ethic was confiscated by the morality of the family. Love, according to Foucault, is desacralized by the mar-riage contract. "It is no longer love which is sacred; marriage is...."[27] Forms of sexual expression which deviate from the reason-able morality of the bourgeois family find themselves relegated to the realm of Unreason.

A similar development holds true for blasphemy, suicide, alchemy, magic, and superstition. Between 1617 and 1649, Fou-cault tells us, thirty-four people were executed for blasphemy. But slowly such executions became less frequent. This is not, however, due to any loosening of laws; blasphemers filled the houses of con-finement. Blasphemy received a new, ambiguous status in the classical age. Categories of the sacred had loosened, and blasphe-my could find no place under any medical category; so as "neither profanation nor pathology,"[28] it fell under the strictures of moral condemnation. Suicide, likewise, having once been sacrilege, now is associated with immorality and, therefore, unreason. Alchemists, magicians, and the superstitious find their home in the houses of confinement, too. Having once been guilty of violat-ing canons of the sacred, in the classical age they are condemned because of their powers of deception. Their place is no longer among obscure, transcendent powers; their place is in a system of errors—the realm of unreason. Briefly, according to Foucault, the classical age carried out a moral revolution. It "discovered a common denominator of Unreason in experiences which had for a long time been remote from one another, forming a halo of culpability around madness. Our scientific and medical knowledge of madness rests implicitly on the anterior constitution of an ethical experience of Unreason."[29]

The birth of the asylum, associated with the work of Tuke and Pinel, is popularly regarded as an act of liberation. The truth of the matter, according to Foucault, is quite to the contrary. Tuke's Retreat served as an instrument of moral and religious segregation. The madman is immersed in a moral community, modeled on the Community of Quakers, where he is forced to take responsibility for his madness, for anything in him that might cause a disturbance of morality and society. "Tuke created an asylum where he substituted for the free terror of madness, the stifling anguish of responsibility; fear no longer reigned on the other side of the prison gates, it now raged under the seals of conscience."[30] The Retreat is a moral milieu dominated by the values of work and family.

Because of his fear that religion contributed to outbreaks of madness, Pinel avoided any religious tenor in his asylum. He did, however, insist upon maintaining the moral content of religion. Pinel's asylum was a "religious domain without religion, a domain of pure morality, of ethical uniformity."[31] The total existence of the inmates and their keepers was organized by Pinel for the sake of bringing about moral uniformity. This was likewise the case, Foucault insists, for the physicians. In the classical age physicians did not function in the houses of confinement. But in the age of the asylum the physician operates at the center of asylum life. In fact, part of the popular mythology maintains that Tuke's and Pinel's "humanitarian liberation" of the insane was founded upon their having introduced medical science into the asylum. According to Foucault, however, introducing physicians into asylum life does not imply the introduction of medical science into the care of the mad. The physician's service is of the moral and social order; "If the medical profession is required, it is as a juridical and moral guarantee, not in the name of science."[32] The physician functioned as a wise person of social and moral responsibility.

B. The Emergence of the Three Genealogical Axes

The metaphor of the lightning flash peppers Foucault's writings of the early 1960s. The recovery of "tragic experience beyond the promises of dialectic" comes like lightning.[33] "That lightning-flash which Nature drew from herself in order to strike Justine" in Foucault's reading of Sade continues to manifest in art the violent transcending of the limitations imposed by reason.[34] Unreason's life in the modern world explodes in the "lightning-flash" of Nietzsche's writings, in those of Hölderlin, Nerval, and Artaud.[35] Was not Nietzsche paving the way for "the lightning flash of being" when he killed God and man?[36] Bataille's transgression erupts "like a flash of lightning in the night."[37]

Perhaps the metaphor simply struck Foucault as particularly appropriate to capture the flashiness of his favorite mad geniuses. Perhaps we ought to read no more into it. The metaphor does, nonetheless, resonate with earlier texts. Nietzsche's Zarathustra proclaims "the lightning out of the dark cloud of man"; the overman is lightning: "Behold, I am a herald of the lightning and a heavy drop from the cloud; but this lightning is called *overman*."[38]

At a crucial juncture in *On the Genealogy of Morals*, moreover, Nietzsche uses the example of the lightning flash to undermine the seductive power of language which lures us into positing a subject or substance underlying action. According to Nietzsche, "the popular mind separates the lightning from its flash and takes the latter for an *action*, for the operation of a subject called lightning.... The popular mind in fact doubles the deed; when it sees the lightning flash, it is the deed of a deed: it posits the same event first as cause and then a second time as effect."[39] We posit a substratum beneath the flux of activity because we prefer substance's familiarity. Like the Stoic who prefers order over chaos and imposes this evaluation on his interpretation of nature, modern men and women impose the formula "cause and effect" to tame nature. For Nietzsche, on the contrary, there is no such thing as a force separated from its expression. There is no substratum "lightning" in itself which undergirds the activity of flashing.

When positive psychiatry or the enlightened medicine of modernity recounts its own history, it begins the story at the end of the eighteenth century and associates its origin with its turning away from theory and toward the perceived; "one narrates how reason or observation had triumphed over prejudices, averted obstacles and brought hidden truths to the light of day."[40] Having abandoned the chimeras of superstition, theoretical constructs, and systems, the enlightened physician could focus his gaze upon the patient's body and disease in all their omnipresent objectivity. Beneath the flashing symptoms, beneath the theoretical systems for classifying these symptoms, beneath the superstitious moral prohibitions, the objectivity of physical or mental illness awaited disinterested observation. The physician need only turn his attention to the lightning of the disease itself undergirding the flashing symptoms and theories in order to pave the way for the psychiatric and medical advances of the nineteenth century. In modern medicine's narrative account of itself, in other words, a transformation in the mode of knowledge occurred which turned medicine's attention to a world of objects that had always been there, waiting patiently to be observed and known.

A central task of Foucault's *Histoire de la folie* and *Naissance de la clinique* is to undermine this mythic history of modern medicine and psychiatry.[41] True, the physician's cool gaze is central to the nineteenth century's medical advances, but this gaze represents, not, essentially, a transformation in the mode of knowledge, but the historical constitution of a world of objects to be known. In spite of the narrative recounted above, "'positive' medicine is not a medicine that has made an 'objectal' choice in favour of objectivity itself.... What has changed is the silent configuration in which language finds support: the relation of situation and attitude to what is speaking and what is spoken about."[42] Rather than a matter of turning one's attention to a preexisting object, positive medicine emerged from a mutation in discourse; its provenance is the practical and discursive constitution of modern individuality and the individual's body as medical object. The individual had to acquire objective status against a background of objectivity.[43] Briefly, Foucault wants to argue in *Histoire de la folie* and *Naissance de la clinique* that, contrary to modern psychiatry's and enlightened medicine's own story which denies any role of an a priori, and contrary to Kant's enlightened story which reveals a transcendental a priori, modern medical and psychiatric perception is undergirded by a concrete a priori which has been practically constituted in history.

The task Foucault sets for himself is the Nietzschean, critical/genealogical one of uncovering the historical conditions of the existence of positivist psychology and medicine. He concerns himself with the "concrete a priori" of clinical experience and medical rationality. But Foucault's critique of medical rationality is Nietzschean, rather than Kantian:

> For Kant, the possibility and necessity of a critique were linked, through certain scientific contents, to the fact that there is such a thing as knowledge. In our time—and Nietzsche the philologist testifies to it—they are linked to the fact

that language exists and that, in the innumerable words spoken by men—whether they are reasonable or senseless, demonstrative or poetic—a meaning has taken shape that hangs over us, leading us forward in our blindness, but awaiting in the darkness for us to attain awareness before emerging into the light of day and speaking.[44]

Especially when *Naissance de la clinique* appeared, Foucault most forcefully was branded a structuralist, but as Dreyfus and Rabinow insist "even at this point he was never quite a structuralist. He was not seeking *atemporal* structures, but '*historical*...conditions of possibility.'"[45] Returning to the metaphor of the lightning flash, Foucault recognizes the objectivity of the lightning, but he recognizes with Nietzsche that it is historically, practically, and discursively constituted, rather than possessing an independent, ahistorical substantiality. Foucauldian "critique of medical 'ontology'"[46] questions the historical, practical, and discursive conditions of the objectivity of the individual's body, thus revealing the concrete, historical a priori of modern, positive medicine.

As early as 1962 Foucault was talking about axes in reference to his *Histoire de la folie*. In his summary of this history in his *Maladie mentale et psychologie* Foucault explicitly recognizes two of the axes operating, but clearly he implicitly recognizes a third.[47] The emergence of the power, truth, and subject axes established the problematic Foucault found himself confronted with that called forth his explicitly Nietzschean, genealogical approach.

1. The Birth of the Asylum

   a. The Power Axis: The Space of Confinement.   Fifteen years after the publication of *Histoire de la folie*, Foucault commented, "When I think back now, I ask myself what else it was that I was talking about, in *Madness and Civilization* or *The Birth of the Clinic*, but power?"[48] Indeed he was, and the functioning of power remained one of his major preoccupations throughout his life. The major elements of his later, more developed understanding of power are present in *Histoire de la folie*. In this early work Foucault reveals power as a "police" affair concerning the ordering of individuals. Although he emphasizes the negative character of power (it excludes, it represses, it confines) in *Histoire de la folie*, he also shows it functioning in a positive manner, practically productive of the objects we encounter.

Finally, in *Histoire de la folie* as in his later writings, power is less to be understood in terms of a Leviathan model in which power is possessed and exercised from the top of a hierarchy; rather, power is revealed as a matter of Nietzschean relations of forces functioning at the level of our cultural practices, especially in transformations of spatial relations. As Foucault later put it in a 1982 interview, "Space is fundamental in any form of communal life; space is fundamental in any exercise of power."[49] Mental illness, for example, is positively produced as the object of psychology by means of the shifting formulas of exclusion, practices of confinement, and the restructuring of this social space.[50]

The reader of *Histoire de la folie* never encounters brutal, dictatorial tyranny in its all-too-familiar forms, but from very early in the text clearly he or she is confronting an account of the exercise of power: "By a strange act of force, the classical age was to reduce to silence the madness whose voices the Renaissance had just liberated, but whose violence it had already tamed."[51] Throughout the text the reader wallows in accounts of subtle movements, apparently harmless—no, apparently benevolent!—shifts in cultural practices. Power is clearly operative, but its form is unfamiliar— yet familiar. According to Foucault, confinement is a "police" matter,[52] or better, "a strange power that the King establishes between the police and the courts, at the limits of the law: a third order of repression."[53] Today we look upon classical age confinement practices as characterizing a more primitive epoch, but as nonetheless in continuity with our contemporary medical understanding of mental illness. Foucault maintains, on the contrary, that "the Hôpital Général had nothing to do with any medical concept. It was an instance of order, of the monarchical and bourgeois order being organized in France during this period."[54] Classical age confinement is a manifestation of police power, not merely in its activity of confining and excluding the Other, but also in its condemnation of idleness and corresponding imperative of labor.

The practice of confinement established an implicit contract with the madman, the poor, the unemployed. Society would shoulder the expenses for his physical sustenance, but he must accept the constraints of confinement and labor. Police power imposes order upon individuals, and order is adequate to virtue; it regiments behavior by imposing repetitive bodily movement. By means of the establishment of the houses of confinement, moral virtue, because of its identification with social order, becomes an affair of the state. Insofar as these institutions attempt to make order adequate to virtue, according to Foucault, confinement entails "a police whose order will be entirely transparent to the principles of religion, and a religion whose requirements will be satisfied without restrictions, by the regulations of the police and the constraints with which it can be armed." Confinement epitomized that police, "the civil equivalent of religion," and thus "conceals both a metaphysics of government and a politics of religion."[55]

Typically, these practices of confinement are interpreted in terms of telos. Confinement, it is assumed, represents a social mechanism with which a social group deals with heterogeneous, asocial elements. A society purchases social solidarity, it is assumed, at the price of eliminating those who fail to conform. Such an interpretation of confinement, according to Foucault, stands in a relation of affinity to one which views madness as a dimension of human nature, as part of the given psychological equipment of human beings. From this vantage point classical age confinement practices would be viewed as an early stage of the apprehension of madness—an apprehension which culminates in our contemporary medical treatment of the mad. This position assumes, in short, that the object of knowledge preexists knowledge.

But Foucault will have none of this, and in response to such teleological interpretations he most explicitly asserts the positive functioning of power. According to Foucault, the very person of the madman "has been raised up by the gesture itself of segregation.... this gesture has been the creator of alienation."[56] Classical age confinement practices ought not be understood in a merely negative fashion, in terms of social exclusion. Confinement practices have also played a positive role of organization, constituting the very being of the madman and establishing a mode of social experience. By these practices of confinement, a coherent perception is formulated, an experience is constituted, which prepares madness as an object for scientific study in our own time. Power and knowledge directly imply one another.

While it is true that a coherent perception of unreason is molded by these practices of confinement, the perception of madness undergoes a regression. The madman in the Renaissance, given the relative hospitality he was offered, played a role in society and thereby attained a certain individuality. He was a unique character among other characters. Under conditions of confinement, however, he is tossed into a more or less undifferentiated mass. Criminals, victims of venereal disease, the unproductive poor, and madmen populate the houses of confinement and meld into a uniform world of unreason. In order for a scientific psychiatry of madness to be made possible, madness must be delivered from these associations and reattain its previous individuality. In order for it to become possible for Pinel to "liberate" the madmen, madness must be freed from these associations. This prior liberation, according to Foucault, is achieved by means of the restructuring of the space of confinement; that is, madness is liberated by the restructuring of space, the transformation of power relations, a change in confinement practices, rather than by intervention of medical knowledge or enlightened reason.[57]

In the nineteenth century a cry of protest arose against confining the mad with criminals. After all, it was said, they are only innocent madmen. Foucault maintains, however, that a similar protest was issued in the eighteenth century, but it was made on behalf of the criminals and other characters who populated the houses of confinement. To be locked up with madmen, it was argued, is cruel and unusual punishment. Separations were made in response to the protest, and madness came to be more thoroughly associated with confinement; with the removal of those characters with whom madmen had previously been associated, the houses of confinement became more completely identified with madness. It is paradoxical. The condition for the attainment of medical status by madness, the condition of its possible "liberation" by Pinel and Tuke, is to embed it more deeply in the abyss of confinement.[58] The initial cries of protest against the injustice of confinement arose on behalf of all those confined—except the mad and the criminals. With the new commitment to reserve confinement exclusively for the mad and criminals, the homogeneity of the world of unreason shatters, the lack of differentiation dissolves, and madness regains its individuality.

This internal restructuring of the space of confinement coincided with external phenomena which contributed to the diminishment of confinement's population and likewise served to isolate madness. Economic and social transformations threw into question traditional politics of assistance to the poor and unemployed, and a new appreciation of poverty emerged. Under a mercantilist economy the poor had no other place but confinement; as neither producer nor consumer he had no socio-economic role to play. But with the emerging industrialization manpower was required, and the confinement of the poor and unemployed lost its meaning. Corresponding to these new economic needs resulting from changing social and economic practices, economic thought likewise transforms itself. The notion of poverty needs to be rethought. Population achieves identification with power. Only the mad and criminals, the perturbers of the labor process, merit confinement.

Thus, two independent movements, one internal to the space of confinement itself, the other external to confinement, restructure the very meaning of madness. The old associations are broken, and madness is isolated and individuated. Long before Pinel came on the scene, madness was freed in an entirely different sense—free from its old associations, "free for a perception which individualized it, free for the recognition of its unique features and for all the operations that would finally give it its status as an object." "Disengaged, not by some intervention of philanthropy, not by scientific and, at last, positive recognition of its 'truth,' but by all this slow work which is effected in the most subterranean structures of experience."[59] At this level power forms the meaning of madness as we know it.

The interpretation of Tuke's activity as liberative could hardly be further from the truth according to Foucault. His retreat maintained the segregation characteristic of the houses of confinement, but the "liberation" involved the establishment of a community resembling as closely as possible that of the Quakers. Sheltered from moral evil the sensitive soul found itself less prone to those passions which cause madness. But more importantly, for Foucault, religion in the Retreat functions as a coercive power; it plays the role of an interiorized counterforce to the power of madness: "religion can play the double role of nature and of rule, since it has assumed the depth of nature in ancestral habit, in education, in everyday exercise, and since it is at the same time a constant principle of coercion."[60]

The constraining power associated with the classical age houses of confinement has its counterpart in Tuke's Retreat. With its benevolent appearance, however, it edges more tightly into the heart of the confined. Fear becomes the essential motivating power in the asylum. An ironic reversal was accomplished: the fear-inspiring madman who led the "humanitarians" to separate him from his former colleagues in confinement is now the one maintained in a constant state of fear.

In the asylum world two practices in particular empower the inspiration of fear in the inmates: Work and the Gaze (le Regard). Since prosperity indicates God's favor, work has a central place in this Quaker religious milieu. Foucault, however, again interprets the role of work in the asylum as a manifestation of the power axis: "work possesses a constraining power superior to all forms of physical coercion, in that the regularity of the hours, the requirements of attention, the obligation to produce a result detach the sufferer from a liberty of mind that would be fatal and engage him in a system of responsibilities."[61] Work orders the disordered life by imposing regimentation upon the body of the mad. Productivity has little or nothing to do with it; in fact, the work is intentionally rendered unproductive. Productivity in the sense of producing normalized individuals has everything to do with it. Work in the asylum functions simply as "a limitation of liberty, a submission to order, an engagement of responsibility."[62]

The gaze, which will play such a central role in Foucault's studies of the birth of the medical clinic and the prison, operated for Tuke in an even more important fashion than work. It related for Tuke with what he called "the need for esteem." The staff of the Retreat would fabricate social situations for the asylum residents in order to observe their behavior. The social situation insisted upon a certain type of behavior, and the constant surveillance by the staff assured conformity to standards. The purpose of the exercise was the imposition of a normalized social personality upon the inmate. According to Foucault, "at the Retreat the partial suppression of physical constraint was part of a system whose essential element was the constitution of a 'self-restraint' in which the patient's freedom, engaged by work and the gaze of others, was ceaselessly menaced by the recognition of guilt."[63] It is important to recognize that madness in these operations is associated with observable behavior; madness is identified with the full positivity of its manifestations. Madness as interior state is silenced.

Pinel wanted to establish a religious institution without religion in his asylum; that is, he wanted to maintain the moral content of religion without any hints of the sacred. Moral uniformity among the inmates stood as his goal—to reduce differences, repress vice, and eliminate irregularities. The power axis manifests itself in Pinel's total administration of the lives of the asylum inhabitants. All behavior of the keepers, physicians, and inmates was ruthlessly organized for the sake of bringing about uniform moral conduct. Foucault points out three power techniques characteristic of Pinel's asylum. First, Pinel imposed silence as a replacement for chains. Having spent twelve years in chains, an excommunicated ecclesiastic who believed he was Christ was one of the first to be released from bondage by Pinel—only to be replaced in a new, more subtle form of bondage. Pinel ordered that a shroud of silence be imposed upon the man; no one was to speak even a word to him: "This prohibition, which was rigorously observed, produced upon this self-intoxicated creature an effect much more perceptible than irons and the dungeon; he felt humiliated in an abandon and an isolation so new to him amid his freedom."[64] It worked; he slowly assumed a more conformist demeanor.

   Pinel's second technique is referred to by Foucault as "recognition by mirror." By means of this technique the madman is brought to observe and recognize his own madness. The keeper's gaze, so important at Tuke's Retreat, now, in Pinel's asylum, is imposed by the madman upon himself. First, the madman was led to observe the manifestation of madness in those around him and to condemn their foolish pretensions. Then he is brought to observe the same manifestations in himself. "He is now pitilessly observed by himself. And in the silence of those who represent reason, and who have done nothing but hold up the perilous mirror, he recognizes himself as objectively mad." Having been freed from its classical age chains, madness in the asylum "imprisoned itself in an infinitely self-referring gaze."[65]

   Finally, Pinel's techniques for dealing with the asylum inmates included perpetual judgment which unified the previous two: "By this play of mirrors, as by silence, madness is ceaselessly called upon to judge itself."[66] Foucault emphasizes the "juridical microcosm" that Pinel established at the asylum. Judge, jury, and executioner must be ever-present on the mind of the inmate; he must be forever conscious of the realm of justice to which he belongs, and omnipresent judgment of his behavior suffices. In a fascinating comparison of "reform" asylum practices and classical age confinement practices, Foucault reveals, in a very Nietzschean manner, the way in which power practices persist from age to age while losing and gaining meaning; the practices persist while their interpretations are transformed.

   During the classical age certain methods intended to be therapeutic, such as baths and showers, were employed for the mad. By a strange and perverse twist, in the age of Pinel the formerly therapeutic and non-punitive practices are transformed into techniques of chastisement.[67] Baths and showers, in the context of classical age understanding of the nervous system, were appreciated as having therapeutic value: refreshment and relaxation had been the hoped for, if not anticipated, result. The same practice, however, attained a purely juridical interpretation under the eye of Pinel: showers and baths became "the habitual punishment of the ordinary police tribunal" which dominated the asylum.[68] According to Foucault, "Everything was organized so that the madman would recognize himself in a world of judgment that enveloped him on all sides; he must know that he is watched, judged, and condemned; from transgression to punishment, the connection must be evident, as a guilt recognized by all."[69]

b. The Subject Axis: One Becomes Mad Because One Wants to Be. How, Foucault asks, was modern individuality fabricated through these confinement practices and the general treatment of the insane? As was the case for the power axis, the moral problematization of madness provides the context for appreciating the role of the subject axis. The moral problematization of madness in history contributes to the constitution of the modern individual of psychological inwardness.

In the fifteenth century the preoccupation of the literary and artistic imagination of Europe shifted. Previously, death had dominated. But toward the end of the century madness replaced death as the prevalent theme. Fear of death and the nothingness of human existence "turns inward." "What is in question," according to Foucault, "is still the nothingness of existence, but his nothingness is no longer considered an external, final term, both threat and conclusion; it is experienced from within as the continuous and constant form of existence."[70] In madness death's nothingness invades human interiority. The central accomplishment of the Renaissance in the history of madness, according to Foucault, was to disengage madness from the world and to link it instead to man, "to his weaknesses, dreams, and illusions." After the Renaissance, "madness no longer lies in wait for mankind at the four corners of the earth; it insinuates itself within man, or rather it is a subtle rapport that man maintains with himself."[71] This relation with himself, self-attachment, provides the foundation of the vices, and thereby, madness's source. The self-attached person willingly accepts error as truth.

The classical age indiscriminately confined personalities that we see as quite diverse; their commonality in the classical age is to be attributed to the moral consciousness that was in the process of being fabricated at the time. The treatment of the poor in the houses of confinement provides a good example to illuminate the subtle procedures by which the modern individual has been shaped. The Catholic response to poverty at this time, like the response of Luther's and Calvin's Reformation, also undergoes an interesting shift. Having come around to accept confinement as an appropriate response to the problem of poverty, the Catholic church made a separation within the realm of poverty.

The medieval church had viewed this world as sacred in its totality, but the church of the classical age distinguished "good paupers" from "bad paupers." The pauper who submitted and lived in conformity with the established order was declared good; the one who was not submissive and who sought to escape from this established order was designated bad. "The first accepts confinement and finds there his repose; the second refuses it, and consequently deserves it."[72] Foucault maintains that this separation of good and bad poverty is essential to the meaning of classical age confinement. Confinement is interpreted as a place of beneficence or as a place of repression depending upon the moral attitude that the poor person manifests, and the same ethical categorization will come to be applied to the mad. "Everyone confined is placed in the field of this ethical valorisation—and well before being an object of knowledge (connaissance) or of pity, he is treated as a *moral subject*."[73]

The relationship between the moral problematization of madness and the constitution of the modern individual emerges more clearly when we examine the role of intentions in the classical age ethical consciousness. The treatment of people with venereal disease provides a good illustration: their treatment is immersed in a whole ceremonial of confession of sin, penance, and moral chastisement. They are dealt with as subjects of correction. The plague, venereal disease, had lost much of the apocalyptic character it once had, and in the classical age it designates a culpability localized in the intentions of the individual. The origin of venereal disease is in the "disordered heart" rather than in the body. The origin of venereal disease is sin; i.e., sin "defined by the deliberate intention to sin.... Evil is no longer perceived in the destiny of the world; it is reflected in the transparent law of a logic of intentions."[74] Madness, too, lost its apocalyptic character. It was no longer sought at the far corners of the world where it had been deposited by the fools' ships. It became localized in human intentions, psychological interiority, the inwardness of the modern individual.

This union of the sins of the flesh and the sins against reason, the association of victims of venereal disease and the mad, renders intelligible the classical age confinement of libertines. Their confinement sheds light on the historical constitution of modern individuality. Foucault calls Bonaventure Forcroy "one of the last of the erudite libertines, or one of the first *philosophes* in the eighteenth century sense of the term," and in Forcroy's case again we see an example of the classical age process of desacralization."[75] Forcroy wrote his *Doutes sur la religion* and *Vie d'Apollonius de Thyane* against the Christian miracle accounts and declared natural law the only true religion. Such libertinage could have expected burning at the stake for blasphemy, but Forcroy was placed in confinement. His crime was not of the religious order; rather, his writings were viewed as bearing a certain relation to immorality and error. Confinement was intended to impose a moral order upon him, and such conditions, it was assumed, would lead him to recognize the truth and the error of his ways.

Libertinage became part of the uniform world of unreason. In the eighteenth century libertinage did not imply freedom of thought or freedom of morals, according to Foucault. Instead, it connoted a condition of servitude whereby reason becomes the servant of desires. Libertinage meant that reason had become the heart's servant. Thus is born, Foucault tells us, "the great theme of a madness which follows, not the free path of fantasy, but the line of constraint of the heart, of the passions, and finally of human nature."[76] Madness is being wedged more deeply into the interior of man: "For a long time the mad had borne the marks of the inhuman. One finds now an unreason very near man, faithful to the determinations of his nature, an unreason which is the abandonment of man to himself."[77]

In the context of emphasizing the minimal role played by medicine in the judgment regarding madness, Foucault reveals the contrast between the juridical consciousness of madness and the practical experience of madness embodied in its chief resource, the house of confinement. According to the juridical consciousness of madness, the madman is treated as a subject of law in a system of obligations. As such, the madman is considered absolved of responsibility to the degree to which he is mad.[78] In contrast, the practical experience of madness embedded in the house of confinement involves regarding the individual as a social being. From this perspective the madman must be seen in terms of the moral relations that justify his exclusion from the free community. While as a subject of law the madman is viewed as free of responsibility insofar as he is mad, the justification of his confinement requires that he be appreciated in a context of culpability. Each of these forms of consciousness of madness operates in the eighteenth century preparing our contemporary medical experience of madness as mental illness.

It is essential for Foucault that one understand that in the classical age "madness becomes perceptible in the form of the ethical."[79] This is crucial for understanding the subject axis because the moralization of madness inserts the problem ever more deeply into human interiority, constituting that interiority. During the classical age, "It is in the quality of the will, and not in the integrity of reason, that finally resides the secret of madness.... Throughout the Middle Ages, and for a longtime through the course of the Renaissance, madness had been linked with Evil, but under the form of imaginary transcendences; henceforth, it communicates with them by the most secret way of individual choice and of evil intention."[80]

In the world of confinement, unlike in the world governed by judicial consciousness, madness excuses nothing. Instead, by an act of will, by the individual's evil intention, madness complies with evil, multiplies it, and makes it more dangerous. Judicial consciousness drew a distinction between inauthentic and authentic alienation so as to avoid punishing someone whose crime is due to madness. In the houses of confinement no such distinction is made; both are viewed as of the same origin, and one passes from one to the other by means of an act of individual will. In the practical consciousness of madness encrusted in the houses of confinement, the constitution of culpability and of individuality walk hand in hand. One becomes mad because one wants to be.

And the madman is judged as mad in an immediate, spontaneous apprehension of the common citizen who recognizes the difference. It is simply good sense that reveals madness in difference. Because madness has been moralized, moreover, the common citizen's reaction to madness's difference is one of scandal. Deviant behavior directs the citizen's attention to its origin in the perverse will, the corrupt intention, and thus, according to Foucault, "Psychological interiority has been constituted from the exteriority of the scandalized consciousness."[81] Individual psychology results from the eruption of scandal in social consciousness: "The purely moral space, which is then defined, gives the exact measurements of that psychological inwardness where modern man seeks both his depth and his truth."[82]

In a somewhat controversial analysis[83] Foucault argues that there is a counterpart, expressed in philosophical literature, to this localization of madness in the perversity of the will. The individuality being constituted in classical age confinement practices has its counterpart in Cartesian subjectivity. In Descartes' method of doubt and its steady progression toward the truth, madness is powerless. Madness fails to sabotage the movement of doubt because, insofar as the doubt is methodic and therefore willed, madness is excluded by the methodological decision of the philosopher. Madness may linger and tempt, just as sleepiness and sloppiness may tempt, but insofar as the doubt is methodical it "is enveloped in this will to alertness which is, at each instant, willingly tearing out the complacency of madness." Methodical doubt systematically excludes "the Nietzschean possibility of the mad philosopher."[84] Thus, the doubt and alertness of Cartesian meditation and the quest for truth are themselves products of individual will, personal intention. The Cogito itself is an implication of the will; the Cogito itself is the result of a prior choice between reason and unreason. All serious thought has as its basis a moral intention on the part of the individual to will against unreason.[85] Madness is likewise a choice which emerges from the intention of the moral individual.

The "liberation" effected by Tuke and Pinel, according to Foucault, simply forwarded the interiorization of madness. The fear which prevailed in classical confinement is interiorized in the modern asylum.[86] The anguish of responsibility inserted into the interior of the madman transforms him into his own keeper. The fabrication of the morally normalized individual is the asylum's task.

 c. The Truth Axis: The Critical Experience of Madness. Our contemporary experience of madness has lost much of this moralistic tone. Even the word "madness" rarely surfaces in polite conversation; what previous generations referred to as "madness" we now call "mental illness." The phenomenon is now a medical, not a moral, problematic. How did madness come to be so problematized? How did madness become a problem of psychology rather than morality? How did it come to be problematized in terms of truth? Based upon the prior constitution of madness as a moral experience, according to Foucault, modern man has been authorized to found our science of man, psychology.

 An apparent coherence characterizes Renaissance expressions concerning madness. There seems to be a consistency, whether these expressions take a plastic or literary form; *Narrenschiff* names both Bosch's painting and Brant's poem. According to Foucault, however, we ought not be misled by this apparent coherence. "Between word and image," he maintains, "between what is depicted by language and what is uttered by plastic form, the unity begins to dissolve."[87] What emerges, even this early, is the opposition between a cosmic/tragic experience of madness and a critical experience of madness. Renaissance painting expressed the tragic proximity of madness—the experience of being drawn to madness's fascinating power. The literary experience of madness, on the other hand, is characterized by irony and a critical distance; discourse disarms madness's fascination. "Whatever obscure cosmic manifestation there was in madness as seen by Bosch," Foucault tells us, "is wiped out in Erasmus."[88] And by the early seventeenth century and the emerging classical age of confinement the confrontation between the cosmic experience and the tragic experience of madness was decided. More and more, madness became immersed in discourse and thereby domesticated. By the middle of the seventeenth century the critical experience of madness triumphed. Banished from the light of day, madness nonetheless survives, flashing on the fringes in the works of Sade, in Van Gogh's visions, in Nietzsche's final postcards.

The practical experience of madness embedded in the houses of confinement entails treating the madman as a social being. In order to justify the madman's exclusion from the free community, he must be seen in terms of a set of moral relations and culpability for having transgressed the code governing such relations. In contrast, according to the juridical consciousness of madness, the madman is viewed as a subject of law, and he is considered absolved of responsibility to the degree to which he is mad. Throughout the classical age, according to Foucault, "The law will indefinitely refine its analysis of madness; and, in a sense, it is just to say that it is on the ground of a juridical experience of alienation that the medical science of mental illness is constituted."[89] So as not to punish unjustly the one whose crime arose from the affliction of madness rather than from choice, it was necessary for the law rigorously to distinguish authentic and inauthentic madness. The truth of madness became a crucial issue for the juridical consciousness, and many of the structures of later psychopathology already appear in the formulations of seventeenth-century jurisprudence. Mental illness, which is here being constituted as an object for medical perception and science, according to Foucault, slowly emerges "as the mythical unity of the juridically incapable subject, and of the man recognized as a perturber of the group: and this under the political and moral thought of the eighteenth century."[90]

Foucault distinguishes the structures of the reasonable from the structures of the rational. In a new form of consciousness which emerged in the course of the classical age, he tells us, a new double relationship was established between reason and madness. On the one hand, madness exists *par rapport* to the structures of the reasonable; i.e., madness exists and is recognized in relation to the anonymous mass who represent the reasonableness of common sense. It is recognized by contrast, as the other of reason par excellence; it is reason's negative. On the other hand, madness exists "*sous le regard*" of the structures of rationality; in full positivity, individualized, with its own proper characteristics, behavior, and language, madness stands under the gaze of rationality.

What takes place in the eighteenth century, however, according to Foucault, is "a slipping of perspectives:" "the structures of the reasonable and those of the rational are inserted into one another, in order to form, finally, a web in which it will no longer be possible for a long time to distinguish them from one another."[91] And here we see the distinctive characteristic of the eighteenth century in unreason's history. The negative moral judgment of reason against madness offers a full positive content to medical rationality. The moral problematization of madness thus gives way to the problematization of madness in terms of truth: "Pure difference, stranger *par excellence,* 'other' to the second power, the madman, in this recoil itself, will become the object of rational analysis, plenitude offered to knowledge (*connaissance*), evident perception; and it will be this [the object of rational analysis—positivity] in the measure precisely in which it is that [difference, stranger, other—negativity]."[92] Madness remains the absence of reason, but an absence in the form of positivity.

"The eighteenth century perceives the madman," according to Foucault, "but deduces madness."[93] Paradoxically, the perceived negativity of the madman is being reconstituted as full positivity, as a fully natural and logical domain to be studied as one studies nature itself. The eighteenth century is in the process of detaching itself from a metaphysic of evil as privation. The language of "morbific substances" replaces the notion of "illness by privation." "In order to give a particular content to the illness," Foucault tells us, "it is necessary to address oneself to real, observable, positive phenomena by which it is manifest."[94] Moral negativity is dissected and classified in terms of its truth.

> If it is true that from the side of man, illness is a sign of disorder, of finitude, of sin, from the side of God who created them, which is to say from the side of their truth, illnesses are a reasonable vegetation. And medical thought ought to give itself to the task of escaping these pathetic categories of chastisement, in order to have access to those, really pathological, from which illness discovers its eternal truth.[95]

Among the categories employed in the eighteenth century for the classification of madness, one in particular stands out: the category of delirium. With tremendous synthetic power it unifies the experience of madness. The problem was that the task of organizing illnesses was never accomplished at the level of the madman and his madness. Madness itself, Foucault tells us, "cannot bear witness to its own truth."[96] Madness could only be approached by some form of mediation; that is, the intervention of either a moral judgment or a physical causal analysis was necessary. But a moral judgment implies that madness be approached in terms of liberty, and a physical causal analysis implies an approach in terms of necessity. Foucault assures us, however, that the antinomy is only apparent. By means of the category of delirium "the moral and the mechanical, liberty and the body, passion and pathology"[97] are localized and unified in the imagination. The imagination is the locale of madness's errors, yet equally the place of synthesis of the body's mechanisms. The perturbed body and the guilty mind unify in the common classical age theory of the imagination as delirious. The category of delirium carries such synthetic power that Foucault speaks of "a transcendence of delirium."[98] And in delirium, according to Foucault, "which is of both body and soul, of both language and image, of both grammar and physiology,... all the cycles of madness conclude and begin. It is this delirium whose rigorous meaning organized them from the start. It is madness itself, and also, beyond each of its phenomena, its silent transcendence, which constitute the truth of madness."[99]

With his analysis of delirium Foucault emphasizes that madness is not a substance which awaited detection throughout history. The transcendence of delirium, instead, provided unity and coherence for multiple images, qualities, and phenomena allowing their problematization in terms of truth. Such is likewise the case for mania and melancholy:

> If mania, if melancholia henceforth assumed the aspects our science knows them by, it is not because in the course of centuries we have learned to "open our eyes" to real symptoms; it is not because we have purified our perception to the point of transparency; it is because in the experience of madness, these concepts were organized around certain qualitative themes that lent them their unity, gave them their significant coherence, made them finally perceptible.[100]

The procedure was not a movement from perception to explanation. Instead, the syntheses were accomplished by means of images. The organizing power of images "made possible a structure of perception, in which at last the symptoms could attain their significant value and be organized as the visible presence of truth."[101]

Another stage in the problematization of madness in terms of truth occurred in the middle of the eighteenth century. What Foucault calls "the great fear" arose, and once again the synthetic agents consisted not of theoretical or medical categories but of fantastic images. A mysterious disease was said to have spread from the houses of confinement to the cities. The air was said to be the culprit, which fits quite well with the moral and medical mythology concerning the benefits of pure country air prevailing at the time. Much of the imagery of the age of leprosy returned, and with the great fear unreason and disease are unified at last. According to Foucault, "it is in the realm of the fantastic and not within the rigor of medical thought that unreason joins illness and draws closer to it. Long before the problem of discovering to what degree the unreasonable as pathological was formulated, there had formed, in the space of confinement and by an alchemy peculiar to it, a mélange combining the dread of unreason and the old specters of disease."[102] Madness was confronted by medical thought and problematized in terms of its truth, not because of advances in the field of medicine, but because of the reactivation of images long forgotten with the closing of the leprosariums. Regression rather than progress accounts for medicine's appropriation of madness. Regression contributes to the constitution of madness as a truth problematic.

At Tuke's Retreat the physical constraint of the houses of confinement gave way to an interiorized self-restraint. Perpetual observation and the regimentation of work regulated the patients' behavior. We saw in our study of the subject axis just how important intentionality was in the houses of confinement. In Tuke's Retreat intentions are irrelevant. Madness in the Retreat "is judged only by its acts; it is not accused of intentions, nor are its secrets to be fathomed. Madness is responsible only for that part of itself which is visible. All the rest is reduced to silence. Madness no longer exists except as *seen*."[103] This reduction of madness to the visible, according to Foucault, is the condition of the possibility of dealing with madness as a truth problematic, the condition of the possibility of the positivist psychology of madness of the nineteenth century. Observation and classification characterize the science of mental illness as developed in the asylum, and in order for such a science to exist madness had to be reduced to merely the observable and classifiable.

2. The Birth of the Clinic

Nietzsche the philologist, according to the Foucault of 1966, was "the first to connect the philosophical task with a radical reflection upon language,"[104] and in his own critique of medical ontology Foucault turns his attention to discourse on disease: "The research that I am undertaking here therefore involves a project that is deliberately both historical and critical, in that it is concerned— outside all prescriptive intent—with determining the conditions of possibility of medical experience in modern times.... It is a structural study that sets out to disentangle the conditions of its history from the density of discourse, as do others of my works."[105] Foucault reveals that the emergence of anatomo-clinical medicine resulted from a much more complex and disparate historical process than enlightened medicine's own narrative would allow. The reorganization of medical practices, transformations in medical discourse, and changes in social attitudes toward sickness and health all converged to bring about a *"formal* reorganization, *in depth,"* that made clinical experience possible.[106]

In the first sentence of the "Preface" to *Naissance de la clinique* Foucault starkly declares his program: "This book is about space, about language, and about death; it is about the act of seeing, the gaze."[107] In a rudimentary form what Foucault will later refer to as the three genealogical axes—power, truth, and the subject—operate in this 1963 work in his discussions of space, language, and death. First, as we saw in the discussion of *Histoire de la folie,* power functioned in the spatial reorganization of the houses of confinement. Similarly, in *Naissance de la clinique* the spatialization of disease offers access to the power axis. Secondly, language provides a wedge into the truth axis. In order for Western man to constitute himself as a positive object for a true science of medicine, he had first to grasp himself within his own language and give himself, "in himself and by himself, a discursive existence."[108] Thirdly, according to Foucault, by the introduction of autopsy into medical practice death made possible the constitution of the individual as the object of science. Death is the "concrete *a priori"* of a medical experience in which modern man is both subject and object of his own knowledge.

a. The Power Axis: The Spatialization of Disease. Foucault characterizes eighteenth-century medicine as a medicine of species, typified by the classification of diseases. In order for the clinical medicine of the nineteenth century to be made possible, the three ways in which classificatory medicine of species was spatialized had to undergo a transformation. The primary spatialization of disease in eighteenth-century medicine involved mapping the diseases on the nosological table, thereby identifying their species. The individual patient was accidental to the disease, and the physician's task entailed disregarding any unique features of the particular patient in order to allow that which was essential in the disease to manifest itself. Classification of disease on the noso-logical table demanded the disease's free development, and this entailed abstracting the patient's uniqueness, as well as any unau-thorized intervention of the physician. In the primary spatializa-tion of disease physician and patient are tolerated as unavoidable disturbances.

Secondary spatialization, in contrast, exaggerates the role of the individual patient. The space of classificatory medicine is flat and homogeneous, yet the disease is actually concretely embodied in a living organism with mass and volume. The problem of sec-ondary spatialization of the pathological concerns the relation between the species of the disease and the particular organism in which it is located. An attention to the individual and the qualities of phenomena in the particular organism is required in this sec-ondary spatialization of disease: "A subtle perception of qualities, a perception of the differences between one case and another, a deli-cate perception of variants—a whole hermeneutics of the pathologi-cal fact, based on modulated, coloured experience, is required; one should measure variations, balances, excesses, and defects."[109] As the source of qualitative variations in the course of the illness, the individual patient drew renewed attention from the physician mak-ing possible a transformation of medical perception itself.

Tertiary spatialization refers to the social space of medical institutions and medical practices;[110] it includes "all the gestures by which, in a given society, a disease is circumscribed, medically invested, isolated, divided up into closed, privileged regions, or dis-tributed throughout cure centres, arranged in the most favorable way." It is the locale where the micro-practices of the power axis are most clearly observed, where disease is inserted into social, politi-cal, and economic space. In his discussion of tertiary spatialization Foucault reveals how medical space came to coincide with social space, how medical space came to "traverse" and "wholly penetrate" social space, how the medicalization of society as a whole was accomplished.[111] As Foucault put it in a 1976 interview, "Medical power is at the heart of the society of normalization."[112] Transforma-tions in tertiary spatialization, according to Foucault, overturned the whole of medical experience "and defined for its most concrete perceptions, new dimensions, and a new foundation."[113]

Consistent with the notion that the uniqueness of the individ-ual patient was accidental to the disease, eighteenth-century medicine of species required a simple and free social space which would allow the disease to run its true and natural course, thereby revealing its essence for classification. Inserted into a more complex social space disease takes on the complexity and fails to run its natural course. The higher the degree of civilization reached, it was thought, the more the health of the population diminishes. In a complex society diseases unite, complicate one another, and conceal their essences.

Similarly, the hospital provides a much too complex social space for eighteenth-century theory of disease. An artificial space which places diseases in the presence of one another, the hospital causes crossbreeding and conceals the essence of each disease. The hospital, moreover, endangers the health of each patient by situating him in a space of exposure to innumerable other diseases. Eighteenth-century medical theory required a natural social space—the family: "gentle, spontaneous care, expressive of love and a common desire for a cure, assists nature in its struggle against the illness, and allows the illness itself to attain its own truth."[114] And the distribution of public assistance followed this logic. The hospital foundations' funds, originally intended to assist the poor in large institutions, were redistributed in a "generalized system of assistance."[115] Families rather than hospitals became the beneficiaries.

But an interesting inversion was thereby accomplished. The sick, once grouped in centralized institutions, are distributed throughout the society as a whole, and medical care and assistance must follow. The national task of public health penetrates the very fabric of society, threading its way into the structure of the family. The redistribution of the sick, and the corresponding redistribution of health care and assistance, require a "generalized vigilance."[116] The national task of public health demands the general medicalization of society. "The medicine of individual perception, of family assistance, of home care," according to Foucault, "can be based only on a collectively controlled structure, or on one that is integrated into the social space in its entirety."[117]

Further penetration of medical perception into the social body developed with a growing consciousness of epidemics, and a new spatialization of disease emerged. Since, in itself, an epidemic did not differ essentially from an individual disease except in terms of quantity, the number of times it struck in a particular time and place, time and space came to determine the "essential basis" of the epidemic. The epidemic's essential basis is, for example, Marseilles in 1721, Bicêtre in 1780, or Rouen in 1769.[118] This new spatialization of disease creates a new analysis and a deeper intrusion of medical perception into society. "The analysis of an epidemic," according to Foucault, "does not involve the recognition of the general form of the disease, by placing it in the abstract space of nosology, but the rediscovery, beneath the general signs, of the particular process, which varies according to circumstances from one epidemic to another, and which weaves from the cause to the morbid form a web common to all the sick, but peculiar to this moment in time and this place in space."[119]

The epidemic's temporal and spatial uniqueness demands corresponding complexity in its observation: "Being a collective phenomenon, it requires a multiple gaze; a unique process, it must be described in terms of its special, accidental, unexpected qualities. The event must be described in detail, but it must also be described in accordance with the coherence implied by multi-perception...."[120] With greater organization, further dispersion of physicians into society, and communication with centralized authorities, this new type of medical experience became institutionalized. The fulfillment of this new medical experience, however, only is realized with the complete penetration of the social body by a police. Surveillance of treatment of the dead, of transactions involving food and housing, directives concerning personal hygiene and dress, information gathering, all became tasks assigned to a widely dispersed police force. According to Foucault, this resulted in "the definition of a political status for medicine and the constitution, at state level, of a medical consciousness whose constant task would be to provide information, supervision, and constraint, all of which 'relate as much to the police as to the field of medicine proper.'"[121]

Further police activity included the establishment of the Royal Society of Medicine, essentially intended for gathering and disseminating medical information concerning epidemics but with the added responsibility of policing medical practitioners. "Thus," according to Foucault, "a double check was set up: that of the political authorities over the practice of medicine and that of a privileged medical body over the practitioners as a whole."[122] As the Society's role expanded, it centralized knowledge and medical authority, required registration, and exercised judgment over medical practice. Medical space more deeply penetrates social space: "One began to conceive of a generalized presence of doctors whose intersecting gazes form a network and exercise at every point in space, and at every moment in time, a constant, mobile, differentiated surveillance."[123]

Two apparently contradictory myths circulated around the time of the Revolution, but Foucault insists that the two are in fact isomorphic. First, the "myth of a nationalized medical profession" in which the physician would function for the body in a manner analogous to the clergy's relation to the soul, and secondly, the "myth of a total disappearance of disease in an untroubled, dispassionate society restored to its original state of health."[124] These myths, according to Foucault, merely represent two sides, the positive and negative, of the same coin.[125] From the point of view of either myth the physician's first task is political: to penetrate the fabric of society and to battle bad government. Because they have thoroughly penetrated the social body in line with the first myth, physicians are prime candidates for judging governmental structures, as suggested by the second myth.[126] This creates "a spontaneous and deeply rooted convergence between the requirements of *political ideology* and those of *medical technology*."[127]

Eighteenth-century medicine of species was characterized by classification of diseases in order to negate these infirmities—what Foucault refers to as "the dubious negation of the negative."[128] With the transformations in medicine and society which occurred late in the century, and with the spatial reorganization of medical practice, medicine took on a positive significance. Although he is not explicitly stating the case at this stage of his work, in *Naissance de la clinique* Foucault's analysis of the power axis clearly reveals power's positive functioning. No longer merely negating negations, late eighteenth-century medicine is positively constituting a definition of the model human being. It prescribes a positive regime of living to ensure health and virtue: "In the ordering of human existence it assumes a normative posture, which authorizes it not only to distribute advice as to healthy life, but also to dictate the standards for physical and moral relations of the individual and of the society in which he lives."[129] Its investigations and prescriptions intervene in all aspects of common life: from the workplace to the marriage bed, from the library to the theater, from the kitchen to the dining room, medicine orders human existence. And since the functioning of its power is neither negative nor repressive, medicine's prescribed regime of living receives a warm welcome from the social body.

   b. The Truth Axis: The Verbalization of Disease.   The distinction between symptoms and signs provided a key to the observation of disease in eighteenth-century medicine of species. Symptoms, while not identical with the essence of the disease, are closest to it; the disease presents itself in symptoms, and the physician's task is to decipher the essence from the presented symptoms. Disease shows itself in its symptoms. Signs, however, maintain a greater distance from the essence of the disease. Signs announce rather than make visible. Late in the eighteenth century, however, the distinction—sign, symptom, essence—collapses.[130] With the collapse of this distinction, so central to eighteenth-century medicine of species, disease becomes completely visible to clinical observation; it is nothing more than the aggregate of its symptoms. Decipherment of its essence from its manifest symptoms is no longer necessary; the disease itself is available for complete description.

But Foucault's central point is not to be missed. He is not simply recounting enlightened medicine's own story of its development, whereby medicine advanced by means of a renewed respect for the empirical beneath the confusion of theory and superstition. In fact, Foucault claims that philosophical theory and medical practice, late in the eighteenth century, coincided and came to be dominated by the model of language. "The doctor's discursive, reflective perception and the philosopher's discursive reflexion on perception come together in a figure of exact superposition, since *the world is for them the analogue of language.*"[131]

Foucault recounts the three stage process whereby the sign/symptom/essence distinction collapsed and disease emerged into the light of language. First, the symptom no longer functions as "sovereign indicator"[132] because the disease itself comes to be completely identified with phenomena. Physicians no longer search for essences beneath the symptoms. Instead, symptoms, as pure, immediate phenomena manifesting change from the state of health, are observed in opposition to non-pathological phenomena. "By this simple opposition to the forms of health," according to Foucault, "the symptom abandons its passivity as a natural phenomenon and becomes a signifier of the disease, that is, of itself taken as a whole, since the disease is simply a collection of symptoms."[133] Secondly, with a new sensitivity on the part of the physician to "difference, simultaneity or succession, and frequency" symptoms become signs.[134] For a physician with honed skills, symptoms can be read like a primitive, natural language. Finally, through the intervention of the descriptive act the "fundamental isomorphism" of the structures of the disease and of language manifests itself; "To the exhaustive presence of the disease in its symptoms corresponds the unobstructed transparency of the pathological being with the syntax of a descriptive language."[135] A fundamental isomorphism of the "to be seen" and the "to be spoken" is established. The world itself having become the analogue of language, the complete unity of the visible and the expressible is rendered possible. "The gaze of observation and the things it perceives communicate through the same Logos...."[136]

In the clinic the place of encounter of physician and patient is laden with discourse in which the truth of disease manifests itself. Examination procedures relied from the start on the use of questionnaires, ensuring a role for language in the examination. A to-and-fro of observation and interrogation of the patient, combined with precise description, characterize the physician-patient encounter. In this play of speech and gaze, according to Foucault, "the disease gradually declares its truth...."[137] In the spirit of Condillac's goal of an ideal language as the key to an ideal science, medical practice committed itself to precise designation and exhaustive description whose purpose was an "exhaustive and complete passage from the *totality of the visible* to the *over-all structure of the expressible*."[138]

With this dovetailing of speech and gaze, of the visible and the expressible, the clinic reveals its virtues as a pedagogical domain. The coincidence in the clinic of both observation and teaching results from the underlying postulate which structures clinical experience: "that all that is *visible* is *expressible*, and that it is *wholly visible* because it is *wholly expressible*."[139] The manifestation of the disease's truth, put into discourse, renders possible initiation into this truth.[140] At this point, we cannot be further from eighteenth-century medicine of species. There is no discernment of essences, no deciphering of symptoms, no burrowing beneath phenomena. Disease has been dragged into the light of day—or better, to use Foucault's expression, "the light of language."[141]

Appearances suggest enlightened medicine's own narrative of its origins: that physicians at last liberated themselves from superstition, from theory, and allowed the unprejudiced gaze free reign. Foucault's analysis, however, insists on the reverse. The fundamental transformation does not entail "an act of psychological and epistemological purification"; instead, the "forms of visibility" have undergone transformation.[142] The new coincidence of the visible and the expressible forms the historical, concrete a priori of modern medical perception. For modern medical perception to become possible it was necessary "to open up language to a whole new domain: that of a perpetual and objectively based correlation of the visible and the expressible."[143]

The correlation of the visible and the expressible echoes an earlier identification formulated in antiquity between the beautiful and the intelligible. Nietzsche called it aesthetic Socratism whose law is, "'To be beautiful everything must be intelligible,' as the counterpart to the Socratic dictum, 'Knowledge is virtue.'"[144] In the hands of Euripides aesthetic Socratism drove one of the final nails into the coffin of Greek tragedy. Foucault claimed in *Histoire de la folie* that the refusal, the silencing, the forgetting of tragedy stands at the foundation of Western culture, and here in *Naissance de la clinique* we encounter what is at least a suggestion that in this work, too, Foucault continues to trace the history of this silencing of tragic experience.

   c. The Subject Axis: Death and the Individual. "Death left its old tragic heaven and became the lyrical core of man."[145] In this cryptic comment Foucault captures his insight into the constitution of the individual as the object of medical perception.

   Enlightened medicine's own narrative of its origins insists that its progress was hindered by religious, moral, and superstitious prohibitions against the performance of autopsies. Medicine's scientific basis in pathological anatomy could be won only by circumventing these obstacles. Tales are told of grave robbing and surreptitious autopsies performed in cemeteries. "With the coming of the Enlightenment," however, "death, too, was entitled to the clear light of reason, and became for the philosophical mind an object and source of knowledge."[146]

   Foucault maintains, however, that the historical data cannot sustain this account. Autopsies were not uncommon, and were in fact encouraged, in the mid-eighteenth century. Institutional obstacles to the dissection of corpses were minimal.[147] Foucault insists the obstacles were not external but internal to medical practice itself. Physicians engaged in medicine of species simply could not see the relevance of lesions in a corpse for determining the essence of a disease. The essence of a disease could only be deciphered from the observation of surface symptoms. Only with the collapse of the sign/symptom/essence distinction could clinical practice and pathological anatomy achieve alignment.[148]

   The individual played no role in the primary spatialization of disease in eighteenth-century medicine of species. Allowing the essence of the disease to manifest itself entailed treating the individual as accidental to his own infirmity. But with the restructuring of clinical experience (cases) and with the integration of pathological anatomy (death) the status of the individual undergoes a transformation. The Aristotelian prescription against a science of the individual is overcome, and the individual body is given to knowledge.

With the abandonment of the search for essences, clinical medicine gave up its attempt to attain the perspective of the ideal observer. In eighteenth-century medicine of species the task was to determine qualities of diseases; a mathematical model of knowledge was irrelevant to such a task. At the end of the eighteenth century, however, probabalistic reasoning was introduced with the collapse of the sign/symptom/essence distinction. "This conceptual transformation was decisive," according to Foucault: "it opened up to investigation a domain in which each fact, observed, isolated, then compared with a set of facts, could take its place in a whole series of events whose convergence or divergence were in principle measurable."[149] The ideal of knowledge entailed the accumulation of individual events; the series of individual pathological facts required examination. Numerous physicians examine series of concrete, individual cases. In other words, all that medicine of species ignored in its quest for essences becomes the focus of late eighteenth-century clinical medicine. Multiple observers replace the transcendent Ideal Observer. The individual patient as a complex pathological event takes center stage in the new clinical medicine.

The integration of death into clinical experience provides the fulcrum for the definitive insertion of the individual into medical knowledge. This, according to Foucault, constitutes "the great break in the history of Western medicine."[150] In autopsy the invisible depths of the individual body can be brought to light; it enables what was once merely a surface gaze to penetrate to the hidden interior. Death provides "the point of view from the height of which disease opened up onto truth."[151] Medicine's problem until the end of the eighteenth century, according to Foucault, consisted of finding a way to articulate the relation between disease and life. Death intervened, through pathological anatomy, to provide the third term between life and disease, forming a new conceptual trinity. "It is not because he falls ill that man dies; fundamentally, it is because he may die that man may fall ill;"[152] thus Foucault concretely expresses the conceptual transformation in the life/disease/death relation. "From the moment death was introduced into a technical and conceptual organon, disease was able to be both spatialized and individualized. Space and individual, two associated structures deriving necessarily from a death-bearing perception."[153]

With the integration of pathological anatomy into clinical experience, medical practice, especially diagnostic practices, became, in a sense, an attempt to anticipate the autopsy. The notion of a sign obtains a new meaning: a sign is no longer something that is read; instead, signs are indicators which enable the physician "to constitute a *projective pathological anatomy.*"[154] Since the physician encountering an individual patient deals with a three-dimensional space, the surface gaze no longer suffices. The senses of hearing and touch must be added. Because the living patient obviously cannot undergo the autopsy that would manifest his disease, the physician's ear and touch must break into the depths of the body to perceive what the autopsy would reveal.

Although now plurisensorial, nonetheless, clinical practice remains characterized by the gaze: "The tactile and auditory dimensions were not simply added to the domain of vision. The sensorial triangulation indispensable to anatomo-clinical perception remains under the dominant sign of the visible." This plurisensorial perception anticipates what is to be revealed eventually to the gaze on the occasion of the autopsy, and hearing and touch merely substitute temporarily for sight. The physician's ear and hand are merely "substitute organs until such time as death brings to truth the luminous presence of the visible."[155] This gaze, according to Foucault, is "that which establishes the individual in his irreducible quality. And thus it becomes possible to organize a rational language around it. The *object* of discourse may equally well be a *subject*, without the figures of objectivity being in any way altered."[156]

Michel Foucault, the licensed psychologist/psychopathologist, in 1962 declared the psychologist's questions no longer his own.[157] In 1954 he wanted to reveal the roots of mental pathology "in a reflection on man himself";[158] in 1962 he wants to reveal these roots "in a certain relation, historically situated, of man to the madman and to the true man."[159] The project of 1954 endeavored to make psychology scientifically rigorous; his 1962 rewrite drops all references to scientific rigor.[160] This real, true man who provided the unifying focus for Foucault's rigorously scientific psychology of 1954 comes to be perceived in 1962 as a moral and historical construct.[161] In 1954 Foucault sought "the concrete forms that mental illness could take in the psychological life of an individual"; in 1962 he seeks "the concrete forms that psychology has been able to assign to it."[162] The "real conditions" of mental illness concern him in 1954; "Psychopathology as a fact of civilization" captures his attention in 1962.[163] Foucault's turn to history and his revelation of the moral orchestration of madness account for these transitions.

The task Foucault originally set for himself in *Histoire de la folie* was to question Western culture concerning what he calls its "limit-experiences."[164] This is not a matter of following the horizontal course of reason's triumphal march but of tracing through time that "constant verticality" which confronts our culture with what it is not. According to Foucault, a culture rejects that which for it is perceived as the Exterior, the Foreign, and this rejection constitutes the limits of that culture, reveals its essential choices, designates its values; "it makes the separation that gives it the visage of its positivity."[165] Nietzsche revealed the central rejection of Western culture: the moralization of tragedy.[166]

Foucault employs an expression to characterize the condition of madness in history that one commentator refers to as "striking by turns for its apparent inappropriateness, inadequacy, and excess."[167] Perhaps. At least we can say that Foucault's choice of expression is odd. Madness in history, according to Foucault, is characterized in terms of *"l'absence d'oeuvre."*[168] Madness' history is characterized as *l'absence d'oeuvre* in the sense that its history is less than history, and this "less" is the focus of Foucault's investigation. According to Foucault, "history is possible only on the absence of history, in the middle of this great space of murmurs which silence watches over, as its vocation and its truth."[169] History is possible only upon the foundation of that which disrupts history's reasonable course. History, as characterized by continuity, causality, and teleology, is possible only upon the silencing of those permanent, eternal forces which resist such domestication. A history of madness, then, intends to reveal the inadequacy of a dialectical analysis. Madness' very excess defies dialectics.

Thus, Foucault's "history of madness" begins with the confession that such a history is impossible. The very nature of the subject matter, as that which resists molding in terms of continuity, causal connections, and teleological progression, remains unavailable to historical narrative because of rationalist history's dependence upon the very notions of continuity, causality, and teleology. Such history depends upon the already accomplished triumph of reason over that which resists a reasonable account. A history of madness would be a continuous, causally connected, teleological account of that realm "which is controlled by neither the teleology of truth nor the rational sequence of causes, since causes have value and meaning only beyond the division."[170] Reason silences all that which resists interpretation in terms of continuity, causality, and teleology; it silences all that resists homogeneous explanation by the Cartesian constitutive subject. And upon this enforced silence of the heterogeneous, the temporal continuity of a dialectical analysis can proceed.

This silencing of tragedy, however, is never total. Its structures are immobile, and it persists through our history, long before Bosch's "wise fools" and will continue long after the last postcards of Nietzsche. "The great work of the history of the world," according to Foucault, "is ineradicably accompanied by an absence of the work, which is renewed at each instant, but which runs unaltered in its inevitable void throughout the length of history."[171]

From the emptying of the leprosariums at the end of the Middle Ages, to the establishment of l'Hôpital Général in the classical age, to the birth of the asylum and "liberation of the insane," Foucault has shown the historical process by which the moralization of madness was accomplished. The three axes along which this moralization occurs establish the problematic that will govern Foucault's future work.

3

LANGUAGE, TIME, AND THE DEATH OF MAN

Les mots et les choses is the centerpiece of Foucault's writings of the mid-1960s, a rich period for Foucault during which his reputation soared.[1] While his writings at this time span diverse fields, from literary criticism to philosophy to history, a unity of these apparently disparate projects appears centering on three Nietzschean concerns: the relationship between language and knowledge, the problem of time and history, and the question of man.

At this point Foucault's attention focuses particularly upon the truth axis. Truth emerges, especially from his investigation of the clinic, as radically problematic. His literary studies revealed the construction of knowledge as intimately entwined with the question of language. As Nietzsche had argued, many of our most cherished truths result from the unquestioned words we have inherited and from our sedimented grammar. *Les mots et les choses* arises from Foucault's pursuit of the problematic relationship between words and things. His discussion of what he calls the "archaeological" level of discourse in *Les mots et les choses* manifests the linguistic paralysis that characterizes our thought. Secondly, perhaps moved by the significant role played by language as revealed in his research on the birth of clinical medicine, Foucault followed that study with a series of essays, including a book-length work,[2] on Nietzsche-influenced literature.

In a rudimentary form the other two genealogical axes, the power axis and the subject axis, pervade this work. Having examined the role of space in *Histoire de la folie* and *Naissance de la clinique* as Foucault's preliminary formulation of the power axis, we now continue our discussion of his post-Nietzschean transcendental aesthetic by examining the similar position of time in *Les mots et les choses*. The power of time constitutes internally the objects of the human sciences—life, labor, and language—in a manner similar to the spatial constitution of madness and *homo psychologicus* as the objects of psychology. Rather than viewing time as part of our transcendental subjectivity, Foucault reveals time as a Nietzschean force constitutive of the objects of our experience.

"Man" occupies the place in *Les mots et les choses* that will later be formulated as the subject axis. In *Histoire de la folie* Foucault revealed that psychology was not a science of man but a science of a historically constituted *homo psychologicus*—a being whose constitution owed much to psychology's own discourse. In *Les mots et les choses* "real man"—man as opposed to this discursively constituted object of psychology, man as the true object of discourse Foucault wanted to approach in *Maladie mentale et personalité*—becomes problematic. Man, too, is revealed as historically and discursively constituted, "an invention of recent date" without much future to anticipate.[3] Heidegger made us comfortable in thinking of man's temporality. Foucault, as Bernauer points out, pushes us to think of him as temporary.[4] A central task of *Les mots et les choses* is the critical, genealogical one of uncovering the historical conditions of man's emergence. And the critical distance provided by genealogy leads us to ask whether his persistence or disappearance better serves our thought.

A. Language and Knowledge

Of all the characters who populate *Les mots et les choses*—life, labor, language, man, resemblance, order, etc.—language is the "hidden protagonist."[5] Foucault argues in this work that language possesses such sovereignty in human reflection that to question language amounts to questioning thought itself.[6] Language for Foucault is constitutive of our categories of thought and, thereby, of the perceptions these categories order. In *Les mots et les choses* Foucault argues that we are confined by historically and discursively constituted codes: "we are already before the very least of our words, governed and paralysed by language."[7] Both Michel Serres and James Bernauer maintain that the intended effect of *Les mots et les choses* is catharsis, "a comprehension and purgation of the conditions that determine contemporary forms of knowledge."[8] Confronting the internal conditions of our discourse enables us to account for our contemporary modes of thought and to identify obstacles to a more adequate thinking of our condition.

Except for *Naissance de la clinique* almost all of Foucault's writings at this time, from 1962 to 1966 and the publication of *Les mots et les choses*, fall under the general heading of literary criticism. Three of the authors about whom he writes, moreover, are self-proclaimed Nietzscheans. Having seen the manner in which the three genealogical axes function in *Naissance de la clinique* in terms of language, space, and death, we will examine the role played by these three in Foucault's literary writings of this period. In this way we hope to gain insight into the growing influence of Nietzsche on Foucault's thought. In the light of the linguistic paralysis revealed in *Les mots et les choses* we will see the significance for Foucault of a tragic and sacred "language in the space of death," a transgressive language called forth by Nietzsche to combat the paralysis imposed by anthropology and dialectics.

1. The Linguistic Paralysis of Thought

Foucault's claim concerning our linguistic paralysis emerges from his exploration of the archaeological level of discourse and his discovery of what he came to call the episteme or epistemic domain. This is a difficult realm to grasp, so we will approach it from three different angles with the hope that each will shed some light.

First, Foucault distinguishes his own archaeological excavation from a doxology. One could write a history of thought starting with an explication of all the intellectual controversies which flourished in any given age thematically guided by the play of these debates. This would entail a history of opinions, would sort out the dominant issues, and would offer an account of the intellectual choices made by the participants in the controversies. The historian of opinions might delineate the issues of a given historical period and paraphrase the positions and arguments of, for example, Hobbes, Berkeley, Hume, and Condillac. An archaeological analysis, on the other hand, would not focus upon the famous controversies of an age. Instead, the archaeologist "must reconstitute the general system of thought whose network, in its positivity, renders an interplay of simultaneous and apparently contradictory opinions possible."

An archaeological analysis, according to Foucault, excavates "this network that defines the conditions that make a controversy or problem possible, and that bears the historicity of knowledge."[9] Foucault engages in critique; he investigates the historical a priori of these controversies rather than the controversies themselves. *Les mots et les choses* reveals the historical conditions of the existence of the various discourses referred to as human sciences in the course of the last four centuries. It concerns, for example, the "network that made possible the individuals we term Hobbes, Berkeley, Hume, or Condillac."[10] As Michael Shapiro suggests, when dealing with Foucault one must "reverse the familiar notion that persons make statements, and say that statements make persons."[11]

In his 1970 Inaugural Lecture Foucault employs an expression which he borrowed from George Canguilhem—"within the true." Prior to being pronounced either true or false, there are numerous other conditions a statement must fulfill in order to be within the true, that is, in order even to be considered in terms of true or false. Take, for example, the following passage from the astronomer Francesco Sizi quoted by Carl Hempel. Claiming that Galileo could not possibly have seen satellites circling Jupiter, Sizi argued as follows:

There are seven windows in the head, two nostrils, two ears, two eyes and a mouth; so in the heavens there are two favorable stars, two unpropitious, two luminaries, and Mercury alone undecided and indifferent. From which and many other similar phenomena of nature such as the seven metals, etc., which it were tedious to enumerate, we gather that the number of planets is necessarily seven.... Moreover, the satellites are invisible to the naked eye and therefore can have no influence on the earth and therefore would be useless and therefore do not exist.[12]

During the Renaissance, whose episteme sanctioned argument in terms of Resemblance, Sizi's argument would warrant examination. The evidence proffered could be tested and the statement declared either true or false. Had Sizi, or someone, offered this same argument during the classical age, whose episteme sanctioned Representation, or in our own time, his statement could not even be considered in terms of truth or falsehood. It would not even be "within the true." "It is always possible one could speak the truth in a void"; Foucault tells us, "one would only be in the true, however, if one obeyed the rules of some discursive 'police' which would have to be reactivated every time one spoke."[13] Foucault's concern for the archaeological level of discourse, the epistemic domain, is an interest in revealing these rules of discursive police. It is a concern for those historical conditions that determine whether or not a given statement stands within the true at a particular time in history.[14]

A third approach might lend more clarity. When asked in 1968 to define his work Foucault responded, "I have tried to disengage an autonomous domain which would be that of the unconscious of science, of the unconscious of knowledge (savoir), which would have its own rules, like the unconscious of the human individual similarly has its rules and determinations."[15] The archaeological level of discourse, according to Foucault, is the locale of the positive, as opposed to the negative, unconscious of knowledge. The traditional historian of science elucidates the controversies and processes of discovery, but he or she also attempts to bring to light whatever may have eluded scientific consciousness: "the influences that affected it, the implicit philosophies that were subjacent to it, the unformulated thematics, the unseen obstacles."[16] These elements of the scientific consciousness Foucault refers to as the negative unconscious of knowledge. He, instead, pursues the positive unconscious of knowledge, "a level that eludes the consciousness of the scientist and yet is part of scientific discourse, instead of disputing its validity and seeking to diminish its scientific nature."[17] Unformulated "rules of formation" of discourse operate throughout the various disciplines during a given period of history, governing theories and concepts and defining the objects for study, and Foucault's task is to formulate these rules and to make them explicit. The archaeological level, the level of the episteme, sets the conditions of the modes of discourse within which the human sciences can express themselves.

Foucault is concerned with the internal conditions of our discourse, as opposed to transcendental conditions. The a priori rules of formation of discourse are internal to discourse rather than in the transcendental structures of the mind, and are, therefore, historical, rooted in the tumultuous history of what has been said.

2. Language in the Space of Death: Transgression

"Foucault disconcerts": thus Charles Taylor begins an essay, and never has the matter at hand been captured quite so concisely.[18] Taylor had his own concerns in mind. The disconcerting character of Foucault's work that presents itself to us resides in his mode of expression. At crucial junctures, after a lengthy, painstaking analysis, his style often becomes positively poetic, what one critic less kindly referred to as "his obscure, arrogant, sensationalist, and opaque form of discourse, which by his own admission is a 'labyrinth into which I can venture...in which I can lose myself.'"[19] The reader schooled in the discursive style of the Western philosophical tradition easily sinks into the quaqmire of Foucault's turgid prose. Foucault, the reader might conclude, disconcerts.

In an excellent essay, David Carroll has revealed Foucault's "reliance on and an identification with" some work of fiction in almost all of his major works: the writings of Shakespeare, Cervantes' *Don Quixote,* and Diderot's *Neveu de Rameau* in *Histoire de la folie;* a passage from Jorge Luis Borges in *Les mots et les choses;* and Diderot's *Les Bijoux indiscrets* in *La volonté de savoir.* According to Carroll, "any analysis of the conditions of Foucault's critical perspective must inevitably confront the problem of the place of a certain 'sovereign form of discourse' in his work, the disruptive, excessive, transgressive role he assigns to a certain poetic or fictional practice of writing and with which he *identifies* his own critical perspective."[20] By examining Foucault's writings on literature of the early 1960s we will see why this discourse plays such a role, why his works do not read like those of Kant, why, in short, Foucault disconcerts.

According to Foucault, death reigned in the Renaissance as the tragic experience par excellence. Toward the end of the Renaissance madness, for a short time before its domestication by dialectics, occupied the space once held by death, revealing the tragic character of human existence. The painting of Bosch, Brueghel, Dürer, Thierry Bouts, and Grünewald attested to this tragic experience of madness. In our own time, language, in the hands of Foucault's mad geniuses, succeeds madness; the language of madness, of death and sexuality, the language of Georges Bataille and his "desperate and relentless attack on the preeminence of the philosophical subject," Maurice Blanchot "who has made possible all discourse on literature," and Pierre Klossowski, "another major and excessive sign"[21] stands in continuity with those Renaissance paintings. The "immobile structures of the tragic" persist in our own time insofar as language occupies the space once held by death.

Our discussion of *Histoire de la folie* entailed interpreting it as a repetition of Nietzsche's *Birth of Tragedy.* As Euripides' aesthetic Socratism rendered tragedy intelligible and thereby murdered it, a moral-critical discourse on madness, characterized by the writings of Erasmus and definitively by Descartes, dissipated the tragic experience of madness manifest in the painting of

Bosch, Brueghel, *et alii.* This tragic experience resides in the place
once occupied by death, according to Foucault.[22] When literature
occupies this space once reserved for death, it maintains ties with
that tragic experience preserved in the painting of the Renaissance
artists. In fact, according to Foucault, the title "literature" ought to
be reserved exclusively for such language in the space of death.[23]
Once conceived as a protection against death and the creator of
immortality, writing has undergone a transformation in our
time—Flaubert, Proust, and Kafka attest to it—and now is "linked
to sacrifice and to the sacrifice of life itself, it is a voluntary oblit-
eration of the self...."[24] Such tragic literature in the space of death,
since the end of the eighteenth century, only manifests itself "in
the lightning-flash of works such as those of Hölderlin, of Nerval,
of Nietzsche, or of Artaud."[25]

Or of Bataille, Blanchot, and Klossowski.

Bataille's appeal for the author of *Histoire de la folie* and
Naissance de la clinique is obvious. If we reflect a moment on
Bataille's notion of "the heterogeneous," a central category in his
thought, his affinity with Foucault's commitments comes clear.
Jürgen Habermas concisely captures the spirit of the concept of
the heterogeneous as revealed in Bataille's "The Psychological
Structure of Fascism": the heterogeneous refers to

> all those elements that resist assimilation to the bourgeois
> form of life and to the routines of everyday life, just as they
> evade the methodical grasp of the sciences. In this concept
> Bataille condensed the basic experience of the surrealist writ-
> ers and artists who wanted to call attention to *the ecstatic
> forces of intoxication and of dream-life* against the impera-
> tives of utility, normality, and sobriety, in order to shake up
> conventionally set modes of perception and experience. The
> realm of the heterogeneous is opened up only in explosive
> moments of fascinated shock when those categories fall apart
> that guarantee in everyday life the confident interaction of
> the subject with himself and with the world.[26]

Habermas grasps that Bataille's concern is not merely with otherness for its own sake; his concern resides with the immobile structures of the tragic, the figures of Dionysian intoxication and Apol-
lonian dream-life.

The discussion of the moral problematization of madness in
the previous chapter traced the process by which the sacred was
reduced to the status of a merely moral problem. Madness under-

went a process of "civilization" that domesticated its sacred, tragic character. In the words of Michel Beajour, "Such key words as 'sovereignty,' 'evil,' 'transgression,' 'excess,' and 'consummation,' with their connotation of barbaric ritual, bespeak Bataille's refusal of 'civilization': to him literature belongs outside the law, it challenges order. Through writing, modern man attempts a return to the primitive darkness of violence and eroticism. Literature must seek the antipodes of reason and culture, or sink into nothingness."[27] Because positivistic reason's imperialism homogenized all that made life tragic, sacred, and thrilling, only transgression of the order imposed by rational discourse affords access to the tragic, the sacred, the thrilling. "Profanation in a world which no longer recognizes any positive meaning in the sacred—is this not more or less what we may call transgression?" Foucault asks. "In that zone which our culture affords for our gestures and speech, transgression prescribes not only the sole manner of discovering the sacred in its unmediated substance, but also a way of recomposing its empty form, its absence, through which it becomes all the more scintillating."[28]

Transgression, for Bataille, is linked through history to the tradition of Christian spirituality and mysticism. In mysticism and eroticism he perceives "the fundamental unity of all movements whereby we escape the calculations of interest."[29] In this tradition of Christian mysticism, sexuality enjoyed a "more immediately natural understanding" and a "greater 'felicity of expression'" than at any other time. The Christian mystical tradition, according to Foucault's Bataille, maintained the continuum "of desire, of rapture, of penetration, of ecstasy, of that outpouring which leaves us spent" flowing without rupture to "the heart of a divine love."[30] Moreover, while conventional wisdom affirms sexuality for the sake of reproduction and claims access to the sacred by means of dogma, eroticism and mysticism transgress such limits of utility and law.

That most excessive act of transgression, the killing of God, is less an act directed against God or religion than an encroachment against our "limited and positivistic world" inscribed by discourse.[31] As Foucault put it in an essay on Hölderlin, "More than simply an event that affected our emotions, that gave rise to the fear of nothingness, the death of God profoundly influenced our language."[32] Trailing the announcement that God is dead, Foucault's Bataille, with his transgressive language which absorbs our sexuality, reestablishes a paradoxical access to the sacred.

What calls forth this transgressive language? According to Foucault, it was Nietzsche, responding to the anthropological and dialectical space opened by Kant—or rather, the space once opened then closed by Kant.[33] Kant, according to Foucault, opened a space in his critique of reason in which thought could once again proceed, but he closed this same space by reducing all critique to the anthropological question, what is man? Moreover, Kant suspended metaphysics' death sentence by introducing dialectics. Critique's questioning of metaphysics and the limits of reason was superceded by the dialectical interplay of contradiction and totality. "To deny dialectically," according to Foucault, "is to make that which one denies enter into the anxious interiority of the spirit."[34] "To awaken us from the confused sleep of dialectics and of anthropology," according to Foucault—or in Bataille's words, to help us "flee from the horror of reducing being to totality"—"we required the Nietzschean figures of tragedy, of Dionysus, of the death of God, of the philosopher's hammer, of the Superman approaching with the steps of a dove, of the Return."[35] Discursive language, nearly silent before these Nietzschean figures, must give way, and the new philosophical task becomes the exploration of that extreme, nondiscursive language of Bataille, Blanchot, and Klossowski—a language in the space of death. In other words, the task is to seek a nondialectical language to function for transgression in a manner analogous to the function dialectics played for contradiction.

In his essay "Le langage à l'infini" Foucault comments that "death is undoubtedly the most essential of the accidents of language (its limit and its center)."[36] The space of death is a space of absence, and at the center of this absence is the disappearance of the philosophical subject. A "dedialectized language" entails an "attack on the preeminence of the philosophical subject."[37] The point, ultimately, of this nondiscursive, nondialectical language is to allow the transgression of the philosopher's own philosophical being. Such a language creates the possibility of the "mad philosopher."[38]

It is all very disconcerting, indeed, but it expresses Foucault's consistent understanding of the task of thought. This transgression of the philosophical subject entails what Foucault intended throughout his writing career. In one of his very last works, he makes a similar claim, expressed less cryptically, about the task of genealogical thought:

> After all, what would be the value of the passion for knowledge if it resulted only in a certain amount of knowledgeableness and not, in one way or another and to the extent possible, in the knower's straying afield of himself? There are times in life when the question of knowing if one can think

differently than one thinks, and perceive differently than one
sees, is absolutely necessary if one is to go on looking and
reflecting at all.... But, then, what is philosophy today—
philosophical activity, I mean—if it is not the critical work
that thought brings to bear on itself? In what does it consist,
if not in the endeavor to know how and to what extent it
might be possible to think differently, instead of legitimating
what is already known?[39]

B. Time: From Classical Order to Modern History

One of the tasks of *Les mots et les choses* is to trace the epistemic
rupture occurring at the end of the eighteenth century that made
the transition from classical order to modern history possible. Foucault chose to devote *Les mots et les choses* to theories of classification, wealth, and language because in these discourses the archaeological network and its ruptures manifest themselves most
clearly.[40] The key to this epistemic rupture in each of these disciplines is the introduction of a temporal element into their discourse. Time, like Nietzschean relations of forces, internally constitutes the objects studied by the human sciences and, like space,
functions as a paradigmatic example of what Foucault will later,
more generically, call power.

1. From Natural History to Biology

Typical intellectual histories attribute an emerging curiosity to
thinkers of the seventeenth and the eighteenth centuries which
accounts for their discovery of the life sciences, opening the way
for the rise of modern biology. With the privileged status given
observation in the Baconian scheme of things, the invention of the
microscope, the new appreciation of rationality modeled on the
physical sciences of light and motion, the historians tell us, the
road was paved for advances in the life sciences. As we saw in our
discussion of *Naissance de la clinique*, it is assumed that enlightened practitioners turned their attention from theory, chimeras,
and superstitions and renewed their respect for the perceived.
Some historians see a battle raging between a theological worldview, with its universe permeated by God's providence, and a
newly emerging scientific worldview insisting on nature's autonomy. In short, Foucault maintains,

Historians want to write histories of biology in the eighteenth century; but they do not realize that biology did not exist then, and that the pattern of knowledge that has been familiar to us for a hundred and fifty years is not valid for a previous period. And that, if biology was unknown, there was a very simple reason for it: that life itself did not exist. All that existed was living beings, which were viewed through a grid of knowledge constituted by *natural history*.[41]

What actually accounts for the rise of natural history in the seventeenth century, according to Foucault, was a transformation of the relationship between signs and things. With the breakdown of resemblance as the governor of the Renaissance episteme, observation could be distinguished from document and fable. Until the late sixteenth century a history was a seamless garment; it entailed a description of a plant's or animal's organs, its resemblances with other things, its virtues, the fables told of it, its uses, and its place in the documents of the ancients. With an epistemic domain governed by resemblance signs and things were one. In the seventeenth century, in contrast, signs became modes of representation instead of signatures of resemblance, and observation, document, and fable could be distinguished. "Thus arranged and understood," Foucault tells us, "natural history has as a condition of its possibility the common affinity of things and language with representation; but it exists as a task only in so far as things and language happen to be separate."[42]

The condition of the possibility of modern biology cannot be attributed to the advance of natural history's classifications in terms of identity and difference. Biology became possible only because of an epistemic shift as dramatic as that which separates the Renaissance world of resemblance from the classical order of representation. The trip from natural history to biology was a two stage process. First, an attempt was made to save the system of representation by introducing new concepts into it. In the second stage the system of representations shattered. As we saw in *Naissance de la clinique* the key task of classical age thought was one of classification in terms of genus and species. Toward the end of the eighteenth century (1775–95), the first stage of the transition occurred when the movement from the description of structure to classification in terms of character became problematic. The essential modification concerned the relation between the visible, describable structure and a newly introduced criterion of identity, organic structure, internal to the organism in question and irreducible to that which is visible and, therefore, representable. With the introduction of organic structure, the notions of life and function move to the center of the classification process. Even in this first stage of the transition, with the notions of life and function, time enters the interior of representation's classificatory space.

Stage two of the transition Foucault attributes to Cuvier who transformed the mode of being of all that had been represented in natural history. First, Cuvier subordinated organ structure to organ function. "What to Classical eyes were merely differences juxtaposed with identities must now be ordered and conceived on the basis of a functional homogeneity which is their hidden foundation," Foucault tells us. "When the Same and the Other both belong to a single space, there is *natural history*; something like *biology* becomes possible when this unity of level begins to break up, and when differences stand out against the background of an identity that is deeper and, as it were, more serious than that unity."[43]

This deeper, more serious identity is Life, purely functional, unavailable to perception and representation, which from then on will make possible any classification. While Lamarck's name is typically associated with evolutionism and Cuvier, because of the "fixist" label his explicit theory received, is usually viewed as an obstacle to evolutionism, Foucault argues that from an archaeological point of view, from the critical point of view concerned with the conditions of the possibility of discourse, Cuvier's innovation made evolutionary biology possible.[44] The condition of the possibility of modern thought (biology, in this case) is not time as an unchanging transcendental structure of human consciousness, but time as a quite recent (contemporary with Kant) historically and discursively constituted, quasi-transcendental a priori.

2.   From the Analysis of Wealth to Political Economy

Typical histories of political economy see this discipline as having slowly emerged after a process of conceptual clarification. For years, these historians suppose, the moral problematics of fair price and usury hindered the progress of a truly scientific economics. The conceptual confusion of money and wealth, value and market price, in mercantilism further slowed the development of political economy. But in the eighteenth century, such historians tell us, some essential distinctions were forged which could later be taken up by the positivist economists with their highly refined techniques. With the discoveries of Smith, Ricardo, and Say concerning the division of labor, the role of capital, and economic laws, it is supposed, political economy attained its true field of study and conceptual coherence.[45]

Foucault sees things differently. From the perspective of the archaeological level, political economy, even in a nascent form, could not exist in the seventeenth and eighteenth centuries. In the classical age, "there is no political economy, because, in the order of knowledge, production does not exist."[46] In the same way that there could be no classical age biology because life did not exist, the absence of production rendered political economy impossible. Just as the classical age was limited to natural history and could not do biology, so it was bound to the analysis of wealth instead of political economy. Moreover, just as the classical age archaeological network built on representation made life impossible, this same network excluded production.

Precious metal, in the sixteenth century, had the character of a visible signature of wealth.[47] Its price was founded on this; it could function as a measure of prices because of this, and on this basis it could function in any exchange. Classical age economic thought had to break down this configuration based on resemblance and to constitute a domain of wealth as the object of its reflection. This was accomplished by turning Renaissance analysis upside down; i.e., classical thought asserted the priority of function to character rather than character to function. A precious metal's character as a visible sign of wealth came to be viewed as dependent upon its ability to function in an exchange. Its value no longer governed by resemblance, precious metal came to be understood in terms of representation: "money for the mercantilists had the power of representing all possible wealth, because it was the universal instrument for the analysis and representation of wealth, because it covered the entire extent of its domain leaving no residuum."[48] According to Foucault, "Whatever its economic determinations and consequences, mercantilism, when questioned at the level of the *episteme*, appears as the slow, long effort to bring reflection upon prices and money into alignment with the analysis of representations. It was responsible for the emergence of a domain of 'wealth' connected to that which, at about the same time, was opened up to natural history...."[49]

As in the case of the transition from natural history to biology, a two-stage process accounts for the introduction of a temporal element into economic thought making possible the move from the analysis of wealth to political economy. Moreover, as in the case of the transition from natural history to biology, the move from the analysis of wealth to political economy is accomplished only with the shattering of the archaeological network of representation.

Adam Smith, we are often told, introduced the concept of labor into economic thought and thereby doomed all previous analyses of wealth to oblivion. Modern political economy, we are told, became possible when Smith introduced labor into economic reflection. According to Foucault, Smith's innovation constituted merely the first stage, and not the decisive one, in the transition from the analysis of wealth to political economy. In fact, Foucault insists, Smith's work is not significantly different at the archaeological level from the analyses of his predecessors and contemporaries.[50] Nonetheless, by introducing labor as a temporal element, according to Foucault, Smith's work stands as an "essential hiatus" in the midst of his contemporaries.[51] While still within the analysis of wealth, and thus within the analysis of representation, Smith introduces labor as toil and time which cannot be reduced to the analysis of representation.[52] With his sense of temporality and finitude Smith stretches the limits of representation beyond their capacity. As early as Smith, then, we can see dimly the anthropology (the concern for man, his finitude, temporality, and death) and the notion of production (labor and capital) which will become central to the episteme of our modernity.

Actually, Foucault maintains, Ricardo's work marks the decisive stage in constituting the conditions of the possibility of modern political economy. Because of his bondage to the network of representation Adam Smith confused labor as productive activity and labor as a commodity. Ricardo's contribution is decisive because he explodes the notion of labor. It is not merely the introduction of the concept of labor into economic thought that allows political economy to emerge. Rather, the network of representation must first be shattered by establishing the centrality of time in economic thought. Ricardo accomplishes this by destroying Smith's confused notion of labor; he "singles out in a radical fashion, for the first time, the worker's energy, toil, and time that are bought and sold, and the activity that is at the origin of the value of things."[53] After Ricardo, labor no longer stands as the measure of value, the representation of wealth, but as the source of value. Value is conceived as the product of labor, no longer a sign, and, thus, must be understood in terms of its temporal development. The possibility of exchange for Ricardo comes to be grounded in labor as productive activity. Foucault's major point is that this new understanding of labor, by introducing time into economic thought, shattered the network of representation which had governed classical age analysis of wealth.[54] The condition of the possibility of modern thought (political economic thought, in this case) is not time as an unchanging transcendental structure of human consciousness, but time as a quite recent (contemporary with Kant) historically and discursively constituted a priori.

3. From General Grammar to Philology

Once the condition of all knowledge, resemblance in the seventeenth century comes to be bound up with error; it reflects an immaturity bypassed with reason's triumph. Francis Bacon with his idols—of the den, the theater, the tribe, and the marketplace—spearheads the attack against the seductions of resemblance. In Descartes' *Regulae* resemblance is overruled, giving way to comparison in terms of identity and difference. Analysis replaces analogies, complete enumeration of analyzed elements stands in lieu of the infinite interplay of resemblances, the openness of interpretation gives way to absolutely certain knowledge, discrimination displaces the tendency to draw things together, and science, grounded in intuitions, separates itself from history, the erudition derived from classic texts.[55] The basis of this epistemological rupture is an epistemic transformation of the being of language: "language is no longer one of the figurations of the world, or a signature stamped upon things since the beginning of time. The manifestation and sign of truth are to be found in evident and distinct perception. It is the task of words to translate that truth if they can; but they no longer have the right to be considered a mark of it. Language has withdrawn from the midst of beings themselves and has entered a period of transparency and neutrality."[56] Foucault suggests that, while the massiveness of language overwhelmed Renaissance thought, language did not even exist in the classical age. Instead, it functioned; its entire being was bound up with its representative function.[57]

Classical age language provides a spontaneous, successive analysis of any simultaneous representation. Its very nature prohibits simultaneous expression of simultaneity; it is limited to arranging phenomena in a successive, linear order—"to my gaze, 'the brightness is within the rose'; in my discourse, I cannot avoid it coming either before or after."[58] The discipline that studied this relation of successive discourse to the simultaneity of thought the classical age called general grammar: "General grammar is the study of verbal order in its relation to the simultaneity that it is its task to represent."[59] It studies the artificial sequence relative to simultaneous representations as this sequence is embodied in what Foucault calls the "quadrilateral of language": theories of the proposition, articulation, designation, and derivation.[60] In contrast to the Renaissance when "language spoke," in the classical age all reflection on language centers on the simple idea that "language analyses."

The notion of inflection functions for the study of language in a manner analogous to organic structure in the transition from natural history to biology and to labor in the transition from the analysis of wealth to political economy. The notion of inflection introduces a temporal element into language, contributes to the breakdown of the network of representation, and makes possible the transition from general grammar to nineteenth-century philology.

Toward the end of the eighteenth century the comparison of languages with one another took center stage, and the role of inflection was highlighted; it was becoming apparent in these linguistic confrontations that inflectional modifications corresponded to modifications of grammar, syntax, or meaning. While, at the time of its introduction, the concern with inflection was consistent with an interest in language's representational value, according to Foucault, "already, through the inflectional system, the dimension of the purely grammatical is appearing: language is no longer constituted only of representations and of sounds that in turn represent the representations and are ordered among them as the links of thought require; it is constituted also of formal elements, grouped into a system, which impose upon the sounds, syllables, and roots a regime that is not that of representation."[61] Just as labor and organic structure, having been introduced into a system of representations, could not be reduced to representational content, so inflectional system was similarly irreducible to representations.

The importance of inflection is that it introduced time into the interior of language. The condition of the possibility of modern thought (philology, in this case) is not time as an unchanging transcendental structure of human consciousness, but time as a quite recent historically and discursively constituted a priori. A word, it is true, continues to represent, but its representative content or function no longer accounts for the being of the word, its "essential architecture."[62] Instead, the "grammatical totality" with its own internal history to which a word belongs constitutes the being of the word. The word is displaced from its role as a name, as representation, and finds its function determined by its place in a larger linguistic coherence. It becomes an element in a complex grammatical structure. Language in the late eighteenth century, according to Foucault, is "thickening"; it is "taking on a peculiar heaviness"; it is losing its transparency to its representations.[63]

While the Port Royal Grammar saw language as a sign analogous to a portrait or a map, at the end of the eighteenth century a musical note provides a more appropriate analogy. With its own coherence, complexity, and history a language now requires internal analysis. No reference need be made to events external to language itself; principles of evolution are internal to languages themselves. Summarizing, Foucault declares, "the independent analysis of grammatical structures, as practised from the nineteenth century, isolates language, treats it as an autonomous organic structure, and breaks its bonds with judgements, attribution, and affirmation. The ontological transition provided by the verb *to be* between speaking and thinking is removed; whereupon language acquires a being proper to itself. And it is this being that contains the laws that govern it."[64]

Inflection introduced time into the interior of language and transformed the very being of language. Production transformed the being of wealth by introducing time into it. Organic structure inserted time into the interior of living beings and made life possible. Time, therefore, first, is not a transcendental form of experience as Kant would have it, but a historical and discursive construct. Since Nietzsche connected the philosophical task with a radical reflection on language, the transcendental aesthetic is historicized. Secondly, time in *Les mots et les choses*, like space in *Histoire de la folie* and *Naissance de la clinique*, foreshadows the appreciation of power that Foucault develops in the 1970s. Time, like power, is immanent in relations of forces, discursive and nondiscursive practices; it is historically and discursively introduced into the interior of the entities we experience.

C. The Birth and Death of Man

1. The Birth of Man in the Age of Critique:
Kant and the Analytic of Finitude

At the end of the classical age with the emergence of the quasi-transcendentals life, labor, and language, man comes into being as the one who lives, labors, and speaks. Prior to that time man did not exist; i.e., "there was no epistemological consciousness of man as such"; no epistemic domain existed that was specifically proper to man.[65] Human nature, obviously, received discussion, but man remained unknown: "Classical thought, and all the forms of thought that preceded it, were able to speak of the mind and the body, of the human being, of how restricted a place he occupies in the universe, of all the limitations by which his knowledge or his freedom must be measured, but...not one of them was ever able to know man as he is posited in modern knowledge."[66] Man appears only with the birth of the sciences of biology, political economy, and philology as the being who lives, labors, and speaks in accordance with their laws and knows himself through knowing these laws. These sciences with their new time-laden objects of life, labor, and language carved out a space in which man could erupt, in which man had to erupt, and thereby opened the space of our modernity. The collapse of the epistemic network of representation requires man as both the "sovereign subject" and "difficult object" of these knowledges.[67] He arises as a "strange empirico-transcendental doublet, since he is a being such that knowledge will be attained in him of what renders all knowledge possible."[68]

Man's entry into scientific discourse is hardly triumphal. He exists as a "figuration of finitude"[69] condemned to labor in order to survive, bound toward death as his limit, required to think in a language that precedes him and which he is incapable of mastering. Man is sovereign subject and difficult object of knowledge, but he is such as "enslaved sovereign, observed spectator."[70] Each of these knowledges reveals man as reeking of finitude. But in the hands of Kant and his contemporaries the apparent disadvantage of man's finitude is twisted into a positive advantage; "since Kant philosophical discourse is the discourse of finitude rather than that of the absolute...."[71] Since Kant, according to Foucault, "the infinite is no longer given, from now on there is only finitude, and it is in this sense that the Kantian critique carried with it the possibility—or the peril—of an anthropology."[72] Man's finitude ultimately triumphs as classical analysis gives way to the analytic of modernity. An analytic of finitude replaces classical analysis of representations; with Kant, "the limits of knowledge provide a positive foundation for the possibility of knowing."[73]

Anthropology, the analytic of man, is constitutive of the thought of modernity. This comes clear from the time of Kant when in his *Logic* he added a fourth question to his original three to which these three would henceforth be referred: "What can I know?" "What must I do?" "What may I hope?" are referred to the question "What is man?"[74] As we saw earlier in our discussion of Foucault's literary criticism, Kant, when he inaugurated the critique of reason, opened a space in which thought could again proceed, but he closed this same space by reducing all critique to the anthropological question, what is man? By introducing dialectics Kant suspended metaphysics' death sentence. Critique's questioning of metaphysics and the limits of reason was superceded by the dialectical interplay of contradiction and totality. Having awakened us from our dogmatic slumber, Kant allows us to roll over and comfortably enjoy an anthropological sleep.

Foucault provided a glimmer of his objection to modern anthropological thought as early as *Histoire de la folie* and his extended attack on modernity's theory and practice of systematically excluding our otherness and reducing it to the categories of the same. Anthropological thought is characterized by a pursuit of this otherness which Foucault here calls "the unthought."[75] The task modern thought sets for itself is the reconciliation of man's other with himself, to make alterity constitutive of identity. While Dreyfus and Rabinow are correct that Foucault objects to anthropological thought because it is boring, his more serious objection is that such thought is reductionistic.[76]

Kantian critique is a two-edged sword. By identifying thinking with anthropology, by reducing all significant questions to the question of man, Kantian critique divides dogmatism into two;[77] a dogmatism of the empirical (e.g., positivism) undergirds and limits the transcendental while a dogmatism of the transcendental (e.g., dialectics) undergirds and limits the empirical. By the same token, however, Kantian critique throws representation into question and opens a new space for thought. By questioning the limits, the foundation, and the origin of representation, Kantian critique reveals the field of representation as näive, dogmatic metaphysics and sanctions thought's venture outside representation's limits. Kantian critique is less a philosophy in its own right than the opening of a space for thought; "it makes possible those philosophies of Life, of the Will, and of the Word, that the nineteenth century is to deploy in the wake of critique."[78] By raising the question Kant made possible a renewal of the general critique of reason. In spite of the fact that it established anthropology and dialectics as the space of modern thought, Kantian critique made Nietzsche possible, and it is Nietzsche "who burned for us, even before we were born, the intermingled promises of the dialectic and anthropology."[79]

2. The Death of Man and the Realization of Critique: Nietzschean Genealogy and the Counter-Sciences

The liberation of thought from anthropological sleep requires us to overcome man, and that is why Nietzsche attains such stature in *Les mots et les choses*. Nietzsche's genealogies, his "philological critique," and biologism, revealed the unity of man and God. As Foucault put it in an exchange with Jean-Paul Sartre, "The man-subject, the subject of his own freedom, conscious of his own freedom, is at bottom a sort of image correlative to God. The man of the nineteenth century is God incarnated in humanity. There has been a sort of theologization of man, the redescent of God on earth which has in some fashion made the man of the nineteenth century theologized."[80] The death of God and the disappearance of man, thus, as Nietzsche showed, are synonymous. His proclamation of the *Ubermensch* signaled for us soon to expect man's demise. But Nietzsche proclaims the death of man as both promise and task, and thereby, he "marks the threshold beyond which contemporary philosophy can begin thinking again; and he will no doubt continue for a long while to dominate its advance."[81]

If we dispose of man, Foucault maintains, philosophy, having been declared dead, has a chance at new life. The absence of man would carve out a space in which thought would once again be possible. And in the meantime,

> To all those who still want to talk about man, about his reign or his liberation, to all those who still ask themselves questions about what man is in his essence, to all those who want to take him as their starting-point in their attempts to reach the truth, to all those who, on the other hand, refer all knowledge back to the truths of man himself, to all those who do not want to formalize without anthropologizing, who do not want to mythologize without demystifying, who do not want to think without immediately thinking that it is man who thinks, to all these warped and twisted [*gauches et gauchies*] forms of reflection one can only oppose a philosophical laugh—which means, to a certain extent, a silent one.[82]

Nietzsche showed us, according to Foucault, that "the rediscovery of the dimension proper to language is incompatible with man."[83] By connecting our philosophical task with a radical reflection on language, Nietzsche removed man from the center of thought and opened a space in which thinking could proceed.

In Nietzsche's wake the various projects characteristic of the twentieth century appeared: man finds himself decentered in Russell and Whitehead's project of a "universal formalization of all discourse," in Heidegger's project of "an integral exegesis of the world which would at the same time be its total demystification," in Saussure's "general theory of signs."[84] Perhaps most interesting for Foucault is the task Mallarmé set for himself of "a transformation without residuum, of a total reabsorption of all forms of discourse into a single word, of all books into a single page, of the whole world into one book." Mallarmé perceived that in his own time "poetry has been visited by some nameless and absolute flash of lightning...revealing that, in general, all books contain the amalgamation of a certain number of age-old truths; that actually there is only one book on earth, that it is the law of the earth, the earth's true Bible."[85] The task of poetry, then, moves toward the fashioning of a single Word. Mallarmé was keenly aware of the density and opacity of language. To name a thing, he maintained, risked drawing one away from the uniqueness of the reality one experienced. Naming leads one into the more comfortable, but impoverished, world of common and useful concepts and definitions; "Speech is no more than a commercial approach to reality."[86] Not even poetry, he feared, could communicate the depth or expansiveness of its own undergirding, inspiring experience.

Mallarmé's work, according to Foucault, ought to be read as a direct reply to Nietzsche's central question in *On the Genealogy of Morals*:

> For Nietzsche, it was not a matter of knowing what good and evil were in themselves, but of who was being designated, or rather *who was speaking* when one said *Agathos* to designate oneself and *Deilos* to designate others.... To the Nietzschean question: 'Who is speaking?,' Mallarmé replies—and constantly reverts to that reply—by saying that what is speaking is, in its solitude, in its fragile vibration, in its nothingness, the word itself—not the meaning of the word, but its enigmatic and precarious being.[87]

Decentered by the density of the word, by the "unique and difficult being" of language, Mallarmé constantly effaced himself in his poetic expression; he refused to play the role of intending subject of his own expression, preferring instead to provide a space in which "the discourse would compose itself."[88] The dialogue between Nietzsche and Mallarmé signaled the disappearance of transparent, representational discourse, discovered "the vast play of language," and orchestrated "a leap towards a wholly new form of thought as to draw to a close a mode of knowing constituted during the previous century."[89] With this decentering of the subject and the opening of a space for deanthropological thought, Foucault two years later would answer Nietzsche's question with Samuel Beckett's question: "What matter who's speaking?"[90]

With the human sciences seesawing between positivism and dialectics Foucault searches for the spirit of the Nietzsche-Mallarmé dialogue in the "counter-sciences" of psychoanalysis, ethnology, and linguistics. According to Foucault, "nothing is more alien to psychoanalysis than anything resembling a general theory of man or an anthropology."[91] Ethnology, moreover, "like psychoanalysis, questions not man himself, as he appears in the human sciences, but the region that makes possible knowledge about man in general."[92] Similarly, "linguistics no more speak of man himself than do psychoanalysis and ethnology."[93] These disciplines "dissolve man."[94] The counter-sciences offer a critique of all that is apparently established by the human sciences; they lure the human sciences into an investigation of their own foundations and, thereby, undermine the anthropological project.

Psychoanalysis investigates, not man, but the unconscious that establishes his limits. While the human science of psychology, primarily reliant upon the categories of function and norm borrowed from the recently established science of biology, attempts to represent man's experience as a living being, psychoanalysis pushes psychology to its limit with its great theme of Death. Sociology, with its categories of conflict and rule on loan from economics, represents man as laboring, consuming, and in conflict; but psychoanalysis seeks the conditions of these in its theme of Desire. Psychoanalysis draws the linguistic study of signification and system to its limit by imposing its own great theme of Law. Psychoanalysis opens a region in which the representations of the human sciences stand in suspense, a region in which "we find outlined the three figures by means of which life, with its function and norms, attains its foundation in the mute repetition of Death, conflicts and rules their foundation in the naked opening of Desire, significations and systems their foundation in a language which is at the same time Law."[95] Because of its concentration on Death, Desire, and Law at the limits of human finitude psychoanalysis cannot provide a general theory of man; that is why psychoanalysis is a praxis, the working out of the therapeutic relationship. The three great themes of psychoanalysis pertain not to man, but to the limit-conditions of the possibility of all knowledge about him.

Ethnology, or social anthropology in the English-speaking
world, does not question man but the conditions of the possibility
of any knowledge of man.[96] "[S]ituated within the particular relation that the Western *ratio* establishes with all other cultures,"
ethnology does not take at face value the representations that people of other cultures provide of themselves.[97] Unconscious structures of cultures, instead, preoccupy the ethnologist: the norms
governing life's functions, the rules governing needs, the systems
which subtend all significations.[98] Psychoanalysis and ethnology
are counter-sciences in relation to the human sciences. They draw
the human sciences into confrontation with their own epistemological foundations, their conditions of possibility, the historical *a priori* which fail to provide the sought-after firm grounding, and
thereby they "undo" man.[99]

And finally, linguistics, according to Foucault's vision, would
complement psychoanalysis and ethnology by providing a formal
model for them. "Like the two other counter-sciences, it would
make visible, in a discursive mode, the frontier-forms of the
human sciences; like them, it would situate its experience in those
enlightened and dangerous regions where the knowledge of man
acts out, in the form of the unconsious and of historicity, its relation with what renders them possible."[100] Linguistics penetrates
the realms of each of the other two counter-sciences and treats language as autonomous so that man need not hold sway. Its focus
upon the being of language establishes linguistics as an ally of the
literature with which we began this chapter. By giving preeminence to the being of language both linguistics and literature displace man as the central problematic of our thought.

4

THE NOTION OF GENEALOGY

Given the emergence of Foucault's problematic in terms of three axes, what resources did he find in the works of Nietzsche? What did Foucault discover in these writings such that he would explicitly label his own work "genealogy"? The first part of this chapter delineates the central elements of Nietzsche's notion of genealogy. What did he intend in his project of a genealogy of morals? What did he hope to find in his quest for "origins"? Nietzsche's more explicit methodological statements appear in his confrontations with adversaries where he clarifies the lapses and wrong turns he wants to avoid in his own genealogical approach. Since he never explicitly says what he means by genealogy, we need to tease out the elements from his genealogical studies and oblique references to his method. The first essay of *On the Genealogy of Morals* clarifies the sense in which genealogy is to be understood as a form of critique, revealing the critical power of Nietzsche's unique mode of questioning.

Nietzsche understands historical narrative as oriented toward the enhancement of life. The second of Nietzsche's *Untimely Meditations*, "On the Uses and Disadvantages of History for Life," manifests the manner in which enhancement of life functions for Nietzsche as the criterion of value. There are three legitimate types of historical narrative for Nietzsche—monumental, antiquarian, and critical—and each is both potentially life-enhancing and potentially life-destroying.

Genealogy as a search for origins is not unusual in the history of philosophy. The unusual feature of Nietzsche's genealogy is that his search for origins assumes that, to put it as baldly as possible, no thing is to be found at the origin. While others search out origins to find something in its pristine purity, untarnished by culture and history, Nietzsche denies the notion of the substratum in all the forms it has taken in the history of philosophy (substance, subject, the soul, the thing-in-itself, etc.). Any thing, person, event is construed by Nietzsche to be a matter of historical, cultural, practical interpretation, and beneath the series of interpretations there is nothing, no thing.

The second part of this chapter examines Foucault's understanding of genealogy. Foucault emerged from his earlier researches on madness, the clinic, and words and things with his own list of "the prejudices of philosophers," and as in part I, we will begin by clearing the ground with a discussion of these prejudices. Secondly, Foucault specifies Nietzsche's notion of genealogy as a search for origins without assuming a substratum at the origin; it is in this sense that genealogy is to be understood as critique. Genealogy is critique in that it reveals and questions historical conditions of existence; it manifests the historical a priori. Genealogy is critique as a historical investigation into the events that have led us to constitute ourselves and to recognize ourselves as subjects of what we are doing, thinking, saying. Finally, critique is genealogical; i.e., genealogy is history oriented toward the future. Genealogy separates out, from the contingency that has made us what we are, the possibility of no longer being, doing, or thinking, what we are, do, and think.

PART I: Friedrich Nietzsche's Notion of Genealogy

Nietzsche's notion of genealogy is best illumined in contrast to two alternative modes of thought. First, in *Beyond Good and Evil* Nietzsche offers a sustained reflection "On the Prejudices of Philosophers" which stipulates the task Nietzsche sets for himself and the philosophical pitfalls he wants to avoid in his genealogical approach. Secondly, the key elements of Nietzschean genealogy emerge in opposition to an alternative genealogical approach: that of Paul Rée and the English psychologists with whom Nietzsche associates Rée.

A. On the Prejudices of Philosophers

Values, for Nietzsche, are those notions that the Western tradition, rooted in Platonism and Christianity, conceives of as deserving of reverence: for example, good as opposed to evil, altruism as opposed to egoism, truth rather than falsehood. The primary task of genealogy is to trace the descent of these values. In Nietzsche's last four books we encounter various forms of tracing the descent of values. Part One of *Beyond Good and Evil* is especially interesting for our purposes because it provides both a justification of Nietzsche's genealogical approach, and at the same time, it is an example of this approach as applied to philosophy as dogmatism.

There is no value, for Nietzsche, without an evaluation, an act of will, which proceeds from a perspective. "Through esteeming alone is there value," in the words of Zarathustra, "and without esteeming, the nut of existence would be hollow."[1] In Nietzsche's words, "Whatever has *value* in our world now does not have value in itself, according to its nature—nature is always value-less, but has been *given* value at some time, as a present—and it was *we* who gave and bestowed it."[2] Truth, for example, is a value, is deserving of respect, therefore, only if related to an evaluation, an act of will. Gilles Deleuze describes this insight of Nietzsche's as a recognition of the "critical reversal" implicit in the very notion of value. According to Deleuze's reading of Nietzsche, "On the one hand, values appear or are given as principles: and evaluation presupposes values on the basis of which phenomena are appraised. But, on the other hand and more profoundly, it is values which presuppose evaluations, 'perspectives of appraisal', from which their own value is derived." Thus, the basic presupposition of genealogy is that the will is the only root of values. The origin of ideals is not in some higher Platonic world of forms, nor in the nature of things, but in the will expressing itself in this world, our world. Given this basic presupposition, genealogy is to be understood as a method for discovering the origin of ideas and ideals in an act of willing.

Genealogy focuses upon the specific quality of the will at the origin of values. For example, Nietzsche would reinterpret a statement such as "Truth is a value" or "Truth deserves reverence" into the more accurate statement, "I will truth instead of error." Genealogy, then, is the study of the way in which the will wills. Is it a weak or strong will? Is it a noble or a servant will? Is it creative-active or revengeful-reactive? Is it a life-affirming or a life-denying will?

In the first part of *Beyond Good and Evil* Nietzsche focuses his attention upon the prejudices of philosophy. The first prejudice, already mentioned, is that truth is to be revered. This section is especially important because here Nietzsche is doing a genealogy of philosophy (i.e., he is asking the genealogical question of philosophy: what is it that the philosopher's will to truth really wills?), he reveals the moral evaluation which underlies the allegedly autonomous search for truth, and he demonstrates the essentially conservative character of this evaluation.

Nietzsche denies any opposition between that which is instinctive and consciousness. He maintains that conscious thinking is mistakenly thought of as independent of the instinctive element, and this prejudice is especially prevalent among philosophers when they reflect upon their own thinking. Against this prejudice, Nietzsche maintains that "most of a philosopher's conscious thinking is secretly directed and compelled into definite channels by his instincts."[3] Fundamentally, the instinct of self-preservation underlies the philosopher's will to truth. The philosopher prefers, for example, the definite over the indefinite, the unchanging over the changing, the one over the many. Behind the acceptance of truth as an ideal, behind the will to truth, is a moral evaluation. The moral drive in this philosophy is a drive to maintain a certain type of life. The will here is preservative, conservative. In Nietzsche's words, "such valuations as these could, their regulatory importance for *us* notwithstanding, be no more than foreground valuations, a certain species of *niaiserie* which may be necessary precisely for the preservation of beings such as us."[4]

The moral evaluation underlying the allegedly pure and autonomous search for truth is evident in the short examples Nietzsche offers of Stoicism and modern physics. The Stoics maintained that their ethics arose from the pure contemplation of nature. Their imperative: live according to nature. Their ethical practice is alleged to be an inference from their theoretical approach to nature. Nietzsche, however, argues that the opposite is in fact the case.

> The truth of it is, however, quite different: while you rapturously pose as deriving the canon of your law from nature, you want something quite the reverse of that, you strange actors and self-deceivers! Your pride wants to prescribe your morality, your ideal, to nature, yes to nature itself, and incorporate them in it; you demand that nature should be nature 'according to the Stoa' and would like to make all existence exist only after your own image....[5]

The Stoics' claim to mirror nature is itself based on a moral evaluation. It is the product of a will which evaluates nature in terms of the predominance of order over chaos. Their very approach to nature arises from a prior moral evaluation of nature which views order as good and chaos as evil. In contrast, Nietzsche proposes a counterview of nature: "prodigal beyond measure, indifferent beyond measure, without aims or intentions, without mercy or justice, at once fruitful and barren and uncertain...."[6]

The case is similar with physicists. Pretending to offer an explanation of the world, the physicist loses sight of the fact, apparent to Nietzsche, that he or she is offering, not an explanation, but an interpretation, an arrangement of the world according to human, all too human, requirements. Physicists like to refer to "nature's conformity to law,"

> But, as aforesaid, that is interpretation, not text; and someone could come along who, with an opposite intention and art of interpretation, knew how to read out of the same nature and with regard to the same phenomena the tyrannically ruthless and inexorable enforcement of power-demands—an interpreter who could bring before your eyes the universality and unconditionality of all 'will to power' in such a way that almost any word and even the word 'tyranny' would finally seem unsuitable or as a weakening and moderating metaphor—as too human—and who none the less ended by asserting of this world the same as you assert of it, namely that it has a 'necessary' and 'calculable' course, but not because laws prevail in it but because laws are absolutely lacking, and every power draws its ultimate consequences every moment.[7]

Thus, thought in either case, that of Stoicism or of physics, is not a mirroring; it is creation. The will to truth is a symptom of the will to virtue.

We have inherited our concepts and values from our ancestors, and philosophers tend to regard these as self-evident and unconditionally binding. For Nietzsche, however, "What is needed above all is an absolute skepticism toward all inherited concepts."[8] In contrast, the genealogist searches for the origins of these concepts and values in the cultural practices and conditions from which they emerged. The genealogist traces the history of the present in order to undermine the self-evidences of the present. Such new philosophers "have found their task, their hard, unwanted, unavoidable task, but finally the greatness of their task, in being

the bad conscience of their age" and in "laying the knife vivisection-
ally to the bosom of the very *virtues of the age....*"⁹ It is in this sense
that the new philosopher's meditations are always "untimely."

In the winter of 1876–77 Nietzsche shared a house in Sorren-
to with Paul Rée. The fruits of that winter were Nietzsche's
Human, All Too Human and Rée's *The Origin of Moral Sentiments.* According to Nietzsche it was Rée's book which first stimulated him to publish some of his own hypotheses regarding the
genealogy of morals. The stimulation that came from Rée's book,
however, was not that which comes from the discovery of a com-
panion moving in one's own direction. Although Nietzsche had
once considered Rée to be a potential colleague, Rée ultimately
failed to adopt the "better method" to which the very nature of his
own study should have compelled him.¹⁰ The fundamental wrong-
ness of Rée's work first stimulated Nietzsche to publish. Referring
to Rée's *The Origin of Moral Sentiments,* Nietzsche asserted, "Perhaps I have never read anything to which I would have said to
myself No, proposition by proposition, conclusion by conclusion, to
the extent that I did to this book...."¹¹ Nietzsche labels Rée's project "genealogical," but it is genealogy in an "upsidedown and perverse" form.¹²

The first hint of the perversity of the English approach to
genealogy arises in Nietzsche's Preface to *On the Genealogy of
Morals* in an oblique reference to the coloring of the two types of
genealogy: English genealogy, and that of Rée, is blue, whereas
Nietzschean genealogy is gray. English genealogy is blue in the
sense of looking about haphazardly, in a directionless fashion—as
if one were looking "into the blue." Nietzschean genealogy is, in
contrast, documentary gray; it is concerned with "what is documented, what can actually be confirmed and has actually existed,
in short the entire long hieroglyphic record, so hard to decipher, of
the moral past of mankind."¹³ In his allusive discussion of Rée's
genealogy Nietzsche focuses his criticisms upon two related
aspects of Rée's endeavor: the lack of historical sense and the lack
of psychological sense in Rée's analysis.

Like the Nietzschean genealogist, Rée is searching for the
origin of morals. Rée's first error is in searching human interiority
for this origin rather than searching the documented evidence
from history, especially history as presented to the philologist. The
English genealogists, among whom we can include Rée, are psychologists. They look to the "inner world"; they look for the origin
in "the *partie honteuse* of human beings," "in the *vis inertiae* of
habit, for example, or in forgetfulness..., creeping around men and

into men."[14] They should have taken their clue from the etymology of our moral categories and sought their origin in history. The English genealogists-psychologists, moreover, are poor psychologists. Briefly, they lack the psychological sense to distinguish reactive ressentiment from noble, creative activity. According to Nietzsche's account of English genealogy,

> "Originally"—so they decree—"one approved unegoistic actions and called them good from the point of view of those to whom they were done, that is to say, those to whom they were *useful*; later one *forgot* how this approval originated and, simply because unegoistic actions were always *habitually* praised as good, one also felt them to be good—as if they were something good in themselves."[15]

The entire analysis is couched in the passive categories of utility, forgetting, habit, and error, and the analysis arises from the standpoint of the passive one *to whom* the actions were done, the one *to whom* they were useful.

Two dimensions of Nietzsche's negative evaluation of the principle of utility can be distinguished: the passive standpoint of the one who judges in terms of utility and the passive character of happiness entailed by the principle of utility. One who judges from the standpoint of the principle of utility, according to Nietzsche, judges from the point of view of a passive third party wanting to be the recipient of benefits of the creative activity of others. In *Beyond Good and Evil* Nietzsche summarizes the typical European virtues—"public spirit, benevolence, consideration, industriousness, moderation, modesty, forbearance, pity"—in terms of their utility for the herd.[16] Secondly, utilitarian happiness, the happiness of this herd, according to Nietzsche, is conceived of as a life of passivity—good sleep and opiate virtues, in the words of Zarathustra.[17] Happiness from this point of view is separated from activity and, thereby, falsified. Since the sundering of happiness from action is the root, not only of the dualism of good and evil, but the root of all dualisms, the passage is worth quoting at length. Nietzsche contrasts the happiness of the active noble with that of the herd:

> The "well-born" *felt* themselves to be the "happy"; they did not have to establish their happiness artificially by examining their enemies, or to persuade themselves, *deceive* themselves, that they were happy (as all men of *ressentiment* are

in the habit of doing); and they likewise knew as rounded men replete with energy and therefore *necessarily* active, that happiness should not be sundered from action—being active was with them necessarily a part of happiness (whence *eu prattein* takes its origin)—all very much the opposite of "happiness" at the level of the impotent, the oppressed, and those in whom poisonous and inimical feelings are festering, with whom it appears as essentially narcotic, drug, rest, peace, "sabbath," slackening of tension and relaxing of limbs, in short *passively.*[18]

In the context of another discussion of the role of utility Nietzsche offers what he calls a "major point of historical method."[19] Nietzsche contrasts his own approach to the history of punishment, which we will examine in detail in our next chapter, with that of the English genealogists. Once the English genealogist claims to have discovered a purpose for punishment he imposes this purpose upon the origin and assumes that he has adequately explained the phenomenon of punishment. According to Nietzsche, however, "the cause of the origin of a thing and its eventual utility, its actual employment and place in a system of purposes, lie worlds apart."[20] Any phenomenon, such as punishment, is interpreted and reinterpreted again and again throughout history. In Nietzsche's words,

> whatever exists, having somehow come into being, is again and again reinterpreted to new ends, taken over, transformed, and redirected by some power superior to it; all events in the organic world are a subduing, a *becoming master*, and all subduing and becoming master involves a fresh interpretation, an adaptation through which any previous "meaning" and "purpose" are necessarily obscured or even obliterated.[21]

The utility of something has no explanatory power. On the contrary,

> purposes and utilities are only *signs* that a will to power has become master of something less powerful and imposed upon it the character of a function; and the entire history of a "thing," an organ, a custom can in this way be a continuous sign-chain of ever new interpretations and adaptations whose causes do not even have to be related to one another but, on

the contrary, in some cases succeed and alternate with one another in a purely chance fashion.... The form is fluid, but the "meaning" is even more so.[22]

B. Nietzsche's Genealogy of Morals

Having cleared the ground of philosophers' prejudices and misguided attempts at genealogy, we can now directly approach Nietzsche's own understanding of genealogy. Since, as mentioned before, he never explicitly states what he means by genealogy, our task is to derive genealogy's elements from his historical studies and passing remarks on methodology.

1. Genealogy is Critique

In the context of his famous discussion of master morality and slave morality Nietzsche introduces what is perhaps the most significant and revolutionary elements in his genealogical approach. He undermines the notion of the substratum (in all the forms it has taken in the history of philosophy—substance, subject, thing-in-itself) by revealing the paralogism at the heart of slave morality. In contrast to "good and bad" which is a formula for a noble way of evaluating, "good and evil" is a distinction made by people of *ressentiment*. Deleuze captures the spirit of *ressentiment* in the following formula: "You are evil therefore I am good";[23] i.e., You are evil, and by compensation I am good because I am the reverse of what you are.

You are evil
I am the opposite of you
Therefore, I am good
Q.E.D.

There is, however, according to Nietzsche, a sophism here. The resentful person's formulation of good and evil is grounded in a falsification. In the formula for good and evil, "You" refers to the active person; "I" refers to the non-active person of *ressentiment*. "You" are a force, a cause, and are evil because of your effects. You could be good by refraining from having effects; that is, you are a force, a cause, which *could* refrain from having effects. A cause, thus, is understood as a neutral entity remaining what it is independent of effects and activity. But for Nietzsche, there is no such thing as a force separated from its expression:

> A quantum of force is equivalent to a quantum of drive, will, effect—more, it is nothing other than precisely this very driving, willing, effecting, and only owing to the seduction of language (and of the fundamental errors of reason that are petrified in it) which conceives and misconceives all effects as conditioned by something that causes effects, by a "subject," can it appear otherwise.[24]

Language seduces the popular mind into doubling phenomena. We say "lightning flashes" and think of a neutral substratum (lightning) which performs the activity of flashing. The lightning is thereby separated from its flashing. "But there is no such substratum; there is no 'being' behind doing, effecting, becoming; 'the doer' is merely a fiction added to the deed—the deed is everything."[25]

In *The Will to Power* Nietzsche affirms the basic principles of Hume's analysis of causality, but he goes beyond Hume in his psychological interpretation of our need for causes. Having observed the constant conjunction of events, human beings tend to label as "cause" the temporally prior event. This labeling, for Nietzsche, is a mnemonic device intended to stabilize our experience. We impose an abbreviated formula (cause and effect) upon our experience, and Nietzsche laments our tendency, our "bad habit," of interpreting this mnemonic formula as an entity, a cause.[26] Nietzsche sees two psychological tendencies at the root of this habit. First, we impose our interpretation of ourselves, as intending subjects, as doers who intentionally perform deeds, upon our experience of events. Here Nietzsche goes beyond Hume:

> That which gives the extraordinary firmness to our belief in causality is not the great habit of seeing one occurrence following another but our inability to interpret events otherwise than as events caused by intentions. It is belief in the living and thinking as the only effective force—in will, in intention—it is belief that every event is a deed, that every deed presupposes a doer, it is belief in the "subject."[27]

Based upon our interpretation of ourselves as causal agents we thought we had in the experience of our own activity a privileged access to causality itself. In *Twilight of the Idols*, Nietzsche sees operative here the "oldest and longest-lived psychology": "every event was to it an action, every action the effect of a will, the world became for it a multiplicity of agents, an agent ('subject') foisted itself upon every event."[28] Thus, the concept of cause is derived from our conviction that we are causes in the sense of neutral subjects who could act or not act, forces separated from what they can do. A falsification resides at the heart of our notion of causality. It is based upon a misinterpretation of the feeling which accompanies *the beginning of the performance* of an action as separate from the action. Upon this separation of ourselves from our actions, upon this separation of doers from deeds, our notion of cause depends. That is why Nietzsche is able to claim that "The concept of substance is a consequence of the concept of the subject: not the reverse!"[29]

The second psychological tendency at the root of our notion of causality is our desire to domesticate experience. We want to normalize experience. Surprise disturbs, and we much prefer the familiar. Like the Stoic who prefers order over chaos and imposes this evaluation on his interpretation of nature, modern men and women impose the formula "cause and effect" to tame nature. Thus, "The supposed instinct for causality is only fear of the unfamiliar and the attempt to discover something familiar in it—a search, not for causes, but for the familiar."[30] Pleasure is the criterion of truth operative here. Since "Danger, disquiet, anxiety attend the unknown—the first instinct is to *eliminate* these distressing states. First principle: any explanation is better than none."[31] We systematically exclude the strange and search our memory for a more soothing and comfortable explanation. When confronted by the strange and unknown, we search our memory for something similar and comfort ourselves by explaining the unknown in terms of the known.

All knowledge, according to Nietzsche, is a function of the will to power, or more explicitly in this context, a function of the will to domesticate and normalize experience. In *On the Genealogy of Morals* Nietzsche asserts the conservative, self-preserving character of the need to believe in a neutral independent subject,[32] but he is even more explicit about this in his aphorisms collected in *The Will to Power.* According to Nietzsche,

> There exists neither "spirit," nor reason, nor thinking, nor consciousness, nor soul, nor will, nor truth: all are fictions that are of no use. There is no question of "subject and object," but of a particular species of animal that can prosper only through a certain relative rightness; above all, regularity of its perceptions (so that it can accumulate experience)—[33]

Moreover, this need to believe in a neutral subject as an element in the normalization of experience has a physiological effect. The development of the brain and the senses is a function of the conserving, self-preserving need. In Nietzsche's words,

> In order for a particular species to maintain itself and increase its power, its conception of reality must comprehend enough of the calculable and constant for it to base a scheme of behavior on it. The utility of preservation—not some abstract-theoretical need not to be deceived—stands as the motive behind the development of the organs of knowledge—they develop in such a way that their observations suffice for our preservation. In other words: the measure of the desire for knowledge depends upon the measure to which the will to power grows in a species: a species grasps a certain amount of reality in order to become master of it, in order to press it into service.[34]

There are no given facts, according to Nietzsche, only interpretations. Nor is the subject a given fact; "it is something added and invented and projected behind what there is."[35]

In his 1886 Preface to *Daybreak* (1881) Nietzsche refers to himself as a "subterrestial," and he is quite explicit concerning what he was seeking down-under.

> I went down into the deepest depths; I tunnelled to the very bottom; I started to investigate and unearth an old *faith* which for thousands of years we philosophers used to build on as the safest of all foundations—which we built on again and again although every previous structure fell in: I began to undermine our *faith in morals*.[36]

Why is it, Nietzsche asks, that every previous structure has toppled? The modern answer of Kant cannot be more wrong:

> Because they have all neglected the prerequisite, the examination of the foundation, a critique of all reason.... (and one may ask apropos of this, was it not rather strange to demand that an instrument should criticise its own value and effectiveness? that the intellect itself should "recognise" its own worth, power, and limits? was it not even just a little ridiculous?)[37]

The correct answer would have been to see that what all previous philosophy actually sought, while masquerading as the pure search for certainty and truth, was a morality. Nietzsche reveals the will at the root of this allegedly pure search. The real task of *The Critique of Pure Reason* was the establishment of the noumenal order. While Robespierre wanted *"de fonder sur la terre l'empire de la sagesse, de la justice, et de la vertu,"*[38] Kant went even further.

> ...in order to make room for *his* "moral kingdom," he found himself compelled to add to it an indemonstrable world, a logical "beyond"—that was why he required his critique of pure reason! In other words, *he would not have wanted it*, if he had not deemed one thing to be more important than all the others: to render his moral kingdom unassailable by—or, better still, invisible to, reason—for he felt too strongly the vulnerability of a moral order of things in the face of reason.[39]

Regularly contradicted by nature and history Kant's morality had to be protected from their snares.

But Nietzsche, the immoralist, does not claim to be completely immune to morality. He finds himself under a strict moral law, "the last cry of morals which is still audible to us": Life, as opposed to the death proclaimed and pursued by morality, "decayed, outlived, and superseded." Nietzsche refers to his task as "the auto-suppression of morals"; i.e., the last category of morality he is capable of hearing, Life, becomes his weapon for undermining morality.

What motivated Nietzsche to undertake his genealogical project? Rather than idle "hypothesis-mongering" concerning the origin of morality, Nietzsche intended to investigate the value of morality, especially in its modern, Schopenhauerian form. Nietzsche's skepticism was directed toward the value of the "unegoistic" which Schopenhauer had lifted to the status of "value-in-itself."[40] The genealogical project, however, was not merely intended to address Schopenhauer; rather, Nietzsche saw in Schopenhauer's work the expression of "the ultimate illness," nihilism.[41] He saw this unegotistic morality, this new European Buddhism, as symptomatic of the nihilistic spirit of modernity.

The genealogical problematic arose for Nietzsche in its first form when he was a thirteen year-old boy. At that time he devoted his first philosophical effort, his "first childish literary trifle,"[42] to the problem of the origin of evil. Although at that age he attributed the origin of evil to God, he later "learned to separate theological prejudice from moral prejudice and ceased to look for the origin of evil *behind* the world."[43] His education in history and philology and his interest in psychological questions transformed his problematic. Thus he was able to formulate the problem in a more mature fashion: "under what conditions did man devise these value judgments good and evil? *and what value do they themselves possess?*"[44] Have these value judgments contributed to human prosperity, or are they a sign of degeneration?

In *The Will to Power* Nietzsche takes great pains to distinguish these two moments of genealogy: the question of the conditions under which our value judgments originated and the question of the value of these value judgments. He indicates that the first moment is preparatory for the critical second moment; i.e., only in the second moment does genealogy function as critique. According to Nietzsche,

> The inquiry into the *origin of our evaluations* and tables of the good is in absolutely no way identical with a critique of them, as is so often believed: even though the insight into some *pudenda origo* certainly brings with it *a feeling* of a diminution in value of the thing that originated thus and prepares the way to a critical mood and attitude toward it.
>
> What are our evaluations and moral tables really worth? What is the outcome of their rule? For whom? in relation to what?—Answer: for life.[45]

This failure to take the step to critique is, once again, typical of the English genealogists. What distinguishes "our task," the task of Nietzschean genealogy, is to move from the history of origins of our moral evaluations to a questioning of the value of the evaluations.

To learn to ask such questions is to open up a whole new prospective field and to be confronted by a new demand. The genealogy of morals, according to Nietzsche, should be understood essentially as critique: "Let us articulate this *new demand*: we need a *critique* of moral values, *the value of these values themselves must first be called in question....*"[46] This critique necessitates a study of the circumstances under which values came to be, the conditions under which they grew, evolved, and changed. Genealogy as critique requires the study of the different forms in which morality has appeared; "(morality as consequence, as symptom, as mask, as tartufferie, as illness, as misunderstanding; but also morality as cause, as remedy, as stimulant, as restraint, as poison)."[47] Genealogy as critique would constitute a body of knowledge that has never existed before nor ever been desired. To question values in terms of their value is critique in that it entails asking whether values have been progressive or regressive, whether values have contributed to our advancement and prosperity. Nietzsche asks,

> What if a symptom of regression were inherent in the "good," likewise a danger, a seduction, a poison, a narcotic, through which the present was possibly living *at the expense of the future*?... So that precisely morality would be to blame if the *highest power and splendor* actually possible to the type man was never in fact attained? So that precisely morality was the danger of dangers?[48]

This new mode of questioning is constitutive of genealogy's power as critique.

2. Critique is Genealogical: Genealogy as History Oriented toward the Future

Genealogy is history, the search for origins, a searching of the past, that is oriented toward the service of life and activity. In the second of his *Untimely Meditations*, "On the Uses and Disadvantages of History for Life," Nietzsche makes clear that he is concerned with history only to the extent that history serves life. The essay is concerned with *Historie*, as opposed to *Geschichte*; i.e., the essay investigates, not the chronological process of what happened in time, but the historical record, the narrative account of what happened in time. Therefore, Nietzsche is concerned with the way people record, narrate, and explain their own past and with evaluating the effects of various types of historical narration upon life. The intention behind his meditation on the value of history "is to show why instruction without invigoration, why knowledge not attended by action, why history as a costly superfluity and luxury, must, to use Goethe's word, be seriously hated by us.... We need it, that is to say, for the sake of life and action.... We want to serve history only to the extent that history serves life...."[49] It is an untimely meditation in that a questioning of the value of history ran counter to Nietzsche's own age's pride in its cultivation of history. Nonetheless, Nietzsche hoped that his untimely meditation on the value of history, as he hoped for history itself, would be "for the benefit of a time to come."[50]

Section 1 of "The Uses and Disadvantages of History for Life"
argues for a distinction between animals and human beings in
terms of our differing relationships with time. Animals live unhistorically; they do not know the meaning of yesterday and today.
Their lives are characterized by a passive forgetfulness, and upon
this their happiness, so envied by human beings, is based. The
ability to forget, according to Nietzsche, is the essential condition
for happiness, for any kind of action, and even for life. In Nietzsche's words,

> Thus: it is possible to live almost without memory, and to live
> happily moreover, as the animal demonstrates; but it is alto-
> gether impossible to *live* at all without forgetting. Or, to
> express my theme even more simply: *there is a degree of
> sleeplessness, of rumination, of the historical sense, which is
> harmful and ultimately fatal to the living thing, whether this
> living thing be a man or a people or a culture.*[51]

The human task is to develop the capacity to forget actively for the
sake of life. In *The Genealogy of Morals* Nietzsche writes with
great admiration of the French revolutionary Count of Mirabeau
as exemplifying the strength of character that results from this
capacity to forget actively. Mirabeau "had no memory for insults
and vile actions done him and was unable to forgive simply
because he—forgot." Unlike the animal's forgetfulness, which is a
matter of passively failing to remember, Mirabeau's forgetfulness
is an active, creative power "to form, to mold, to recuperate and to
forget" his experience for the sake of serving life.[52]

Every civilization, according to Nietzsche, has what he calls
its own "plastic power," its own way of actively and creatively
interpreting its own past. "I mean by plastic power the capacity to
develop out of oneself in one's way, to transform and incorporate
into oneself what is past and foreign, to heal wounds, to replace
what has been lost, to recreate broken moulds."[53] This plastic
power entails both an active, creative remembering and an active
forgetting which establish a horizon around oneself, and the life,
health, and activity of a person or culture are dependent upon the
proper establishment of this horizon. One must be able actively to
forget as well as actively to remember when appropriate. According to Nietzsche, "the unhistorical and the historical are necessary
in equal measure for the health of an individual, of a people and of
a culture," and the ability to live unhistorically is to be considered
the more vital and fundamental of the two, "inasmuch as it consti-

tutes the foundation upon which alone anything sound, healthy and great, anything truly human, can grow."[54] An active mode of living requires a limited horizon, a limited, actively invented perspective on the world. There can be no new interpretation without a rejection, an active forgetting, of previous interpretations.

There are three types of history, according to Nietzsche, each of which is potentially life-enhancing and potentially life-destroying: monumental history, antiquarian history, and critical history. Each of these modes of history pertains to the living human being: monumental history pertains to him "as a being who acts and strives," antiquarian history pertains to him "as a being who preserves and reveres," and critical history pertains to him "as a being who suffers and seeks deliverance."[55]

The powerful person of great deeds demands a monumental history. Such history is life-enhancing for the person of action by enabling him to avoid despair and by empowering him to act, "For the commandment which rules over him is: that which in the past was able to expand the concept 'man' and make it more beautiful must exist everlastingly, so as to be able to accomplish this everlastingly."[56] The interpretation of the monumental historian is founded upon the will that the great moments in the life of humankind form a continuous, progressive chain. It is founded upon a will to maintain as a living presence each great life-enhancing moment in history. The person of great deeds, moreover, receives from monumental history the knowledge that great deeds were once possible and that such greatness might be possible once again.

Monumental history is the result of an active remembering of humankind's moments of greatness, but it is even more so the result of an active forgetting. "How much of the past would have to be overlooked if it was to produce that mighty effect, how violently what is individual in it would have to be forced into a universal mould and all its sharp corners and hard outlines broken up in the interest of conformity!"[57] In order to manifest the monumental effects in a monumental fashion, monumental history tends to overlook the differences in the causes of actions, the motivation of the actor, the differing instigations of actions. Nietzsche even goes so far as to say that monumental history borders on "free poetic invention," such that in some periods of history it was next to impossible to distinguish the monumentalized past from mythical fiction.[58]

Monumental history can be life-enhancing in the hands of people of great deeds, but it can be destructive in two contexts: at times when in these same hands of great achievers, but it is even more destructive of life when it falls into the hands of the impotent. First, in the hands of the powerful, monumental history "inspires the courageous to foolhardiness and the inspired to fanaticism...."[59] Nietzsche envisions destroyed empires floating in the wake of assassinations, wars, and revolutions. But the destructive capacity of monumental history is even more insidious when it falls into the hands of the impotent. They destroy, not through their own activity, but by stifling the creativity of the powerful. The strong artistic spirit receives the monuments of the past, learns from these monuments, and transforms this learning into a life-enhancing higher practice. In contrast, the impotent erect these monuments as static idols. They stifle the creative potential of the powerful with their characteristic slogan: "Behold, this is true art: pay no heed to those who are evolving and want something new!"[60] They condemn the contemporary for lacking the authority of history. Moreover, "their instincts tell them that art can be slain by art: the monumental is never to be repeated, and to make sure it is not they invoke the authority which the monumental derives from the past. They are connoisseurs of art because they would like to do away with art altogether...."[61] When monumental history falls into the hands of the impotent it becomes

> the masquerade costume in which their hatred of the great and powerful of their own age is disguised as satiated admiration for the great and powerful of past ages, and muffled in which they invert the real meaning of that mode of regarding history into its opposite; whether they are aware of it or not, they act as though their motto were: let the dead bury the living.[62]

The destructive capacity of monumental history blossoms in the soil of "the man who recognizes greatness but cannot himself do great things."[63]

Reverence for the past, piety, and gratitude characterize the antiquarian historian. The antiquarian seeks to preserve his own roots and heritage. "By tending with care that which has existed from of old, he wants to preserve for those who shall come into existence after him the conditions under which he himself came into existence—and thus he serves life."[64] Rather than possessing the goods he has preserved from the past—even those trivial and decaying—the soul of the antiquarian is possessed by them. His soul enters them and bestows dignity upon them. The future orientation of antiquarian history is made explicit by Nietzsche in the words he puts in the mouth of the antiquarian enjoying the history of his own city: "Here we lived, he says to himself, for here we are living; and here we shall live, for we are tough and not to be ruined overnight."[65]

Like monumental history, antiquarian history is character-ized by ignorance, or better, an active forgetting. According to Nietzsche,

> The antiquarian sense of a man, a community, a whole peo-ple, always possesses an extremely restricted field of vision; most of what exists it does not perceive at all, and the little it does see it sees much too close up and isolated; it cannot relate what it sees to anything else and it therefore accords everything it sees equal importance and therefore to each individual thing too great importance. There is a lack of that discrimination of value and that sense of proportion which would distinguish between the things of the past in a way that would do true justice to them; their measure and propor-tion is always that accorded them by the backward glance of the antiquarian nation or individual.[66]

This preoccupied reverence for what is of one's own heritage mani-fests a certain narrowness of vision, but it serves life as a check on the flighty preoccupation with the ever new and allegedly improved. The ignorance of the antiquarian historian is life-enhancing, like the tree's satisfaction with its own soil and roots is life-enhancing.

The potentially destructive power of antiquarian history should already be clear. Age itself bestows value. The new enters unproven; it has yet to pass through the refiner's fire and is, there-fore, casually rejected. According to Nietzsche, the danger for life in antiquarian history is that "everything old and past that enters one's field of vision at all is in the end blandly taken to be equally worthy of reverence, while everything that does not approach this antiquity with reverence, that is to say everything new and evolv-ing, is rejected and persecuted."[67] The antiquarian's senses are prone to hardening, and he mummifies life rather than preserving it. In order to avoid this degeneration the antiquarian historian must remain open to the inspiration of the present and new. More-over, antiquarian history must maintain itself in creative tension with the other types of history.

> For it knows only how to *preserve* life, not how to engender it; it always undervalues that which is becoming because it has no instinct for divining it—as monumental history, for exam-

ple, has. Thus it hinders any firm resolve to attempt something new, thus it paralyses the man of action who, as one who acts, will and must offend some piety or other.[68]

This insight into the potentially destructive power of antiquarian history leads Nietzsche to see the necessity of a third type of history, the critical mode.

For the sake of life and in the name of life human beings must now and then destroy some of the past by condemning it. Essentially, this process of destruction is a matter of attempting to give oneself a past which one prefers to one's actual past. It is impossible to free oneself completely from one's own given heritage by condemning the aberrations of one's past. "The best we can do," according to Nietzsche, "is to confront our inherited and hereditary nature with our knowledge of it, and through a new, stern discipline combat our inborn heritage and inplant in ourselves a new habit, a new instinct, a second nature, so that our first nature withers away."[69] Every past, according to Nietzsche, is open to such condemnation and rejection because of the role played in all things human by violence and weakness. In one of his more shocking comments Nietzsche asserts, "It requires a great deal of strength to be able to live and to forget the extent to which to live and to be unjust is one and the same thing."[70] Our generation is the result of the crimes of previous generations, and although the facticity of this is unchangeable, we can critically reinterpret our past and create an alternative one in which we would prefer to have originated.

*   *   *

The problem of language is at the center of Nietzsche's thought; language embodies its own metaphysics. By problematizing language, Nietzsche made a problem of man. By throwing into question the subject-object grammatical structure of our language, he removed human consciousness from its exalted place at the source of our activity and dismantled the doer-deed model for understanding any event in the universe. By decentering man, Nietzsche shattered the unity which had previously been posited at the source of the entities and events we encounter. This allowed the manifestation of a multiplicity at the origin. Nietzsche's genealogies are meant to trace this multiplicity.

When Nietzsche asserts that there is no value without an evaluation, he assaults some of the metaphysician's most sacred cows. If, as Nietzsche maintains, everything is mediated by the life and consciousness of knowers, the division between the real and the apparent breaks down. He shatters the Kantian notion that self-critical rationality can liberate us from the distortions and simplifications of our grammar and concepts. Even the metaphysician's allegedly pure search for truth is based upon a prior evaluation of truth as that which is to be esteemed. The metaphysician's preference for the definite over the indefinite, the unchanging over the changing, the one over the many, is simply that—a preference, an act of will. These preferences, according to Nietzsche, mask what he considers obvious, that our values, ideas, and concepts all originate in time and multiplicity. There is no such thing for Nietzsche as a thing subsisting independently of its relations with other things. These relations, rather than a metaphysician's substratum, constitute any thing's conditions of existence. Genealogy's task is to bring these concrete, practical, and historical conditions of existence into the open. Because of the concreteness such a task demands, and because of Nietzsche's devaluation of human consciousness, genealogy focuses its historical analyses on the body and its relations.

Nietzsche's genealogy, then, can be viewed as a diagnostic history of the present. The genealogist traces the history of the present in order to undermine its self-evidences and to open possibilities for the enhancement of life.

PART II: Michel Foucault's Notion of Genealogy

L'archéologie du savoir is a strange text and a stumbling block for Foucault's commentators. Perhaps the most extreme interpretation is that offered by Allan Megill; *L'archéologie du savoir* is a parody of Descartes' *Discourse on Method*.[71] If so, it is an awfully long and tedious joke. Deleuze sees *L'archéologie du savoir* as not so much a discourse on Foucault's method as "the poem of his previous work," whatever that means.[72] Sheridan bemoans its striking austerity in contrast to *Les mots et les choses* and calls it not a book in its own right but "an extended theoretical postscript" to *Les mots et les choses*.[73] After completing *L'archéologie du savoir*, according to Sheridan, Foucault discovered the role power played in discourse and "felt impelled to abandon altogether the terms he had fashioned for himself and to adopt, unashamedly, the Nietzschean term 'genealogy.'"[74] According to Barry Smart *L'archéolo-gie du savoir*'s concepts and categories are "almost totally subvert-ed" by Foucault's shift to genealogy, leaving the reader with an either-or option: "Archaeologist of ideas or genealogist of power?"[75] Smart views *L'archéologie du savoir* as a blind alley from which Foucault later recovered. Jeffrey Minson, in contrast, maintains that the reader of Foucault's later genealogies must return to *L'archéologie du savoir* to put genealogy "back on course."[76] Minson leads his readers to believe that genealogy would have been the blind alley if it had not been for the light of archaeology to help it find its way. There is much to be said for those interpretations which see *L'archéologie du savoir* as essentially disruptive. The text introduces a vast new vocabulary which will never again see the light of day in Foucault's work. Its talk of discursive forma-tions, archives, points of diffraction of discourse, the remanence of statements, remains forever bracketed between the covers of this single, unusual text.

François Russo, on the contrary, reads *L'archéologie du savoir* as another consistent step in Foucault's total project: "The author controls his topic; he knows where he is going; he is intent on defining the exact meaning of the notions which he uses and he explains himself with all the precision and rigour that may be asked for."[77] *L'archéologie du savoir*, thus, fits right in, advancing the argument which genealogy will pick up. Bernauer agrees. *L'archéologie du savoir* is not a disruption of Foucault's problemat-ic. "Not since his earliest anthropological writings," according to Bernauer, "has he been so certain of his project and so sure of its importance, not just in terms of its relation to the history of ideas but, of more consequence, to thought itself. Archaeology is the promise of a thought adequate to a culture which is awakening from belief in its dialectical intelligibility."[78]

Dreyfus and Rabinow argue at great length that Foucault's project in *L'archéologie du savoir* founders and turns him away from the theory of discourse and to Nietzsche's genealogy as a new means to developing a method. This new method would enable him "to thematize the relationship between truth, theory, and values and the social institutions and practices in which they emerge."[79] While never completely abandoned—archaeology will henceforth subordinate itself to and serve genealogy—archaeology appears to Dreyfus and Rabinow as an obstacle to be overcome before Fou-cault can get to the serious business of analyzing the relationships among truth, knowledge, and social institutions and practices. There is more than a little difficulty, however, in reading *Histoire de la folie,* Foucault's *archaeology* of madness's silence or *Naissance de la clinique: Une archéologie du regard médical* and still argue that Foucault in his early archaeological writings is simply concerned with autonomous discourse, independent of technologies of power, social practices, and institutions.[80] As Foucault insists with an interviewer, "there is only interest in describing this autonomous stratum of discourse to the measure in which one can put it in relation with other strata, of practices, of institutions, of social and political relations, etc. It is this relation which has always haunted me, and I have wanted, in *Histoire de la folie* and *Naissance de la clinique,* to define the relations between these different domains."[81] And again, "The archaeology of the human sciences has to be established through studying the mechanisms of power which have invested human bodies, acts and forms of behaviour."[82] *L'archéologie du savoir* coaxes its readers to see that "their history, their economics, their social practices, the language that they speak, the mythology of their ancestors, even the stories they were told in their childhood, are governed by rules that are not all given to their consciousness."[83] Archaeology examines the "archive," "that specific discursive configuration which permits a discourse to arise, to exist and to function within the framework of social relations and practices, within modes of institutionalized application and cultural usage."[84]

Discussing the development of Foucault's problematic Lemert and Gillan call *L'archéologie du savoir* an "interruption" rather than "a decisive event." Nonetheless, if we follow their lead we can gain some clarity on the place of *L'archéologie du savoir* in the development of Foucault's problematic. According to Lemert and Gillan, "It is easy, all too easy, to receive *Archaeology of Knowledge* as Foucault's methodological program…. The book is also topical. Its subject is knowledge (savoir), and knowledge's relationship to discourse…. Beneath the description of method, this book is what its title says it is, a book on knowledge."[85] Indeed, we ought to take *L'archéologie du savoir* for what it says it is. The text stands as a mature statement in Foucault's corpus, an essential element in his mature genealogical problematic.

In a 1983 interview Foucault puts it as follows: "three axes are possible for genealogy. All three were present, albeit in a somewhat confused fashion, in *Madness and Civilization.* The truth axis was studied in *The Birth of the Clinic* and *The Order of Things.* The power axis was studied in *Discipline and Punish,* and the ethical axis in *The History of Sexuality.*"[86] After *Les mots et les choses's* explorations along the truth axis in terms of a study of discursive formations, Foucault, in *L'archéologie du savoir*, articulated the principles for exploring such formations and solidified his discoveries from his three previous major works, that discursive practices are inserted into systems of institutional and other nondiscursive practices.

Truth, what a culture takes to be true knowledge, thought itself, for Foucault, is intimately bound up with the fate of language. His explorations in *Les mots et les choses* and solidifying reflections in *L'archéologie du savoir* stand together as his analysis of the truth axis in his genealogical project, revealing, among other things, that discourse is inserted into systems of nondiscursive practices. The continuation of his pursuit of the genealogical problematic will lead him to study how these discursive practices are inserted into systems of institutional and other non-discursive practices. The power axis is, thus, the focus of his lectures on power/knowledge and his study of the birth of the prison.[87] While none of the three axes plays itself out in radical independence—a central point of genealogy—the integrity of the truth axis is not to be missed. *Les mots et les choses* and *L'archéologie du savoir* stand as Foucault's attempt to do justice to this axis.

Attempting to distinguish Foucault's archaeologies from his genealogies, Barry Smart argues that "The archaeological investigations are directed to an analysis of the unconscious rules of formation which regulate the emergence of discourses in the human sciences. *In contrast*, the genealogical analyses reveal the emergence of the human sciences, their conditions of existence, to be inextricably associated with particular technologies of power embodied in social practices."[88] Smart accounts for the transition in terms of a shift in Foucault's "value relationship to his subject matter" from the "relative detachment" of archaeology to "a commitment to critique" characteristic of genealogy. Foucault's commitment to critique is "evident in the opposition expressed 'to the scientific hierarchisation of knowledges and the effects intrinsic to their power.'"[89] For Foucault, however, any critique, in the sense of opposition, is founded upon a more fundamental critique, in the sense of revealing the contingent historical conditions of the existence of, for example, this scientific hierarchisation of knowledges. "A critique does not consist in saying that things are not good as they are," Foucault maintains. "It consists in seeing what kinds of self-evidences, liberties, acquired and non-reflective modes of thought, the practices we accept rest on."[90] The task of genealogy is to reveal the historical conditions of existence (what he will later call "historical ontology"), and an essential element in such a task is an archaeological analysis of discursive rules of formation of objects. Genealogy is critique, a questioning of the historical conditions of existence, a questioning of the historical a priori.[91] Archaeology proceeds along the truth axis, analyzing discursive conditions of existence. Genealogy travels the power axis, examining culturally true discourse's insertion into institutional and other non-discursive practices.

The disputes among Foucault's commentators never commanded his full attention. Although he showed himself to be a compliant respondent to questioning, he rarely directly addressed the relationship between archaeology and genealogy. Instead, he pressed on to the issues that always interested him from the time of *Histoire de la folie*, the relation between knowledge and social practices. In the spring of 1983 the intellectual historian, Martin Jay, asked Foucault about the "shift in the methodological focus" of his work from "the earlier archaeological perspective" to the "genealogical perspective" of the 1970s: "Is this a significant and radical break in your work, or can we conceive of genealogy as basically similar to archaeology...? How would you describe the difference between archaeology and genealogy as an historical method?"[92]

Foucault responded that he employed the expression "archaeological research" in order to differentiate his work from both social history and philosophical hermeneutics. More importantly, he asserted that the difference between archaeology and genealogy is that between method and goal:

> What I mean by archaeology is a methodological framework for my analysis. What I mean by genealogy is both the reason and the target of analyzing those discourses as events, and what I am trying to show is how those discursive events have determined in a certain way what constitutes our present and what constitutes ourselves—either our knowledge, our practices, our type of rationality, our relationship to ourselves or to others.... the genealogy is the finality of the analysis, and the archaeology is the material and methodological framework.[93]

The task of genealogy is to reveal the historical conditions of our existence, and an essential element in such a task is an archaeological analysis of discursive rules of formation of objects. This relationship between archaeology and genealogy emerges most clearly by reading *L'archéologie du savoir* through the prism of Foucault's 1971 essay "Nietzsche, la généalogie, l'histoire," the landmark essay which signals his explicit adoption of Nietzschean approaches.[94] As Foucault himself claims, "my archaeology owes more to Nietzschean genealogy than to so-called structuralism."[95] Such a reading brings out the consistency of his developing genealogical problematic.

A. On the Prejudices of Philosophers

Foucault's *L'archéologie du savoir* of 1969 includes a meditation on his own previous work, concentrating upon *Les mots et les choses, Naissance de la clinique*, and *Histoire de la folie*.[96] In the spirit of *Les mots et les choses*'s revelation of man as the historically and discursively constituted, precarious obstacle to thought, Foucault seeks the erasure of man in all his guises. As Roger Paden puts it, *L'archéologie du savoir* "is a strategic work, aimed at undercutting any anthropological grounding of knowledge."[97] *Naissance de la clinique* dismantled the Enlightenment's own narrative accounts of its progress in knowledge by turning away from theory to the perception of preexisting objects; in that spirit Foucault seeks means to reveal the historical and discursive constitution of objects, concepts, and intellectual strategies. In the spirit of *Histoire de la folie*'s disclosure of the historical constitution of *homo psychologicus* by means of confinement practices, Foucault relentlessly pursues the systems of exclusion which govern our discourse. Foucault's enterprise, then, which he sees imperfectly sketched in his three previous works, entails measuring "the mutation" rather than the continuity in history, questioning the themes and methods of the history of ideas, throwing off "the last anthropological constraints," and revealing the sources of these constraints.[98] The task, then, is "to define a method of historical analysis freed from the anthropological theme,...to define a method of analysis purged of all anthropologism."[99]

It is no surprise that Foucault would devote his work to undermining virtually self-evident unities. His research in *Histoire de la folie* had already shown that the unity of a discipline or science was untenable. The discipline of psychology proved deeply interwoven with social and economic conditions. Psychology's object proved incapable of providing coherence; *Histoire de la folie* revealed madness as much too malleable to unify psychology's discourse. If the object of a discipline could not undergird its coherence, neither could a consistent style or manner of statement shared by practitioners. *Naissance de la clinique* revealed the embeddedness of clinical discourse in the discourse of ethics, politics, and economics. *Les mots et les choses,* finally, precluded any attempt to establish the unity of discourse on the persistence of certain concepts and themes. Natural history had more in common with general grammar and the analysis of wealth than it had with biology.

Like Nietzsche, Foucault maintains that the lives of modern men and women are frighteningly narrow and impoverished. In the spirit of *Histoire de la folie's* study of confinement practices and following his insight from his literary studies that the fate of thought is bound up with that of language, Foucault proposes to analyze the ways in which our discourse contributes to this impoverishment. He advances the hypothesis that "in every society the production of discourse is at once controlled, selected, organised and redistributed according to a certain number of procedures, whose role is to avert its powers and its dangers, to cope with chance events, to evade its ponderous, awesome materiality."[100]

At this point he sees this future work falling under two categories for which he offers a preliminary formulation in his inaugural lecture: works of critique and works of genealogy will "alternate, support and complete each other."[101] Critique attempts to recognize the negative conditions which exclude and rarify discourse; it illumines the conditions which account for the exclusion and limitation of discourse. Critique "deals with the systems enveloping discourse; attempting to mark out and distinguish the principles of ordering, exclusion and rarity in discourse."[102] Genealogy studies the formation of discourses "through, in spite of, or with the aid of these systems of constraint."[103] Genealogy attempts to grasp the formation of discourse "in its power of affirmation,... the power of constituting domains of objects, in relation to which one can affirm or deny true or false propositions."[104]

B. Foucault's Notion of Genealogy

Following Foucault, however, our task requires us to postpone our examination of his explicitly genealogical studies and, first, delve more deeply into this notion of genealogy.

1. Genealogy as Critique I:
Toward the Realization of the Critique of Reason

"Genealogy is gray, meticulous, and patiently documentary. It operates on a field of entangled and confused parchments, on docu-

ments that have been scratched over and recopied many times."[105]
Provisionally Foucault defines genealogy as "the union of erudite
knowledge and local memories which allows us to establish a historical knowledge of struggles and to make use of this knowledge
tactically today."[106] It studies events in their singular uniqueness
without reference to telos or utility. Genealogy especially focuses
on what we typically hold to be ahistorical, self-evident, and substantial in order to reveal its rootedness in history. In a 1977 discussion Foucault refers to his task as "eventalisation": "making
visible a *singularity* at places where there is a temptation to
invoke a historical constant, an immediate anthropological trait, or
an obviousness which imposes itself uniformly on all."[107] Genealogy
as eventalisation breaches the self-evidences and undermines the
apparent necessity which undergird our knowledge and practices.
It was not always self-evident that mad people'suffered from mental illness, that criminals needed incarceration, that individual
bodies required examination to determine the causes of illness.
Instead of sitting satisfied with apparent self-evidences, genealogy
seeks a "causal multiplication";[108] it analyzes events to reveal the
multiplicity of processes by which they are constituted. Genealogy
"disturbs what was previously considered immobile; it fragments
what was thought unified; it shows the heterogeneity of what was
imagined consistent with itself."[109]

Genealogy seeks the historical conditions of the existence of
the entities and events we encounter, but it, nonetheless, distances
itself from the quest for their origins: "A genealogy of values,
morality, asceticism, and knowledge will never confuse itself with
a quest for their 'origins,' will never neglect as inaccessible the
vicissitudes of history."[110] It refuses to take refuge in the philosopher's ideal significations as an escape from the molelike diggings
of the historian, yet it, likewise, refuses recourse in the search for
origins. In his 1972 discussion with Giulio Preti, Foucault contex-
tualized his refusal of the search for origins, and these comments
are worth quoting at some length:

In a few words, I will say that in Nietzsche I find a questioning of a historical type which makes no reference to the "primordial" [*originario*] as do many of the inquiries of Western
thought. Husserl and Heidegger put into question again all of
our knowledge and their foundations, but they do so beginning from what is primordial [*originario*]. This inquiry occurs
however at the cost of any articulated historical content.
What I like instead in Nietzsche is the attempt to put into

question again the fundamental concepts of knowledge, or morality and of metaphysics, having recourse to a historical analysis of a positivistic type without going back to the origins [*origini*].[111]

While clearly Foucault wants to distance himself from the quest for origins, it is not yet apparent why he objects to such a quest. What is it about this quest for origins that sacrifices "any articulated historical content"?

Reflecting on Nietzsche's own texts, Foucault seeks distinctions among various terms typically translated as "origin": *Ursprung, Entstehung, Herkunft, Geburt.* In the Preface to *On the Genealogy of Morals*, according to Foucault's reading, Nietzsche attempted to draw an opposition between *Ursprung* and *Herkunft*, words which he had previously and would later use interchangeably. Critically evaluating his own thought at age thirteen, his "first childish literary trifle,"[112] and Paul Rée's *The Origin of Moral Sentiments*, Nietzsche capsulizes his critique by calling these quests for *Ursprung.* Characterizing his own writings, from *Human, All too Human*, written in the winter of 1876–77 (published the following year) to *On the Genealogy of Morals*, Nietzsche claims that they are governed by his *Herkunfts-Hypothesen*, although he had previously used the word *Ursprung* for these writings. According to Foucault, then, Nietzsche forges an opposition between *Ursprung* and *Herkunft* in 1887 that he did not maintain ten years previously. What could Nietzsche have been getting at in elevating the quest for *Herkunft* and denigrating the search for *Ursprung?*

The pursuit of *Ursprung*, according to Foucault's Nietzsche, is "an attempt to capture the exact essence of things, their purest possibilities, and their carefully protected identities, because this search assumes the existence of immobile forms that precede the external world of accident and succession."[113] One imagines the *Ursprung* as a primordial truth or original identity beneath masks accumulated in history. The true genealogist governed by the *Herkunfts-Hypothesen*, in contrast, turns away from metaphysics and "listens to history"; his quest leads him to the discovery that there is no eternal essence behind things; he discovers "the secret that they have no essence or that their essence was fabricated in a piecemeal fashion from alien forms."[114] Having turned to the history of things, the genealogist finds "not the inviolable identity of their origin," but rather "the dissension of other things." He discovers "disparity."[115]

The genealogist, then, foregoes the search for an original identity and essence unmasked; instead, he cultivates the disparate details, events, and accidents found at any beginning. He pursues history's events, "its jolts, its surprises, its unsteady victories and unpalatable defeats," for it is these that account for any beginning, not an essence in its pristine purity. "History is the concrete body of a development, with its moments of intensity, its lapses, its extended periods of feverish agitation, its fainting spells; and only a metaphysician would seek its soul in the distant ideality of the origin."[116] Only a metaphysician would expect to find an essence at the beginning.

In his 1973 Rio de Janeiro lectures, Foucault draws attention to Nietzsche's repeated use of the term *Erfindung*, invention, and argues that the word is used with a polemical intent. "When [Nietzsche] speaks of 'invention' he has in mind a word which opposes invention, the word 'origin,'" according to Foucault. "When he says 'invention' it is in order not to say 'origin,' when he says *Erfindung*, it is in order not to say *Ursprung*."[117] Nietzsche derides Schopenhauer, for example, for seeking the *Ursprung* of religion in a metaphysical need.[118] Instead, religion was invented.[119] By employing the term "invention," however, Nietzsche is not attributing causal efficacy to an intending subject's free creativity. Instead, according to Foucault, Nietzsche emphasizes the poverty and smallness, even stinginess, involved in the piecemeal fabrication of great things.

Herkunft and *Entstehung* better capture the spirit of genealogy. While typically translated as "origin," *Herkunft* connotes "stock" or "descent" (*la souche, la provenance*).[120] Genealogy as the analysis of descent assists Foucault's project of decentering the subject: "Where the soul pretends unification or the self fabricates a coherent identity,...[t]he analysis of descent permits the dissociation of the self, its recognition and displacement as an empty synthesis, in liberating a profusion of lost events."[121] Instead of unifying in terms of continuity or evolution, genealogy maintains events in their dispersion. Its task is "to identify the accidents, the minute deviations—or conversely, the complete reversals—the errors, the false appraisals, and the faulty calculations that gave birth to those things that continue to exist and have value for us; it is to discover that truth or being do not lie at the root of what we know and what we are, but the exteriority of accidents."[122]

Foucault offers a very allusive comment at this point: "This is undoubtedly why every origin of morality from the moment it stops being pious—and *Herkunft* can never be—has value as critique."[123] In a footnote Foucault directs our attention to the section of *Twilight of the Idols* entitled "Reasons for Philosophy."[124] In these five short sections, five long aphorisms, we encounter genealogy as critique; indeed, we encounter genealogy promising the realization of the critique of reason.

Philosophers, according to Nietzsche, lack historical sense and hate "even the idea of becoming."[125] He characterizes their thought as Egyptianism: they think it a tribute to mummify and dehistoricize. The philosopher's motto: "What is, does not *become*; what becomes, *is* not...." Since all they ever encounter, however, is things in various stages of becoming, they seek reasons to account for the allusiveness of that which is: what we see is illusion; the senses deceive.

> Moral: escape from sense-deception, from becoming, from history, from falsehood—history is nothing but belief in the senses, belief in falsehood. Moral: denial of all that believes in the senses, of all the rest of mankind: all of that is mere "people." Be a philosopher, be a mummy, represent monotono-theism by a gravedigger-mimicry![126]

For Nietzsche, the senses do not lie: "It is what we *make* of their evidence that first introduces a lie into it, for example, the lie of unity, the lie of materiality, of substance, of duration.... 'Reason' is the cause of our falsification of the evidence of the senses." We are bound to persist in error, according to Nietzsche, "to precisely the extent that our prejudice in favour of reason compels us to posit unity, identity, duration, substance, cause, materiality, being."[127] A genealogy of morals, thus, reveals the will at the heart of our preference for reason, at the heart of our falsification of sensual evidence, or our preference for being over becoming. A genealogy of morals, thus, promises the realization of the critique of reason; "every origin of morality from the moment it stops being pious—and *Herkunft* can never be—has value as critique" of reason. The critique of reason, thus, is not a matter of seeking the limits of reason in order to "provide a positive foundation for the possibility of knowing";[128] instead critique is a historical investigation which unveils reason's falsifications and reveals the moral will that undergirds it.

Reason's denial of sensory evidence, manifest in its preference for unity, the unchanging and immobile, directs us to attach genealogy to the body. "Genealogy, as an analysis of descent," according to Foucault, "is thus situated within the articulation of the body and history. Its task is to expose a body totally imprinted by history and the process of history's destruction of the body."[129] Genealogy attaches itself to everything that touches the body, its nervous system and diet, digestive system and climate; in this sense, genealogy resembles medicine more than philosophy. Its approach has more in common with physiology than with philosophy and its tendency to deny the body.[130]

Foucault translates *Entstehung* as emergence. When genealogy searches for emergence, it must take care to avoid the metaphysician's temptation—to impose present needs and the present state of affairs at the point of arising, enabling one to point to a continuous, teleological development culminating in the present. In this way the metaphysician introduces meaning and purpose into history. The genealogist, in contrast, seeks to reestablish the various systems of subjection: "not the anticipatory power of meaning, but the hazardous play of dominations."[131] The genealogist sees the present state of affairs and present needs as another episode; not the result of a meaningful development, but a result of struggle and relations of force and domination: "The domination of certain men over others leads to the differentiation of values; class domination generates the idea of liberty; and the forceful appropriation of things necessary to survival and imposition of a duration not intrinsic to them account for the origin of logic."[132] By avoiding the metaphysician's tendency to impose meaningful intentions into what is actually the struggle of forces, Foucault can claim that "no one is responsible for an emergence; no one can glory in it, since it always occurs in the interstice."[133] As Dreyfus and Rabinow point out, this constitutes a significant difference between Foucault and Nietzsche: "whereas Nietzsche often seems to ground morality and social institutions in the tactics of individual actors, Foucault totally depsychologizes this approach and sees all psychological motivation not as the source but as the result of strategies without strategists."[134] His research for *Histoire de la folie*, first, made him quite skeptical of the psychological approach. His desire to remove the subject from the center of thought, secondly, precluded giving credit to individual agents. "What matter who's speaking?"[135] Finally, power functions in a much too anonymous manner for Foucault to attribute responsibility to individuals.

While genealogy distances itself from metaphysics and opts for history, it likewise rejects history in its traditional form. Traditional history adopts a suprahistorical perspective; its point of view is eternal, outside of time. The traditional historian's suprahistorical perspective, according to Foucault, is made possible "because of its belief in eternal truth, the immortality of the soul, and the nature of consciousness as always identical to itself."[136] In other words, the traditional historian stands in relation to history as Socrates stands to philosophy: "As the demagogue is obliged to invoke truth, laws of essences, and eternal necessity, the historian must invoke objectivity, the accuracy of facts, and the permanence of the past."[137] For the traditional historian the object of knowledge preexists knowledge.

Genealogy, in contrast, is "effective history" insofar as it takes everything the traditional historian sees as eternal and relocates it in its process of becoming.[138] It is rigorously anti-Platonist.[139] Where traditional history sees immutable feelings, a constant instinctual life, and a body governed by the laws of physiology, effective history relinquishes any such constants. Effective history avoids metaphysics by refusing any absolutes; instead, it "distinguishes, separates, and disperses." In an essay on Deleuze Foucault writes of a project they share: "To pervert Platonism is to search out the smallest details, to descend (with the natural gravitation of humor) as far as its crop of hair or the dirt under its fingernails—those things that were never hallowed by an idea."[140] Foucault characterizes effective history as "the kind of dissociating view that is capable of decomposing itself, capable of shattering the unity of man's being through which it was thought that he could extend his sovereignty to the events of his past."[141] Avoiding the categories of continuity, teleology, and destiny, "History becomes 'effective' to the degree that it introduces discontinuity into our very being."[142]

In this notion of effective history, echoes of Foucault's account of what is meant by an archaeological description of the archive can be detected. In *L'archeologie du savoir* Foucault maintains that the description of the archive

deprives us of our continuities; it dissipates that temporal identity in which we are pleased to look at ourselves when we wish to exorcise the discontinuities of history; it breaks the thread of transcendental teleologies; and where anthropological thought once questioned man's being or subjectivity, it now bursts open the other, and the outside. In this sense, the diagnosis does not establish the fact of our identity by the play of distinctions. It establishes that we are difference, that our reason is the difference of discourses, our history the difference of times, our selves the difference of masks. That difference, far from being the forgotten and recovered origin, is this dispersion that we are and make.[143]

This suspension of anthropology's shelters, these taken-for-granted categories of continuity, frees a new field of study: "this field is made up of the totality of all effective statements (whether spoken or written), in their dispersion as events and in the occurrence that is proper to them." The task entails "a *pure description of discursive events* as the horizon for the search for the unities that form within it."[144]

Foucault calls it "archaeology." The term comes from Kant, Foucault tells us, who used it "in order to designate the history of that which renders necessary a certain form of thought."[145] Foucault further links archaeology to his genealogical project by pointing out that the Greek root *archè* means "commencement" or "beginning."[146] This archaeology of discursive events, like Nietzschean philology, assists a genealogy of these unities; it provides a critique, a questioning of the discursive conditions of existence of these unities. Unlike Nietzschean philology, however, archaeology's elementary unit of analysis is not the word but the statement.[147]

2. Genealogy as Critique II: The Historical A Priori

The statement ought not be confused with a sentence, proposition, or speech act—the typical objects of linguistic analysis.[148] It is an existential function of signs. This enunciative function whereby signs group as statements can be identified according to several criteria, each of which emerges from Foucault's suspension of the categories of continuity and remains consistent with the results of his three previous historical studies. If we read these criteria in the light of analogous claims from the tradition of philosophy of language, the Nietzschean tone of Foucault's analyses emerges more clearly.

The relation between the statement and what it states, first, is a unique one, not to be confused with the relation between signifier and signified, name and what it designates, sentence and meaning, proposition and referent. John Searle, for example, calls a "referring expression" any utterance that "serves to pick out or identify one 'object' or 'entity' or 'particular' apart from other objects, about which the speaker then goes on to say something or ask some questions, etc."[149] To determine the truth value of an utterance, then, would entail empirical investigation. Foucault's concern is critical, as opposed to empirical; he seeks the historical and practical conditions of existence. In line with his studies of madness and the clinic, Foucault maintains that a statement is linked to a "referential" that ought not be construed as a permanent object, thing, or fact; rather, a statement's referential is a set of "laws of possibility, rules of existence for the objects that are named, designated, or described within it, and for the relations that are affirmed or denied in it."[150] The referential is that set of historical, practical, and discursive conditions that account for the existence of the object.

The task Foucault sets for himself has more in common with that of Nietzsche. As Tracy Strong puts it, Nietzsche's "focus turns away from behavior and concentrates on that which makes morality (for instance) 'possible,' or, in his language, 'the soil' from which it springs.... What Nietzsche gives us is not, in my reading, a new set of philosophical answers to particular problems; it is, instead, more a form of human archeology, an analysis of the particular 'soil' from which these problems have sprung."[151] As Foucault would have it, "This genre of researches is only possible as an analysis of our own subsoil (*sous-sol*)."[152]

Histoire de la folie made clear to Foucault that a set of rules functioned whereby the objects of psychiatric discourse were constituted, and in *L'archéologie du savoir* he more clearly delineates the realms in which these rules operate. We saw in our first chapter the interplay of diverse factors—economic, political, religious, medical, moral—which brought about the formation of the object, madness. The analysis of its rules of formation entails mapping its surfaces of emergence by which these diverse factors grant it coherence. Archaeology reveals the interplay of these diverse realms which limited, defined, and gave madness its status as an object and, thus, made it "manifest, nameable, and describable."[153] Archaeology, moreover, reveals the interaction of various social authorities in the constitution of madness as an object; medical, legal, religious, literary, and artistic authorities all participated in its formation. Finally, the archaeologist analyzes the "grids of specification," the systems of division and classification of discourse, which polish and lend precision to the object. In sum,

What, in short, we wish to do is to dispense with "things." To "depresentify" them.... To substitute for the enigmatic treasure of "things" anterior to discourse, the regular formation of objects that emerge only in discourse. To define these *objects* without reference to the *ground*, the *foundation of things*, but by relating them to the body of rules that enable them to form as objects of a discourse and thus constitute the conditions of their historical appearance.[154]

Archaeology, thus, effects a dismantling of the substratum that has assured continuity for the Western philosophical tradition. To dispense with things anterior to discourse implies the primacy of interpretation over signs. As early as 1964 Foucault argued that since the nineteenth century, since Nietzsche, Marx, and Freud, interpretation has become an infinite task because there is no thing to interpret. "There is nothing absolutely primary to interpret, because at bottom, everything is already interpretation, each sign is in itself not the thing which is offered to interpretation, but interpretation of other signs. There is never, if you will, an *interpretandum* which is not already an *interpretans*."[155] Signs are interpretations which attempt to mask the fact that they are interpretations. Marx, for example, studies the history of relations of production as an interpretation that posed as natural. Basing his analysis of a patient's symptoms upon what the patient reveals through speech, Freud's "interpretation is the interpretation of an interpretation."[156] Words, for Nietzsche the philologist, do not signify a signified; words impose and preserve an interpretation.

When Foucault declares "everything is interpretation," he is not making a metaphysical claim about the nature of being, about the way the world is in its truth. Contrary to Heidegger's interpretation, in which Nietzsche represents the last metaphysician in the Western philosophical tradition, Foucault reads Nietzsche as revealing the futility of metaphysics. As David Hoy puts it, "instead of making an ontological claim Nietzsche is trying to undercut ontology by exposing the metaphysical fiction of '*the world*' as a determining ground or *hypokeimenon*."[157] When Foucault asserts that "there is never an *interpretandum* that is not already *interpretans*," he is pointing to our immediate practical and discursive handling of life that makes it intelligible and, thereby, constitutes a primordial interpretation. Any other interpretations interpret this first level of interpretation. Our fundamental practical and discursive engagement with the world already constitutes an interpretation, an evaluation.[158]

The relation between the statement and the subject, secondly, is equally peculiar yet consistent with the decentering operation Foucault insists on effecting. A statement's subject is not equivalent to the author of its formulation; rather a space, the position of the subject, determines the relation between statement and subject; the changing position of the physician in the houses of confinement or the medical clinic exemplifies this. "To describe a formulation *qua* statement," briefly, consists in "determining what position can and must be occupied by any individual if he is to be the subject of it."[159] This implies that the interpreter interprets neither the signifier nor the signified; rather one interprets the one who imposes the interpretation. Interpretation now is always "interpretation for the 'who?'"[160] Particularly in his research for *Naissance de la clinique* Foucault became aware of the importance of the position of the subject of discourse, and the rules governing this subjective position call for analysis. Who has the qualifications, the prestige, the status to speak a certain type of discourse, and from what institutional site does he or she speak? As we saw in our discussion of clinical medicine, the institutional sites of discourse fluctuate, and these transformations require analysis. Foucault's concern with the speaker's institutional site does not entail an interest in his or her power in any traditional sense. Statements are not necessarily proclamations of the great and near great. Comments from a low-level magistrate can have more importance than presidential addresses because the magistrate's remarks indicate the operation of the statement at the level of concrete, everyday practices.

John Searle lends a primacy to the subject of discourse, but Foucault's concern for the subject could not be further from his. For Searle the meaning intended by the speaking subject and the grasping of this intended meaning by the hearer are determinative of the successful performance of a speech act.[161] Foucault, in contrast, is not concerned with transcendental or psychological subjectivity but a "space of exteriority" which situates the speaker and lends validity to his or her discourse. Far from indicating the synthetic function of a unifying subject, Foucault's analysis reveals the speaker's dispersion in his status, the institutional sites he occupies, his position. Foucault is intent on continuing the decentering operation effected by Nietzsche.

The practical, historical, and discursive conditions constitutive of madness, the world of medical objects, life, labor, and language make it apparent to Foucault that the statement only operates in conjunction with this associated domain of conditions. This relation, thirdly, characterizes the enunciative function.[162] Refusing näively to assume that concepts are the organizing principles of discourse, archaeology treats concepts as elements dispersed throughout discourse that are ordered and whose relations are governed by systems of rules peculiar to the type of discourse in question.[163] These rules account for the formation of concepts. The organization of concepts, objects, and statements into themes, theories, and intellectual strategies is similarly governed by sets of rules, and these rules, according to Foucault, account for the formation of these strategies. Themes, theories, and intellectual strategies do not result from a fundamental project or from opinions; they emerge from discursive rules of formation.

Finally, a repeatable materiality is constitutive of the statement. While it is true that "a statement must have a substance, a support, a place, and a date,"[164] this spatio-temporal character bears less importance than the institutional character it carries. A formulation's institutional setting, whether asylum, clinic, university, or senate floor, is constitutive of its efficacy as a statement. Archaeological analysis investigates the formulation of signs as statements in their social and historical existence.[165] Clearly, then, a statement never functions in isolation; its social and historical character implies its rootedness in a system of statements which Foucault refers to as a "discursive formation." Statements governed by the same "rules of formation" belong to a single discursive formation. In accordance with these rules, the objects, concepts, and theoretical strategies with which we are familiar are constituted; these rules are their conditions of existence. A central task of archaeology is to make these conditions explicit in their historical and practical functioning.

Following the speech act theories of J. L. Austin and John Searle, Jürgen Habermas coins the expression "institutionally bound speech actions."[166] Speech actions such as betting, christening, and appointing are bound to norms and standards typical of particular social institutions, and these norms determine the successful or unsuccessful performance of speech acts. Foucault's research on the asylum and the clinic provided him with a deep sense of what might be called discourse's institutional bondage, but the operations he discovered there were less a matter of institutional norms than Nietzschean relations of forces—power. Institutional practices did not simply regulate the successful performance of speech acts; asylum and clinical practices positively constituted psychiatry's and medicine's objects of analysis.

In his research for *Histoire de la folie* Foucault discovered that the discipline of psychiatry emerged early in the nineteenth century due to conditions apparently extrinsic to the discipline itself. The formation of psychiatry's concepts and strategies occurred in conjunction with transformations in confinement practices; modes of hospitalization; techniques of social exclusion; and judicial, moral, and economic factors. While these apparently extrinsic factors provided the conditions for the emergence of psychiatry, moreover, psychiatry infiltrated legislation, literature, philosophy, political decisions, and the common discourse of everyday life. Foucault's research on the asylum and the clinic led him to conclude that

in a society such as ours, but basically in any society, there are manifold relations of power which permeate, characterise and constitute the social body, and these relations of power cannot themselves be established, consolidated nor implemented without the production, accumulation, circulation and functioning of a discourse. There can be no possible exercise of power without a certain economy of discourses of truth which operates through and on the basis of this association. We are subjected to the production of truth through power and we cannot exercise power except through the production of truth.[167]

In other words, the "discursive formation whose existence was mapped by the psychiatric discipline was not coextensive with it, far from it: it went well beyond the boundaries of psychiatry."[168] This "far from it" designates the realm of the non-discursive dimension of the historical a priori.

With the analysis of these rules of formation—of objects, of the position of subjects, of concepts and strategies—Foucault specifies the conditions of existence of a discursive formation, and these conditions he calls the "historical *a priori*." Since his concern throughout has been with statements actually made, the historical a priori does not reveal the conditions of validity for judgments, but the conditions of reality for statements: "An *a priori* not of truths that might never be said, or really given to experience; but the *a priori* of a history that is given, since it is that of things actually said."[169] Unlike Chomsky's transformational generative grammar, Foucault's archaeology is not interested in the formal possibilities of a language but in the real existence of discourse; "my object is not language but the archive, which is to say the accumulated existence of discourse."[170] In Foucault's words,

As opposed to those called structuralists, I am not very interested in the formal possibilities offered by a system like language. Personally, I am more haunted by the existence of discourse, by the fact that words have been uttered, these events have functioned by relation to their original situation, they have left traces behind them, they subsist and exert, in this very subsistence at the interior of history, a certain number of manifest or secret functions.[171]

3. Critique as Genealogical: Critique as History of the Present

Two intellectual events, according to Foucault, characterize the period during which he wrote, and these events made genealogy a distinctly appropriate mode of research. The "efficacy of dispersed and discontinuous offensives" or the "efficacy of discontinuous, particular and local critique," first, characterizes this period of history.[172] By this he means that "things, institutions, practices, discourses" have been showing an increasing vulnerability—"A certain fragility has been discovered in the very bedrock of existence"—a vulnerability to local and strategic critiques which operate without "any systematic principles of coordination."[173] Such local critique, according to Foucault, is autonomous and non-centralized; it does not depend on established "regimes of thought" for its validation. The anti-psychiatry movement, attacks on traditional morality, and offensives against legal and penal systems provide examples. Corresponding to this efficacy of local critique, secondly, is the discovery of the inefficacy of global or "totalitarian theories"; "the attempt to think in terms of a totality," according to Foucault, "has in fact proved a hindrance to research."[174] This is not to suggest that global theories such as Marxism and psychoanalysis have not been useful for local research and critique. Foucault does want to claim, however, that such global theories have been useful to the extent that their global character, their "theoretical unity," has been "put in abeyance, or at least curtailed, divided, overthrown, caricatured, theatricalised, or what you will."[175]

Related to these two events of the last twenty-five to thirty years is another factor which starkly separates Foucault's project from that of Nietzsche. A culture's plastic power that enables it actively to forget for the enhancement of life, revered by Nietzsche, is the enemy against which Foucault directs his genealogical attacks. The Foucauldian genealogist's task is to afflict the comfortable by dredging up what has been forgotten, whether actively or passively. He or she counteracts the prevailing social amnesia by emancipating subjected historical knowledges. Foucault calls it "an insurrection of subjugated knowledges" by means of which local critique proceeds.[176] By subjugated knowledges Foucault means two things: "the buried knowledges of erudition and those disqualified from the hierarchy of knowledges and sciences."[177] First, in his research on the birth of the asylum, for example, Foucault discovered historical contents that had been covered over by functionalist and systematizing histories. Such historical contents enabled him to produce an effective critique of the asylum. They made possible the rediscovery of "the ruptural effects of conflict and struggle" that characterized the asylum's emergence. By subjugated knowledges, secondly, Foucault means "a whole set of knowledges that have been disqualified as inadequate to their task or insufficiently elaborated; naive knowledges, located low down on the hierarchy, beneath the required level of cognition or scientificity."[178] Such subjugated knowledges are popular (*"le savoir de gens"*)—the common knowledge of the patient, the nurse, or the doctor. It is not a matter of common sense but rather a knowledge that is regional, specific to a particular domain, which cannot be unanimous. Critique functions, Foucault maintains, by means of the insurrection of such regional knowledge. Subjugated knowledges, both in the form of buried erudition and in the form of disqualified, regional knowledge, maintain the memory of historical struggles; their insurrection resurrects the memory of hostile encounters.

Foucault's task entails writing "the history of the present."[179] His genealogies are "retrospective disciplines" that find "their point of departure in our actuality."[180] In an interview with John Simon, Foucault asserts that he has always been concerned with phenomena of the past;

But I was interested in them—in fact, profoundly interested in them—because I saw in them ways of thinking and behaving that are still with us.

I try to show, based upon their historical establishment and formation, those systems which are still ours today and within which we are trapped. It is a question, basically, of presenting a critique of our own time, based upon retrospective analyses.[181]

Using the medical language reminiscent of Nietzsche, Foucault refers to his own work as diagnostic and curative. Since Nietzsche, according to Foucault, philosophy has the mission of diagnosing the present, "to say what we are today, what it means to say what we say."[182] His archaeological "labor of excavation beneath our own feet" allows him to call himself a philosopher because such work characterizes philosophy since Nietzsche wrote.[183]

The question, then, concerns the nature of philosophy. Is it inevitable that philosophy find its task in thinking the totality? For the past century since Hegel, according to Foucault, philosophy, indeed, proposed such a task for itself, but this is a relatively recent notion. Prior to Hegel, he claims, philosophy maintained no such pretense of thinking the totality, and since Nietzsche philosophy no longer pretends to totalize. "According to Nietzsche," Foucault tells us,

> to philosophize was a series of acts and operations which pertained to diverse locales: to describe a Greek tragedy was to philosophize, to occupy oneself with philology or with history was to philosophize. Then, Nietzsche discovered that the peculiar activity of philosophy was to diagnose, as we have already said: what are we today? What is this "today" that we are living?[184]

"I am not a prophet," he once told an interviewer, "at most a diagnostician";[185] yet he wants genealogy to go beyond diagnosis "to become a curative science," "to prescribe the best antidote."[186] Genealogy is critique as a historical investigation into the events that have led us to constitute ourselves and to recognize ourselves as subjects of what we are doing, thinking, saying. Moreover, critique is genealogical; that is, genealogy is history oriented toward the future. Genealogy separates out, from the contingency that has made us what we are, the possibility of no longer being, doing, or thinking what we are, do, or think.[187]

Conclusion

The problem of language resides at the center of the work of both Nietzsche and Foucault. Nietzsche emphasizes language's capacity to regularize our experience; for example, the concepts 'cause' and 'effect' tame experience by locating it under the horizon of previous experience. Without language everything would appear to us as it does to an infant, like William James's booming, buzzing confusion. Language allows entities and a world to be; it is the condition for the existence of a world, so Nietzsche's concern with language is an attempt to make these conditions manifest. In this sense, his work is critical as opposed to empirical. Borrowing a term Dreyfus and Rabinow made much of, Nietzsche's work is an analytics as opposed to an analysis; he is concerned with the conditions of existence rather than existence.

Foucault maintains that our thought is confined by historically and discursively constituted codes: "we are already before the very least of our words, governed and paralysed by language."[188] Focusing upon the statement as the elementary unit of analysis,

Foucault continues this attempt to decenter the subject with a more sustained, sophisticated, and detailed analysis of discourse than that found in Nietzsche's work. Foucault's study of discourse, like Nietzsche's, is critical rather than empirical; it is an analytics as opposed to an analysis. He analyses a statement's 'referential' (the historical, practical, and discursive conditions for the existence of the 'referent') rather than the referent. His concern with the relation between the subject and the statement focuses on the site from which the speaker speaks, rather than on his or her psychological subjectivity. His analysis of concepts treats them in terms of the discursive rules that govern their relations rather than as discrete units. Finally, he examines the statement's embeddedness in social, cultural, and institutional practices. By these means he reveals the historical and practical conditions under which a statement can be considered, not true or false, but *in terms of* truth and falsehood.

Nietzsche primarily objects to the subject-object grammatical structure of Western languages; it allows the separation of the doer from the deed, the dancer from the dance, the lightning from its flash. This results in an overvaluation of consciousness and subjectivity. Thus, by making language the problem, he makes man the problem. Foucault is committed to this same problematization of language in order to make man the problem. Kant introduced the critique of reason but closed the possibility of such a critique by reducing thought to the question "what is man?" Nietzsche, according to Foucault, made philosophy once again possible by decentering man. In Heidegger's words, "Anthropology is that interpretation of man that already fundamentally knows what man is and hence can never ask who he may be."[189] By decentering man, Nietzsche, according to Foucault, opened a space in which thought might once again proceed and human possibilities might open.

It is a truism that Nietzsche committed himself to overturning metaphysics, and Foucault, unlike Heidegger, maintains that Nietzsche succeeded. A hostility to what is transient, changing, contradictory, and upsetting of a sense of security most obviously characterizes metaphysics for Nietzsche. It refuses to accept what Nietzsche considers obvious, that values, ideas, concepts, and man himself emerged from particular historical circumstances. Instead, metaphysical thinking yearns for the unconditioned, for freedom from contradiction, for being rather than becoming. That everything originates in time and history might be the most consistent wellspring of Nietzsche's thought from as early as *The Birth of*

Tragedy. The crucial error committed by the metaphysician, from Nietzsche's point of view, is to separate the actor from the activity; the metaphysician posits a spiritual causality that resides in the will or intention of the agent. Such a separation entails a subject or substratum as the one, single source of the activity or event, rather than a multiplicity, complex relations of forces, at the origin. Nietzsche's decentering of the intending subject as the single source of actions and events calls forth a genealogical approach to manifest the multiplicity at the origin.

Foucault concurs: "It's not a matter of locating everything on one level..., but of realising that there are actually a whole order of levels of different types of events differing in amplitude, chronological breadth, and capacity to produce effects." For this reason, both Foucault and Nietzsche have "recourse to analyses in terms of the genealogy of relations of force, strategic developments, and tactics."[190] For both, history has no constants; both deny any persistent substratum. Their historical writings especially focus upon those entities that are assumed to be ahistorical—the soul, man, the subject. Genealogy focuses on what we typically hold to be ahistorical, self-evident, and substantial in order to reveal its rootedness in history.

Following from the rejection of the distinction between agent and action, Nietzsche likewise rejects the distinction between a thing and its relations to other things. There is no such thing for Nietzsche as a thing subsisting independently of its relations; the positing of a fixed center of such relations results from the metaphysician's will to stabilize the chaotic flux of our experience. A similar insight underlies Foucault's desire to "depresentify" things; in his historical studies he discovered the complex relations of forces that undergird and constitute the entities of our experience. Mental illness, the individual body as object of medical perception, life, labor, language, man himself, and, as we will see more clearly in our next chapter, the modern individual, all result from the complex, historical interplay of spatial adjustments, temporal transformations, and modifications of social practices, all of which fall under Foucault's generic expression, "power." This context, this set of conditions of existence with which they are both concerned, is the realm of power. Both think power outside the confines of a political theory; instead, a relational theory of power operates in the thought of both Nietzsche and Foucault.

But we must avoid misunderstanding. It is not merely that Foucault followed Nietzsche's arguments about the nature of reality and then responded by employing a genealogical method in his own work. Rather, the problematic he discovered and found himself confronting called forth a genealogical approach. From his historical study of the asylum in the early 1960s he saw the interplay of the three genealogical axes. The modern individual, the object of psychology, appeared as a function of the knowledge and power relations in which it became entwined. Power operated in spatial and temporal transformations that constituted the modern individual as the object of psychiatric knowledge. It was less a matter of Foucault's having been convinced by Nietzsche's dialogue with the philosophical tradition, than a matter of seeing a series of problems emerge from his own historical studies and political engagement for which only a Nietzschean approach was adequate. Typically he found the philosophical community oblivious to the issues that drew forth his passion; "neither the philosophical community nor even the political community has been even slightly interested in them. None of the journals, institutionally assigned to register the smallest jolt in the philosophical world, has paid any attention to them."[191] Nietzsche's response to the philosophical tradition interested him less than the angle genealogy offered for his concrete historical and political concerns.

Both Nietzsche and Foucault, then, are committed to genealogical critique, the attempt to reveal the historical context of events, their historical conditions of existence. Both seek to reveal the unquestioned premises of a culture, the practical background from which events and the entities of our experience emerge. Genealogy for both is a quest for "origins," but both assume that no thing is to be found at the origin; there is no original or transcendental signified. Any thing, person, event is construed to be a matter of historical, cultural, practical interpretation, and beneath the series of interpretations there is no thing.

Philosophy for both Nietzsche and Foucault is diagnosis. It is the history of the present. Nietzsche examines the practical, historical context of Greek culture because an understanding of these conditions of existence is essential to understanding modern European culture. The same for Foucault's historical studies. The genealogist traces the history of the present in order to undermine our self-evidences. Genealogy is history oriented toward the future. Nietzsche seeks possibilities for the enhancement of life by means of his genealogical studies. Foucault puts the same goal in terms of creating possibilities for no longer being, doing, thinking what we are, do, think. Thus, Nietzsche is concerned with the conditions under which value judgments were formulated as the first moment of critique; the second moment questions their value for life. Foucault is concerned with the conditions of the existence of statements and the entities of our experience as the first moment of critique in order to throw these statements and entities into question and to open possibilities.

Nonetheless, both are committed to "the radical but unaggressive scepticism which makes it a principle not to regard the point in time where we are now standing as the outcome of a teleological progression."[192] Both deny any role to telos in history; "whatever exists, having somehow come into being, is again and again reinterpreted to new ends."[193] Once a concept, value, or practice originates, it becomes subject to continual reinterpretation in the light of new systems of purposes.

Both Nietzsche and Foucault oppose the division of the world into real and apparent. Everything is mediated by the life and consciousness of knowers. All truth is truth for a form of life. All reason is practical reason. Both, therefore, question any allegedly pure and autonomous search for truth, as manifest for Nietzsche in the Stoics and the modern physicists, for Foucault in the Enlightenment. Any search for truth is inevitably undergirded by a will to truth, a will to knowledge. Thought does not mirror; it creates. Both object to the Kantian notion that self-critical rationality can offer a fulcrum unencumbered by the distortions and simplifications of our conceptual and linguistic apparatus. Their objections to science follow from this refusal to privilege what is merely one perspective among others; both object to the privileging of science to the exclusion of other modes of knowing.

Nietzsche and Foucault reject the Socratic maxim that all that is is intelligible. This is apparent in their respective discussions of tragedy. For Nietzsche, Euripides' aesthetic Socratism rendered tragedy intelligible and thereby murdered it; for Foucault, a moral-critical discourse on madness, characterized by the writings of Erasmus and definitively by Descartes, dissipated the tragic experience of madness. Both Nietzsche and Foucault reject the totalizing and normalizing tendencies of the Hegelian dialectic. Instead, both attempt to find difference in apparent identity.

Genealogy, according to both Nietzsche and Foucault, finally, keys on the body. Nietzsche goes so far as to claim that genealogy has more in common with physiology than with philosophy. Both attempt to reveal the manner in which the modern soul was constituted by means of social practices imposed upon the body.

In their more general, theoretical statements about the nature of genealogy, then, Nietzsche and Foucault stand very close together. It is with regard to this last issue, however, the issue of the role of the body in genealogy, that the significant difference between the two approaches emerges. And this difference is most vivid when we move beyond the theoretical claims about genealogy and examine how Foucault and Nietzsche concretely practice genealogy. David Hoy is correct when he suggests that Foucault's *Surveiller et punir*, "which reads like a historical case study of the theory of punishment in the second essay of the *Genealogy*, is perhaps a better example of historical genealogy than Nietzsche's own work."[194]

5

THE PRACTICE OF GENEALOGY:
THE GENEALOGY OF THE SOUL

"If I wanted to be pretentious," Foucault commented upon the publication of *Surveiller et punir*, "I would use 'the genealogy of morals' as the general title of what I am doing."[1] Having formulated the elements of his Nietzschean approach to the history of the present, then, Foucault turned his attention to the prison system. In the early 1970s, prison revolts flared throughout the world offering a problem worthy of the genealogist's attention. For the thinker concerned with the functioning of power, moreover, the prison system presents a particularly spectacular manifestation. "Prison is the only place," Foucault told Deleuze, "where power is manifested in its naked state, in its most excessive form, and where it is justified as moral force."[2] But Foucault's genealogy of the prison is not primarily a direct history of such institutions; his genealogy is a work of critique, "a critique of relations existing at a minute level,"[3] an attempt to uncover "the concrete, changing soil,"[4] the historical conditions for the emergence of the prison. In answer to the question, why study the prison?, Foucault responded that he wanted "to recover the theme of the genealogy of morals" which would trace changes in concrete "moral technologies," transformations in the day-to-day practices of punishment.[5] "In this piece of research on the prisons, as in my other earlier work," he went on, "the target of analysis wasn't 'institutions,' 'theories,' or 'ideology,' but *practices*—with the aim of grasping the conditions that make these acceptable at a given moment." And by "practices" he means "places where what is said and what is done, rules imposed and reasons given, the planned and the taken for granted meet and interconnect."[6]

The prison has become sedimented in the contemporary mind as the natural and necessary response to social problems. The purpose of Foucault's research on prisons, or better, the practice of imprisonment, is to show how imprisonment came to be viewed as "an altogether natural, self-evident, and indispensable part" of the penal system, and thereby "shaking this false self-evidence, of demonstrating its precariousness, of making visible, not its arbitrariness but its complex interconnection with a multiplicity of historical processes, many of them of recent date."[7] It has come about that we as a culture know what we are doing when we imprison, and we know why we do it. As Foucault once put it, "People know what they do; they frequently know why they do what they do; but what they don't know is what what they do does."[8] In response to this sedimentation of beliefs, Foucault's project in *Surveiller et punir* is "to bring it about that they 'no longer know what to do,' so that the acts, gestures, discourses that up until then had seemed to go without saying become problematic, difficult, dangerous."[9]

It is as if the prison offered itself as the paradigmatic site where Foucault could test his hypothesis about the insertion of discursive practices in systems of nondiscursive practices and could study their relations. A comment in a 1975 interview is worth quoting at some length:

> With the prisons there would be no sense in limiting oneself to discourses *about* prisons; just as important are the discourses which arise within the prison, the decisions and regulations which are among its constitutive elements, its means of functioning, along with its strategies, its covert discourses and ruses, ruses which are not ultimately played *by* any particular person, but which are none the less lived, and assure the permanence and functioning of the institution.[10]

Prison discourse and penal practices intertwine, give rise to one another, produce and support one another, and by examining these relations Foucault seeks to unveil how power and knowledge directly imply one another. He continually insists that the significance of the history of the prison system resides not in the explicit theoretical foundations of punishment, nor within the explicit legal system itself, but in the technology of the penalty, in concrete penal practices. "The longer I continue," he told a group of Marxist geographers, "the more it seems to me that the formation of discourses and the genealogy of knowledge need to be analysed, not in terms of types of consciousness, modes of perception and forms of ideology, but in terms of tactics and strategies of power."[11]

Prison riots and naked power do not alone call forth his genealogy of the prison, however. Like Nietzsche before him, Foucault is interested in tracing the genealogy of the soul. *Surveiller et punir: Naissance de la prison* is as much a genealogy of the modern soul, "the prison of the body," as a genealogy of the penal institution. It is "a correlative history of the modern soul and of a new power to judge; a genealogy of the present scientifico-legal complex from which the power to punish derives its bases, justifications and rules, from which it extends its effects and by which it masks its exorbitant singularity." *Surveiller et punir* is "a history of the modern soul on trial."[12] But why the soul? Because on the soul, on "this reality-reference, various concepts have been constructed and domains of analysis carved out: psyche, subjectivity, personality, consciousness, etc.; on it have been built scientific techniques and discourses, and the moral claims of humanism."[13] Briefly, the issues which emerged from his previous historical studies continue to plague him. "'Anthropologization' is the great internal threat to knowledge in our day,"[14] Foucault concluded toward the end of *Les mots et les choses*, and to undermine the substantiality of the modern soul promises thought's emancipation.

To specify the subject matter more precisely, Foucault's concern at this stage is the genealogy of the modern soul as individuality; his concern is "the political technology of individuals," not what will later interest him, "technologies of the self."[15] He conceives of the individual as a practical, discursive, and historical construct, "one of the prime effects of power," rather than an "elementary nucleus, a primitive atom" which power seizes, subdues, or crushes.[16]

Although the positive productivity of power appeared in Foucault's writings as early as *Histoire de la folie*, as we saw in our first chapter, he begins explicitly to discuss power as positive only in the 1970s. While we did see the positive production of *homo psychologicus* in his early writings, it was also clear that Foucault emphasized the power to exclude and confine. Perhaps his visit to the prison facility at Attica in April of 1972 made possible his explicit formulation of the positive productivity of power. In his initial reaction to this visit, we can detect a certain vacillation in his position. Immediately he perceived the facility as a vast machine which produces nothing; "Attica is a machine for elimination, a form of prodigious stomach, a kidney which consumes, destroys, breaks up and then rejects, and which consumes in order to eliminate what it has already eliminated."[17] His language of elimination, destruction, rejection suggests his appreciation for the negative functioning of power. Foucault characterized his interest in power as the opposite of the Durkheimian problematic; that is, instead of asking how individuals bind together in society, how society constitutes a totality, Foucault wanted to pursue the systems of exclusion and elimination, negation and rejection, which allow a society to function. But when pursued by his interviewer, Foucault admitted that his previous ideas about power as exclusion had been undermined. Attica appeared to him "too complex to be reduced to purely negative functions of exclusion; its cost, its importance, the care that one takes in administering it, the justifications that one tries to give for it seem to indicate that it possesses positive functions."[18]

While perhaps the most effective and most vivid, the prison is only one of many institutions in our time that have the constitution of individuals as their end. Foucault is especially clear on this point in a series of lectures he delivered in Rio de Janeiro in 1973. Although an effect of the institutions he studied throughout his writings—the psychiatric hospital, the medical clinic, the prison— is the exclusion of individuals, "their primary end is to bind them to an apparatus for the normalization of men."[19] And in this way these institutions are isomorphic with others, such as the school and the factory. His study of the prison, then, is less for the prison's intrinsic fascination, than as "the concentrated, exemplary, symbolic form" of a whole series of modern social institutions. The prison, then, is not just the prison; it is "the image of society, its inverted image, an image transformed into menace."[20]

The present chapter is divided into two parts. Part 1 examines the second essay of *On the Genealogy of Morals* in which Nietzsche offers his genealogy of the soul by means of a history of punishment. Two aspects of Nietzsche's genealogy of the soul manifest themselves. When he actually practices genealogy, first, Nietzsche manifests tendencies which characterized English genealogy, as discussed in our previous chapter; i.e., in his history of punishment Nietzsche seeks the origin of the bad conscience, and ultimately of the soul, in human interiority, human instincts. Secondly, Nietzsche emphasizes the relatively enduring quality of punitive procedures and draws attention to the manner in which the meaning of these procedures changes.

Part 2 examines Foucault's genealogy of the modern soul as individuality as presented primarily in his *Surveiller et punir,* what one reviewer refers to as "one of the greatest works of intellect produced in our century."[21] Foucault, first, successfully brackets human interiority; human nature, our instincts, our intentions proffer no explanation. Secondly, the discontinuity among penal practices provides Foucault's starting point. Rather than laying out the continuity of forms of punishment and indicating the transformations of their meaning, Foucault begins with transformations in penal practices and from there interprets the meaning of crime and punishment. This move, to attend to the transformations of penal practices themselves, sustains his focus upon the concrete, practical and historical conditions for the existence of the modern soul as individuality. It enables him to avoid taking recourse to quasi-transcendentals, such as human nature, our instincts, intentions.

PART 1: Nietzsche's Genealogy of the Soul

The task of the second essay in *On the Genealogy of Morals* is to answer the question, what is the origin of the morbid and self-destructive feeling of guilt? It is worth noting at the outset that here, as is typical of his approach, Nietzsche attempts to see difference in apparent identity (the opposite of the spirit of most philosophy). In the present context the apparently identical concepts of responsibility and guilt are not to be taken as identical. Responsibility is rooted in the ability to promise and to remember having promised and in a mastery of the self over time; this differs from morbid, self-destructive guilt. How was it possible for an animal (which has no memory) to become an animal with the right to make promises? "To breed an animal with *the right to make promises*—is not this the paradoxical task that nature has set itself in the case of man? is it not the real problem regarding man?"[22]

Nietzsche emphasizes that the memory, the foundation of the right to make promises, is an active creation, the result of the struggle of self-overcoming. The force which opposes this creation of memory and which must be overcome is an active forgetting. "Forgetting is no mere *vis inertiae* as the superficial imagine; it is rather an active and in the strictest sense positive faculty of repression (*Positives Hemmungsvermogen*)..."[23] without which there could be no happiness. Therefore, the counterforce which bestows the right to make promises must itself be active and robust. This counterforce can be "no mere passive inability to rid oneself of an impression, no mere indigestion through a once-pledged word with which one cannot 'have done,' but an active *desire* not to rid oneself, a desire for the continuance of something desired once, a real *memory of the will*...."²⁴ How did it come about that humans became the animals with the right to make promises?

According to Nietzsche, our right to make promises is the result of two achievements: we had to become calculating animals and calculable animals. In Nietzsche's words,

> To ordain the future in advance in this way, man must first have learned to distinguish necessary events from chance ones, to think causally, to see and anticipate distant eventualities as if they belonged to the present, to decide with certainty what is the goal and what the means to it, and in general be able to calculate and compute. Man himself must first of all have become *calculable, regular, necessary*, even in his own image of himself, if he is to be able to stand security for *his own future*, which is what one who promises does!²⁵

We must have become calculable, regular, and this was achieved by the social imposition of uniformity. The right to make promises and the responsibility this entails are the result of "the labor performed by man upon himself...."²⁶ Nietzsche refers the reader to his early work, *Daybreak*, to appreciate this labor performed upon oneself—what Nietzsche calls the "morality of mores" and what Foucault will later call "techniques of the self." "Self-conquest is required, not by reason of its useful consequences for the individual," according to Nietzsche, "but that custom and tradition may appear to be dominant, in spite of all individual counter desires and advantages. The individual shall sacrifice himself—so demands the morality of custom."²⁷ By means of this "social straitjacket" man made himself calculable.²⁸

So how was a memory created for the human animal? Briefly, by means of punishment, violence, cruelty. The creation of a memory for the human animal was achieved by what Nietzsche calls mnemotechnics: "One can well believe that the answers and methods for solving this primeval problem were not precisely gentle; perhaps indeed there was nothing more fearful and uncanny in the whole prehistory of man than his *mnemotechnics*."²⁹ According to Nietzsche,

> Man could never do without blood, torture, and sacrifices when he felt the need to create a memory for himself; the

most dreadful sacrifices and pledges (sacrifices of the first-born among them), the most repulsive mutiliations (castration, for example), the cruelest rites of all the religious cults (and all religions are at the deepest level systems of cruelties)—all this has its origin in the instinct that realized that pain is the most powerful aid to mnemonics.[30]

Some ideas are selected and lifted out of their competition with other ideas by means of their association with ascetical practices, and they are thereby, by means of these practices, rendered present and unforgettable. For a primitive people whose desires are governed by the immediate demands of the present, social demands must be associated with cruelty in order to become present realities. Having sketched the history of German penal practices—from stoning, to boiling in oil, to flaying alive—Nietzsche indicates the role of these practices in the creation of the German social memory:

With the aid of such images and procedures one finally remembers five or six "I will not's," in regard to which one had given one's *promise* so as to participate in the advantages of society—and it was indeed with the aid of this kind of memory that one at last came "to reason"! Ah, reason, seriousness, mastery over the affects, the whole somber thing called reflection, all these prerogatives and showpieces of man; how dearly they have been bought! how much blood and cruelty lie at the bottom of all 'good things'![31]

Thus, the social memory is a result of punishment, of cruelty against native spontaneity.

The English genealogist, looking about in the blue, consulting his own merely modern experience and interpreting this experience into the past, attributes the origin of the guilty conscience to an innate sense of justice. He imposes upon primitive humankind our modern sense that "the criminal deserves punishment *because* he could have acted differently"; i.e., the criminal *intended* his action, is therefore *responsible* for his action, and is therefore *deserving* of punishment. In contrast, Nietzsche maintains that "a *high* degree of humanity had to be attained before the animal 'man' began even to make the much more primitive distinctions between 'intentional,' 'negligent,' 'accidental,' 'accountable,' and their opposites and to take them into account when determining punishments."[32]

The Nietzschean genealogist, documentary gray in approach, again finds his clue in etymology: the concept *Schuld* (guilt) originates from the concept *Schulden* (debts). It is rooted in the debtorcreditor relationship, and in "the idea that every injury has its *equivalent* and can actually be paid back, even if only through the *pain* of the culprit."[33] According to Nietzsche,

> To inspire trust in his promise to repay, to provide a guarantee of the seriousness and sanctity of his promise, to impress repayment as a duty, an obligation upon his own conscience, the debtor made a contract with the creditor and pledged that if he should fail to repay he would substitute something else that he "possessed," something he had control over; for example, his body, his wife, his freedom, or even his life.... Above all, however, the creditor could inflict every kind of indignity and torture upon the body of the debtor; for example, cut from it as much as seemed commensurate with the size of the debt—and everywhere and from early times one had exact evaluations, *legal* evaluations, of the individual limbs and parts of the body from this point of view, some of them going into horrible and minute detail.[34]

It entails an odd logic. The debtor, in lieu of repayment in equivalent cash, material goods, or services, offers the creditor what, according to Nietzsche's conjecture, must have been appreciated as a kind of pleasure—"the pleasure of being allowed to vent his power freely upon one who is powerless, the voluptuous pleasure '*de faire le mal pour le plaisir de le faire*,' the enjoyment of violation."[35] Nietzsche asks: "to what extent can suffering balance debts or guilt? To the extent that to *make* suffer was in the highest degree pleasurable, to the extent that the injured party exchanged for the loss he had sustained, including the displeasure caused by the loss, an extraordinary counterbalancing pleasure: that of *making* suffer...."[36] The linking of guilt and suffering is not governed by some telos—for utility's sake, for the sake of revenge or deterrence. Instead, punishment originated in a festival of cruelty, inherently pleasureable, administered for the sake of the sheer joy of it. Only later was the form of punishment utilized for some purpose, reinterpreted, and given new meaning. Thus, from the debtor-creditor relationship active human memory, the memory of the will, emerged. Moreover, Nietzsche suggests, thinking as such emerged from the social practices involved in the debtor-creditor relationship.[37]

Nietzsche distinguishes two dimensions of punishment, an enduring dimension and a fluid dimension: "on the one hand, that in it which is relatively *enduring*, the custom, the act, the 'drama,' a certain strict sequence of procedures; on the other, that in it which is *fluid*, the meaning, the purpose, the expectation associated with the performance of such procedures."[38] Nietzsche assumes that the procedure antedates its employment for some purpose. The purposeful employment of punitive procedures "is *projected* and interpreted *into* the procedure." This meaning imposed upon the procedure is "supplemental," "accidental."[39] The relatively enduring procedure of punishment, according to Nietzsche, is repeatedly overlain by the fluid element, the imposed meaning, and by the time a culture reaches later stages the procedure will possess a synthesis of meanings. The fluid multiplicity of meanings "finally crystallizes into a kind of unity that is hard to disentangle, hard to analyze and, as must be emphasized especially, totally *indefinable*. (...all concepts in which an entire process is semiotically concentrated elude definition; only that which has no history is definable.)"[40] A wide variety of meanings have been imposed upon the procedure of punishment—"Punishment as a means of rendering harmless...as recompense...as isolation of a disturbance...as a means of inspiring fear...as a kind of repayment...as the expulsion of a degenerate element...as a festival...as the making of a memory...as payment of a fee...as a compromise with revenge...as a declaration of war..."—and at various times in history one or more of these meanings predominates over the others.[41]

Punishment is overladen with multiple utilities, and the English genealogist, along with the popular mind, selects one of these utilities and dubs it the predominant one. The English genealogist supposes that the function of punishment is to instill a bad conscience, a feeling of guilt, in the wrongdoer. This hypothesis, however, manifests the English tendency to gaze about in the blue rather than to examine the documentary gray evidence. Where, they should wonder, is there less of a sense of guilt than among criminals and convicts? The evidence makes clear that punishment hardens and actually hinders the development of a sense of guilt. According to Nietzsche,

we must not underrate the extent to which the sight of the judicial and executive procedures prevents the criminal from considering his deed, the type of his action *as such*, reprehensible: for he sees exactly the same kind of actions practiced in the service of justice and approved of and practiced with a good conscience: spying, deception, bribery, setting traps, the whole cunning and underhand art of police and prosecution, plus robbery, violence, defamation, imprisonment, torture, murder, practiced as a matter of principle and without even emotion to excuse them, which are pronounced characteristics of the various forms of punishment—all of them therefore actions which his judges in no way condemn and repudiate *as such*, but only when they are applied and directed to certain particular ends.[42]

Thus, the origin of the bad conscience is not to be sought in penal practices.

The genealogy of punishment, nonetheless, does provide a clue to the origin of the bad conscience. While punishment fails to instill the sense of guilt, it does tame people. At this point Nietzsche offers the claim toward which he has been building in his genealogy of punishment in "a first provisional statement of my own hypothesis concerning the origin of the 'bad conscience.'"[43] The bad conscience emerged when human beings finally incorporated in societies of peace. This brought on the most fundamental change human beings had ever endured, and Nietzsche likens it to the trauma endured by sea animals forced to become land animals. The trauma endured by human beings, at this point "semi-animals," when they entered society was due to the devaluation of their aggressive, warlike instincts: "they no longer possessed their former guides, their regulating, unconscious and infallible drives: they were reduced to thinking, inferring, reckoning, co-ordinating cause and effect, these unfortunate creatures; they were reduced to their 'consciousness,' their weakest and most fallible organ!"[44] In spite of this change, however, their old instincts continued to make demands. Reduced to dependence upon consciousness for his survival while his aggressive instincts continued to insist upon recognition and expression, man was forced to permit this aggressive expression of instinct by redirecting it—upon himself. This, according to Nietzsche, constitutes the genealogy of the modern soul: "All instincts that do not discharge themselves outwardly *turn inward*—this is what I call the *internalization* of man: thus it was that man first developed what was later called his 'soul.'"[45] Human interiority's origin and development was a function of the social inhibition of the outward expression of aggressive instinct. Nietzsche's hypothesis presupposes that this change could not have been gradual and organic but must have been a rupture—"a break, a leap, a compulsion, an ineluctable disaster which precluded all struggle and even all *ressentiment*"[46]—which can only be understood as the result of acts of violence.

Two points need to be made before we proceed to Foucault's practice of genealogy. In spite of this last reference to a rupture in human evolution, first, Nietzsche emphasizes the relatively enduring procedures of punishment that undergird a fluid multiplicity of interpretations of these procedures. From the opening pages of Foucault's *Surveiller et punir*, in contrast, where Foucault juxtaposes a brutal, eyewitness account of a 1757 public execution with the daily schedule of a mid-nineteenth-century prison, transformations in punitive practices themselves clearly stand at the center of Foucault's analysis. Secondly, when Nietzsche proposes the etymology of the concept *Schuld*, rooting it in the debtor-creditor relationship, he most vividly practices genealogy in accordance with his few methodological assertions. By means of this etymology he argues that practical and economic demands forced man to make himself a calculating and calculable animal. His speculations about the pleasure of venting one's power freely upon the powerless, on the other hand, manifest a blue, English hue. His hypothesis that the soul is the effect of man's having internalized his aggressive instincts, likewise, entails some of that "idle hypothesis-mongering" of which he accused Paul Rée. In contrast, Foucault's analysis remains documentary gray throughout because his concern always remains focused upon concrete penal practices.

Unlike Kantian critique, genealogical critique does not attempt to reveal transcendental conditions of possibility; instead, genealogy is critique in the sense of an attempt to reveal the concrete, historical, and practical conditions of existence. As we saw in chapter 3 Foucault emphasizes that the archaeological level of discourse that interests him is a place of exteriority. His concern is with rules embedded in our discursive and nondiscursive practices which provide the concrete, historical conditions for the existence of the entities and events we encounter, rather than with transcendental conditions, the structure of the mind, or human nature. If the human subject, as both Nietzsche and Foucault maintain, is constituted practically and historically from very concrete conditions, then Foucault's asceticism, honed in *L'archéologie du savoir*, in limiting his analysis to external conditions and practices, ought to be rewarded. Instead of taking recourse to instincts, as Nietzsche did, or some other dimension of human nature, it is more consistent with the problematic of both Nietzsche and Foucault to bracket any such explanations.

PART 2: Foucault's Genealogy of
the Modern Soul as Individuality

In his study of the evolution of punishment, Emile Durkheim
argues that a less developed society with centralized power is more
apt to employ a more intense form of punishment than a more
developed society with dispersed power. As societies develop, moreover, deprivation of liberty tends to become the normal means of
social control.[47] As individualization increases so does leniency in
punishment. Western societies, by employing incarceration as punishment, thus show their advanced state of development. Foucault,
in contrast, maintains that greater individualization is the effect,
not the cause of newly required power tactics. "My hypothesis,"
Foucault told an interviewer of 1975, " is that the prison was linked
from its beginning to a project for the transformation of individuals."[48] And again, the following year, "it's my hypothesis that the
individual is not a pregiven entity which is seized on by the exercise
of power. The individual, with his identity and characteristics, is
the product of a relation of power exercised over bodies, multiplici-
ties, movements, desires, forces."[49] One who approaches the history
of punishment in a Durkheimian fashion "runs the risk of positing
as the principle of greater leniency in punishment processes of individualization that are rather one of the effects of the new tactics of
power, among which are to be included the new penal mechanisms."[50] In order to avoid Durkheim's risk, and following insights
and discoveries from his own previous historical researches, Foucault posits four general rules to guide his genealogy of punishment. At this point it is clear to him that power does not simply
negate, repress, or exclude; it positively constitutes the entities of
our experience. Therefore, first, his study attempts to tease out the
positive effects of penal tactics. Following from this first rule, then,
penal tactics are to be viewed "as techniques possessing their own
specificity."[51] Emerging from his insights into the relationship
between power and knowledge, thirdly, *Surveiller et punir* seeks a
common matrix, "a single process of 'epistemologico-juridical' formation," for the history of penal law and that of the human sciences; that is, "make the technology of power the very principle
both of the humanization of the penal system and of the knowledge
of man."[52] Finally, this genealogy of the soul seeks the soul's descent
in transformations of power relations directed toward the body.

As in his earlier works, Foucault argues that changes in our cultural practices account for the transformation of the empirical realities we encounter, and more importantly in *Surveiller et punir*, these practices account for the constitution of the modern individual. Three sets of penal practices were available at the end of the eighteenth century, and each of these sets of practices embodies an interpretation of what it means to be, to be a crime, a punishment, a person. Rather than viewing punishment as a relatively stable procedure *overlain* by a fluidity of utilities and interpretations, Foucault emphasizes the discontinuities in punitive procedures and the interpretive changes *embedded in* penal practices themselves.

Foucault wants to claim that crime has changed: i.e., criminology's object of study, the focus of penal practices, has been transformed. But, this claim is not to be understood in terms of the truism that some acts which were once crimes are no longer crimes (e.g., blasphemy) and that some crimes are only recently possible (e.g., violation of the speed limit). In fact, in spite of this truism Foucault insists that there has been a certain continuity in the division made between the permitted and the forbidden. Instead, he wants to make a more profound assertion: in spite of this relative continuity of the division between the permitted and the forbidden, crime, the object of penal practices has been substantially changed—"the quality, the nature, in a sense the substance of which the punishable element is made, rather than its formal definition" has been profoundly altered.[53] Crime as illegal behavior has been displaced by the human "soul" as the object of judgment:

> Under cover of the relative stability of the law, a mass of subtle and rapid changes has occurred. Certainly the "crimes" and "offences" on which judgment is passed are juridical objects defined by the code, but judgment is also passed on the passions, instincts, anomalies, infirmities, maladjustments, effects of environment or heredity; acts of aggresssion are punished, so also, through them, is aggressivity; rape, but at the same time perversions; murders, but also drives and desires.[54]

Juridical procedure asks whether or not an act has been established and whether or not it is punishable. But it also asks: "What *is* this act? ...to what field of reality does it belong? ...Where did it originate in the author himself?"[55] These aspects of human interiority, it may be countered, are relevant insofar as they are explanatory, but for Foucault, "behind the pretext of explaining an action, are ways of defining an individual."[56] That comment, in as concise a manner as possible, expresses Foucault's concern: the genealogy of the modern soul as individuality. How did the modern individual come to be constituted?

As we saw in *Histoire de la folie* and *Naissance de la clinique,* judicial, penal, academic, scientific, religious, and therapeutic practices account for the transformation of the empirical realities we encounter and for the constitution of the modern soul, ourselves. Assessing, diagnostic, and prognostic practices, techniques for distributing bodies in space, timetables, surveillance practices, and examinations account for the change in the object of inquiry, the subject of inquiry, and thereby, for changes in the modes of study themselves. The clearest road providing access to the significance of penal practices for Foucault is located at that historical juncture at the end of the eighteenth century when the classical age of representation gave way to the modern age of man. Three competing penal paradigms were vying for dominance at the end of the eighteenth century. These three models of penal practice and an account of the transition from the first to the third provides the central focus of *Surveiller et punir.*

A. The Emergence of Humanity as Legal Limit: From Monarchical to Reform Penal Practices

First, the monarchical model, characterized by the spectacle of public torture, maintained a few adherents in spite of the social anomalies which had emerged from it. Crime was understood at its deepest level as injury to the sovereignty, and thus, penal practice was a ritual liturgy to reconstitute this sovereignty. "The public execution, then, has a juridico-political function," according to Foucault. "It is a ceremonial by which a momentarily injured sovereignty is reconstituted. It restores that sovereignty by manifesting it at its most spectacular."[57] Foucault's interpretation of public execution is not based on the explicit penal or judicial theory of the time, but upon the implicit understanding of what it means to be, to be a crime, to be a punishment, inherent in penal practices themselves. His interpretation of crime and punishment of the time is founded upon the meticulous ritual practices: the court-ordered ceremonial procedure, "processions, halts at crossroads and church doors, the public reading of the sentence, kneeling, declarations of repentance for the offence to God and to the king."[58] What it means to be a crime and a punishment, an injury to the sovereign power and a reconstitution of this power, is inscribed in the penal practices. The practices solidified the understanding of crime as injury to the sovereign: "If torture was so strongly embedded in legal practice, it was because it revealed truth and showed the operation of power."[59]

This set of monarchical practices, however, began to lose its ascendency because it gave rise to self-destructive social anomalies. In the same way that he showed the instability of representation in *Les mots et les choses*, Foucault in *Surveiller et punir* reveals the instability of monarchical penal practices. The primary reason why monarchical penal practices (which made no bones about being brutal) had to give way to penal practices that claimed to be humane is because of the role of the general population inherent in the practices themselves. The people were essential to monarchical penal practices. They were "the main character... whose real and immediate presence was required for the performance."[60] The people were the site of the reconstitution of the sovereign's power because this reconstitution depended upon their witness to and recognition of the power display. The display, however, was unstable:

> If the crowd gathered round the scaffold, it was not simply to witness the sufferings of the condemned man or to excite the anger of the executioner: it was also to hear an individual who had nothing more to lose curse the judge, the laws, the government, and religion.... In these executions, which ought to show only the terrorizing power of the prince, there was a whole aspect of the carnival, in which rules were inverted, authority mocked and criminals transformed into heroes.[61]

Although monarchical penal practices continued through much of the eighteenth century and were, therefore, among the competing paradigms at the end of that century, nonetheless, such unstable practices could not last. A new paradigm was called for. A new set of practices had to emerge. Public execution could no longer be tolerated.

The second set of penal practices available at the end of the eighteenth century was provided by the French reformers, and this set of practices, in true classical age style, could be characterized in terms of representation; "continuity and permanence" rather than "expenditure and excess" would characterize penal practices.[62] Foucault expresses the reformers' effort in the following terms:

...it was an effort to adjust the mechanisms of power that frame the existence of individuals; an adaptation and a refinement of the machinery that assumes responsibility for and places under surveillance their everyday behavior, their identity, their activity, their apparently unimportant gestures; another policy for that multiplicity of bodies and forces that constitutes a population. What was emerging no doubt was not so much a new respect for the humanity of the condemned...as a tendency towards a more finely tuned justice, towards a closer penal mapping of the social body.[63]

Society is the target, representation is the mode of correction, and the criminal's "humanity" is the legal limit of the new penal practices. If we briefly examine each of these three central concepts—society, representation, humanity—the significance of penal practices in the classical age comes to the fore.

First, according to Foucault, society is the target of classical age penal practices. The point of reform punishment is deterrence of crime. Through the intermediary of the criminal, punishment is directed toward the whole of society—particularly any members of society prone to behavior similar to that of the criminal. Therefore, "One must calculate a penalty in terms not of the crime, but of its possible repetition. One must take into account not the past offence, but the future disorder.... One must punish exactly enough to prevent repetition."[64] Foucault's analysis of representational discursive practices (in *Les mots et les choses*) is concretized in his treatment of representational penal practices. Since society as a whole rather than the individual criminal is the ultimate object of penal practices, the effect of punishment must be an ideal effect, a matter of representation. One of the central rules embedded in classical age penal practices, according to Foucault, can be expressed as follows:

If the motive of a crime is the advantage expected of it, the effectiveness of the penalty is the disadvantage expected of it. This means that the "pain" at the heart of punishment is not the actual sensation of pain, but the idea of pain, displeasure, inconvenience—the "pain" of the idea of "pain." Punishment has to make use not of the body, but of representation.[65]

The representation of pain in minds throughout the population, rather than the sensation of pain in the body of the condemned, is the implicit project of penal practices.

Foucault reveals six elements of representational technology embedded in classical age penal practices, six conditions with which these practices conform. First, punishment must be unarbitrary so that a clear association of ideas between the idea of crime and the idea of its punishment might be effected. Make the link between a particular crime and its appropriate punishment so consistent as to appear natural. Secondly, penal practices must play upon the calculus of advantages and disadvantages. The representation of punishment's disadvantage must be more lively ("greater force and vivacity"—Hume) than the representation of crime's advantage. Thirdly, temporality is integrated into penal practices. Unlike monarchical practices for which punishment was brutal but brief, classical age practices, which seek both to establish representations in minds and to transform those minds, must be based upon duration. Fourthly, part of representing punishment as natural is to make it appear to be advantageous to society as a whole. "The ideal would be for the convict to appear as a sort of rentable property: a slave at the service of all."[66] Penal practices— from roadwork to license plate manufacturing—must represent the social interest and make punishment visible and verifiable. Fifthly, the publicity of punishment must represent society's legal structure. "The laws associated a particular crime with a particular punishment. As soon as the crime is committed, the punishment will follow at once, enacting the discourse of the law and showing that the code, which links ideas, also links realities."[67] Publicity by means of posters and placards must be distributed to effect this association of ideas. Finally, penal practices must teach a lesson; they must be representations of moral fables. Crime and punishment must form a narrative structure that can grasp the popular imagination.

The criminal's "humanity" functions as the legal limit of the new penal practices. For our purposes, this is the most significant aspect of reform penal practices because, according to Foucault, a very significant entity, man, is emerging from these practices. After the revolution of 1789, "In the worst of murderers, there is one thing, at least, to be respected when one punishes: his 'humanity.'"[68] The quotation marks around "humanity" are necessary and important because at this point in history humanity is, more or less, a kind of ghost in the machine, a skeleton or framework. It is the abstract legal limit of penal practices. Humanity as something "substantial," as a "positivity," is at this point in history in the process of being constituted by cultural practices. "The day was to come, in the nineteenth century," according to Foucault, when this "man," discovered in the criminal, would become the target of penal intervention, the object that it claimed to correct and transform, the domain of a whole series of "criminological" sciences and strange "penitentiary" practices. But, at the time of the Enlightenment, it was not as a theme of positive knowledge that man was opposed to the barbarity of the public executions, but as a legal limit: the legitimate frontier of the power to punish. Not that which must be reached in order to alter him, but that which must be left in tact in order to respect him.[69]

Later he will refer to these penal practices as part of the process of "anthropological individualization."[70]

What Foucault calls "the rule of optimal specification" which pervaded penal practices in the classical age illustrates the process whereby humanity as legal limit, and ultimately the modern individual, were constituted. Foucault records the collection and classification of data, modeled on the taxonomies of natural history, which characterized penal practices. Since the "idea of the same punishment does not have the same effect on everyone: the rich do not fear fines nor the notorious infamy,"[71] the offender himself must be subjected to rigorous classification similar to the classification of his crime. Foucault sees both the modern individual and the rise of modern psychology as functions of this classification of the criminal. In previous forms of penal practices, he tells us, "The modulation of the penalty belonged to 'casuistry' in the broad sense," and Foucault insists upon the non-individualizing character of casuistry. However, he continues, "what was now beginning to emerge was a modulation that referred to the defendant himself, to his nature, to his way of life and his attitude of mind, to his past, to the 'quality' and not to the intention of his will. One perceives, but as a place yet unfilled, the locus in which, in penal practice, psychological knowledge will take over the role of casuistic jurisprudence."[72] The ethical tone of their rhetoric hides the fact that their practices remove the issue of crime and punishment from the ethical sphere. These practices open up a penal space in which sickness and cure, rather than moral wrong and right, are at issue.

B. The Solidification of Individuality

The third set of penal practices available at the end of the eighteenth century, the set of practices which prevailed, can be called disciplinary practices. These, according to Foucault, represent a hitherto unforeseen form of power, "probably even more important than the constitutional reforms and new forms of government established at the end of the eighteenth century": "It becomes a matter of obtaining productive service from individuals in their concrete lives. And in consequence, a real and effective 'incorporation' of power was necessary, in the sense that power had to be able to gain access to the bodies of individuals, to their acts, attitudes and modes of everyday behaviour."[73] These new practices, according to Foucault, solidify the modern individual that was sketched out by representational practices.

The concern for detail in these new penal practices is even more refined and meticulous. Exercises, not representations, characterize these practices: "time-tables, compulsory movements, regular activities, solitary meditation, work in common, silence, application, respect, good habits." The criminal is "subjected to habits, rules, orders, an authority that is exercised continually around him and upon him, and which he must allow to function automatically in him."[74] In sharp contrast to the spectacle of monarchical practices and the corresponding publicity of representational practices, moreover, the new disciplinary practices require secrecy. While philosophers and jurists speculated on social contracts and the origins of civil society, procedures for coercing bodies developed among military personnel, educators, and in the ascetical practices of religious communities. These developing disciplinary practices, according to Foucault, bore the true and effective political power by their capacity to mold, transform, and constitute individuals. In contrast to Machiavellian tyranny,

> Discipline "makes" individuals; it is the specific technique of a power that regards individuals both as objects and as instruments of its exercise. It is not a triumphant power, which because of its own excess can pride itself on its omnipotence; it is a modest, suspicious power, which functions as a calculated, but permanent economy. These are humble modalities, minor procedures, as compared with the majestic rituals of sovereignty or the great apparatuses of the state.[75]

Discipline's effectiveness, moreover, is due essentially to the simplicity and humility of its instruments, and Foucault delineates three of its central techniques: hierarchical surveillance, the normalizing sanction, and the examination. In Foucault's discussion of these techniques we obtain a clear view of his meticulous concern for detail which, not incidentally, corresponds with the metic-ulous details borne by his subject matter, "the infinitely small of political power."[76]

Foucault's treatment of disciplinary penal practices consists of a series of examples of such practices as they were institutional-ized in military, medical, educational, and industrial establish-ments. "The prison was meant to be an instrument," according to Foucault, "comparable with—and no less perfect than—the school, the barracks, or the hospital, acting with precision upon its indi-vidual subjects."[77] Other examples could have come from tech-niques of colonization, slavery, and child rearing. Thus, Foucault insists that disciplinary penal practices were consistent with gen-eral cultural practices. By distinguishing these cultural practices, Foucault is arguing that types of individuality, or characteristics of modern individuality, were produced by these practices: "A meticulous observation of detail, and at the same time a political awareness of these small things, for the control and use of men, emerge through the classical age bearing with them a whole set of techniques, a whole corpus of methods and knowledge, descrip-tions, plans and data. And from such trifles, no doubt, the man of modern humanism was born."[78] Recalling the critical role played by spatial transformations in *Histoire de la folie* and *Naissance de la clinique* and the role of time charted in *Les mots et les choses*, we can see the continuing importance of space and time in *Surveiller et punir*. The effects of the emerging concern for writing and confession, moreover, contribute to the individualization of modern men and women.

1. Surveillance and the Transformation of Space

"People have often reproached me for these spatial obsessions, which have indeed been obsessions for me," Foucault told a group of geographers in 1976. "But I think through them I did come to what I had basically been looking for: the relations that are possi-ble between power and knowledge."[79] "A whole history remains to be written of spaces—which would at the same time be the history of powers," Foucault commented a year later.[80] In *Surveiller et punir* he classifies the first type of disciplinary practices under the general heading "the art of distributions." The monk's cell is paradigmatic of distribution in space. By means of the enclosure, partitioning, and ranking of individuals discipline prevailed. Such practices as the separation of factory workers according to function, skill, and productivity, and the spatial distribution of school children according to rank was aimed toward the establishment of "presences and absences, to know where and how to locate individuals, to set up useful communications, to interrupt others, to be able at each moment to supervise the conduct of each individual, to assess it, to judge it, to calculate its qualities or merits. It was a procedure, therefore, aimed at knowing, mastering and using. Discipline organizes an analytical space."[81] Briefly, the image Foucault conveys recalls Plato's cave in which chained individuals are isolated from one another making each more available to the manipulative power of the centralized source of shadows.

"A fear haunted the latter half of the eighteenth century." according to Foucault, "the fear of darkened spaces, of the pall of gloom which prevents the full visibility of things, men and truths."[82] Hierarchical surveillance, seeing without being seen, provides the power to coerce without violence. Long before Heisenberg formulated his indeterminacy principle, the classical age already had the basic insight that observation alone could affect behavior. By increasing visibility, moreover, the classical age knew it could transform and control behavior. This desire for increased visibility manifests itself especially in classical age architecture. This is not the age of the palace, "built simply to be seen," nor of the fortress, built "to observe the external space." Instead, the classical age architectural problem was "to permit an internal, articulated and detailed control—to render visible those who are inside it; in more general terms, an architecture that would operate to transform individuals; to act on those it shelters, to provide a hold on their conduct, to carry the effects of power right to them, to make it possible to know them, to alter them."[83] The task was to establish the architectural equivalent of the autopsy. By the very organization of living space, of work, educational, or correction space, the task was to dissect and manifest the interior and the individuals who occupied this space. The goal—to attain "power through transparency,"[84] to enable a single gaze to see everything and, thereby, to control it.

Jeremy Bentham, designer of the panopticon, and for that reason "more important, for our society, than Kant or Hegel,"[85] established the architectural paradigm for hierarchical surveillance. Bentham's architectural problem was "precisely the inverse of the problem faced by the Greeks."[86] The Greek theater had to enable the masses to see a few individuals on stage. With its centralized observation tower encircled by individualized cells, the panopticon enables a single person to see without being seen and, thus, to bring about the effect of a constant surveillance which tends "to individualize the author of the act."[87] Each individual occupies an assigned space in which he can be observed from the front, but side walls prohibit any interaction with fellow inmates. Each prisoner is "the object of information, never a subject in communication."[88] Never knowing whether or not he is observed at a given moment, the prisoner, patient, worker, or student must assume that he is. In the system of surveillance "There is no need for arms, physical violence, material constraints. Just a gaze. An inspecting gaze, a gaze which each individual under its weight will end by interiorising to the point that he is his own overseer, each individual thus exercising this surveillance over, and against himself."[89] The panopticon is, thus, "certainly a form of architecture, but it is above all a form of government."[90]

"Medical power is at the heart of the society of normalization,"[91] according to Foucault, and he maintains that government by individualization proceeded similarly in late eighteenth-century spatial transformations in the hospital. In *Généalogie des équipements de normalisation* a group of researchers under Foucault's direction attempted to answer the question, how did the hospital, once viewed as the place where the poor go to die, come to be viewed as a place of medical assistance? As Foucault revealed in his own history of the medical clinic, spatial transformations were of crucial significance. The hospital, this research group reported in 1976, had previously been a place for "the overdetermination of illness,"[92] a place where diseases crossbred and complicated one another, because the hospital was an overcrowded space with poor air circulation. A corruption of the hospital air, it was thought in the late eighteenth century, complicated people's conditions, making the hospital the space of death. A link was thus forged between sick bodies and architectural space; architectural issues were medicalized, and the therapeutic ends of medicine became questions of architecture.

The research group's most important revelation is that the medicalization of hospital space entailed setting into motion a process of individualization. Questions of air circulation involved determining the air requirements of individual organisms, and the need to avoid the interaction of different illnesses required the establishment of the individualized space of quarantine. In the Academy of Science's 1786 report of its investigation into the hospital space of l'Hôtel-Dieu, according to Foucault's research group, can be found "for the first time a reference to the organism and by this fact a reference to something like individual needs."[93] Once the individual organism manifests its own exigencies, the individual is no longer merely an "arithmetical unity" but is also "a spatial unity at the interior of an architectural and therapeutic strategy."[94]

Such individualization permits a more penetrating government; such individualization in medical space, as in the prison, allows the establishment of the order of surveillance. The management of hospital space is guided by the end of enabling the constant observation of the patient and the changes in his or her illness. But management of space for the sake of surveillance is not limited to the space of the hospital. In 1800 Bichat defined life as "the ensemble of functions which resist death."[95] By thus associating life with health, a generalized concern for the healthiness of the entire population follows, requiring a general extension of the medicalization process from the hospital to the city as a whole. The medicalization of the entirety of urban space follows the medicalization of hospital space.[96] And the normalizing, individualizing power of surveillance penetrates more deeply into the social body.

2. Discipline and the Transformation of Time

Along with these spatializing practices, Foucault reveals a series of temporalizing practices. The timetable, like the prison cell, suggested by the practices of monastic communities, is the paradigm for this second form of activity control. Schools, factories, and hospitals manifested techniques for establishing rhythms, imposing tasks according to time, and regulating cycles of repetition. Time was partitioned in a more detailed fashion—in quarter hours, minutes, and seconds. "A sort of anatomo-chronological schema of behavior is defined," according to Foucault. "The act is broken down into its elements; the position of the body, limbs, articulations is defined; to each movement are assigned a direction, an aptitude, a duration; their order of succession is prescribed. Time penetrates the body and with it all the meticulous controls of power."[97] To appreciate the significance of this for Foucault we ought to recall his discussion of life, labor, and language from *Les mots et les choses*. These three new positivities were constituted by the introduction of a temporal process into the objects of natural history, the analysis of wealth, and general grammar. Similarly, Foucault is trying to show that an "organic individuality" is being produced by disciplinary practices focused upon time. His analysis of time zeroes in to "the point where power reaches into the very grain of individuals, touches their bodies and inserts itself into their actions and attitudes, their discourses, learning processes and everyday lives."[98] As he put it in his 1973 Rio de Janeiro lectures, the problems of space, time, and the body dovetail; that is, the point of the spatial segregation of workers, students, inmates is to exploit time and to discipline the body:

> The primary function of sequestration [spatial segregation] was to exploit time in such a way that the time of men, *el vital*, is transformed into the time of work. The second function consists in converting men's bodies into work force. The function of the transformation of the body into a work force corresponds to the function of the transformation of time into time of work.[99]

Temporal transformations in the late eighteenth-century hospital mirrored those of the prison. In *Généalogie des équipements de normalisation* Foucault's research group reports that, like hospital space and urban space, hospital time, too, was medicalized. Medical administrators established hierarchies in the hospital staff, precisely defined the tasks of each, and governed the time of the performance of each task. Physicians' visits to patients underwent particularly meticulous scrutiny; medical administrators specified the time of day, duration, and frequency of physicians' visitations in order to establish "a medicalized time: time more largely consecrated than previously to the observation of the illness and its evolution; time of constant medical surveillance."[100]

3. Writing and Confession

Discipline employs the sanction as an instrument for normalizing behavior. This normalizing sanction especially attunes to nonconformity, "that which does not measure up to the rule, that departs from it, deviations."[101] Failure to conform to standards of behavior, artificially established but rooted in "nature," entails corrective punishment, usually an appropriate type of exercise; repetitious exercise molds the student's or soldier's behavior in accord with the norm, "So that they might all be like one another."[102] Such normalizing sanctions forward the process of governing individuals by observing them; it is the locale at which knowledge of an individual dovetails with power over the individual. "By assessing acts with precision, discipline judges individuals 'in truth'; the penalty that it implements is integrated into the cycle of knowledge of individuals."[103] And this interplay of knowledge of the individual and power over the individual that he discovered leads Foucault to conclude:

> The juridico-anthropological functioning revealed in the whole history of modern penality did not originate in the superimposition of the human sciences on criminal justice and in the requirements proper to this new rationality or to the humanism that it appeared to bring with it; it originated in the disciplinary technique that operated these new mechanisms of normalizing judgement.[104]

The examination combines hierarchical surveillance and the normalizing sanction. In the ritualized examination we find united "the ceremony of power and the form of the experiment, the deployment of force and the establishment of truth;...it manifests the subjection of those who are perceived as objects and the objectification of those who are subjected."[105] The examination objectifies the examinee; it draws him forth into the light of the examiner's gaze. It renders the examinee into written documentation, sustaining and furthering his identification and individualization. Foucault seizes upon the individualizing capacity of writing, and his remarks are worth quoting at some length:

> Thanks to the whole apparatus of writing that accompanied it, the examination opened up two correlative possibilities: firstly, the constitution of the individual as a describable, analysable object, not in order to reduce him to "specific" features, as did the naturalists in relation to living beings, but in order to maintain him in his individual features, in his particular evolution, in his own aptitudes or abilities, under the gaze of a permanent corpus of knowledge; and, secondly, the constitution of a comparative system that made possible the measurement of overall phenomena, the description of groups, the characterization of collective facts, the calculation of the gaps between individuals, their distribution in a given "population."[106]

The written documentation resulting from the examination solidifies the individual by specifying his own characteristics and by differentiating him from others. Each individual is constituted as a "case."

At this point Foucault forcefully and explicitly makes the claim that was manifest in a rudimentary form in his work as early as *Histoire de la folie* and toward which he has been building throughout his career: "We must cease once and for all to describe the effects of power in negative terms: it 'excludes', it 'represses', it 'censors', it 'abstracts', it 'masks', it 'conceals'. In fact, power produces; it produces reality; it produces domains of objects and rituals of truth. The individual and the knowledge that may be gained of him belong to this production."[107]

Writing played a similar normalizing and individualizing role in the late eighteenth-century hospital. Writing, like the redistribution of medical space and the regimentation of hospital time, emerged as a new medical practice that established the medical function of the hospital. Writing codifies the admission, placement, and treatment of the patient and, thereby, contributes to the patient's individualization and to the normalization of medical procedure. "Means of knowledge, possibility of permanent control, writing answers here to the care for order, subjacent to the reform of the hospital."[108] Written documentation allows the individual patient to be known by the simple reading of a sheet of paper.

We can see why Pierre Rivière's written confession of his crime so intrigued Foucault and his colleagues.

> I, Pierre Rivière, having slaughtered my mother, my sister, and my brother, and wishing to make known the motives which led me to this deed, have written down the whole of the life which my father and my mother led together since their marriage.... I shall then tell how I resolved to commit this crime, what my thoughts were at the time, and what was my intention.[109]

And the manuscript continues for more than a hundred more pages.[110] Written in 1835, Rivière's memoir, according to Foucault, answers a new question. Previously, once it had been established whether or not the accused had performed the criminal act, the case was closed. "'What is this individual who has committed this crime?' is a new question."[111]

In a fascinating essay of 1978 Foucault reveals how judicial practices coincided with penal practices in the formation of the modern individual. He argues that the question, in some form or other, 'who are you?' has become essential to modern judicial procedure—a question that would have seemed out of place to late eighteenth-century legislators and constitutional framers. Beyond admitting to having committed a crime, much more is required of the accused in modern judicial practice; "there must be confession, self-examination, explanation of oneself, revelation of what one is."[112] The identity of the accused provides a "supplementary material" over and above the law, the fact of its having been violated, and the presence of the person responsible.[113] "The magistrates and the jurors, the lawyers too, and the department of the public prosecutor," according to Foucault, "cannot really play their role unless they are provided with another type of discourse, the one given by the accused about himself, or the one which he makes possible for others, through his confessions, memories, intimate disclosures, etc."[114] The essay is concerned with the evolution of the notion of "the dangerous individual," and in his 1973 Rio de Janeiro lectures Foucault draws attention to the significance of this notion: "The notion of dangerous signifies that the individual ought to be considered by society at the level of his habitual tendencies [*virtualidades*] and not of his acts; not at the level of his effective infractions of a law, but of the habitual tendencies [*virtualidades*] toward behavior that they represent."[115] Foucault supports his claim with an anecdote from a contemporary French trial of a capital crime: referring to his client's failure to so disclose himself to the court and to psychiatrists, the defense attorney attempted to throw into question employing the death penalty for his client by asking, "Can one condemn to death a person one does not know?"[116]

*   *   *

From our comparison of Nietzsche's and Foucault's notions of genealogy in chapter 4 and from the juxtaposition of their respective practices of genealogy presented here in chapter 5, it becomes clear that, while Foucault's approach is Nietzschean, it is neither identical nor reducible to its Nietzschean elements. The greater effectiveness of Foucault's practice of genealogy results from his concentration upon the transformations of penal practices themselves and from his refusal of any quasi-transcendental explanations, such as human nature, our instincts or intentions. By these means Foucault sustains his critical attention upon the concrete, practical, and historical conditions for the existence of the modern soul as individuality.

6

THE GENEALOGY OF
THE MODERN SUBJECT

In 1976 the first volume of Foucault's history of sexuality, *La volonté de savoir*, appeared. It led us to expect succeeding volumes governed by the same historical periodization as in Foucault's writings from *Histoire de la folie* and *Naissance de la clinique* through *Les mots et les choses* to *Surveiller et punir*. It led us to expect, specifically, studies of the hysterical woman, the masturbating child, the Malthusian couple, and the perverse adult, as constituted from the seventeenth to the nineteenth centuries.[1] But *L'usage des plaisirs*, the second volume which appeared eight years after the first, studies the discourse of philosophers and physicians of Greek antiquity, the fourth century B.C., and announces a radically restructured project analyzing discourse on sexuality of second-century Rome through the writings of the early Church Fathers.[2] Foucault begins his second volume of the history of sexuality with an explanation for the delay in his publication schedule and for the restructuring of his project that this second volume represents.

Typically, sexuality is thought of as a given, a constant, something without a history. The subject of sexual desire is immersed in a history of repression and interdictions without itself having a history, "a superimposition of, on the one hand, desires which derive from natural instincts, and, on the other hand, of permissive or restrictive laws which tell us what we should or shouldn't do."[3] The historical manifestations of the subject of sexual desire vary according to transformations of modes of repression,

157

but beneath these manifestations the subject of desire remains constant. "What this amounted to, in effect," according to Foucault, "was that desire and the subject of desire were withdrawn from the historical field, and interdiction as a general form was made to account for anything historical in sexuality."[4]

But why a genealogy of the desiring subject?[5] And why abandon the historical periodization Foucault specialized in throughout his career—roughly the Renaissance to the nineteenth century—and enter the morass of literature of and on classical Greek and Roman antiquity? There are several reasons. Primarily, he tells us, because of the common acceptance of the theme of the desiring subject. The desiring subject stands at the center of traditional theories of sexuality as well as theories that seek independence from the tradition. Christian thought on sexuality handed on the theme of the desiring subject to the nineteenth and twentieth centuries. While Foucault maintains that "the experience of sexuality, as a singular historical figure" is quite distinct from the Christian experience of "the flesh," the theme of the desiring subject presides at the center of both. The task he proposed for himself in the first volume, then, of analyzing the constitution of the experience of sexuality from the eighteenth century onward, required, in order to be adequate to the task, a genealogy of the desiring subject, "a historical and critical study of desire and the desiring subject."[6]

Foucault's reflections on where his intellectual journey had brought him reveals a second reason for departing from his familiar turf. While preparing the last volumes of his history of sexuality he began to delineate explicitly his previous historical studies in terms of the three genealogical axes which we have seen operating from as early as 1961. Reminiscing in 1984, Foucault claims that in *Histoire de la folie* and *Naissance de la clinique* he wanted to "analyze the genesis" of

> first, the formation of a domain of recognitions which constitute themselves as specific knowledge of "mental illness" [the truth/knowledge axis]; second, the organization of a normative system built on a whole technical, administrative, juridical and medical apparatus whose purpose was to isolate and take custody of the insane [the power axis]; and finally, the definition of a relation to oneself and to others as possible subjects of madness [the subject axis].[7]

As we have seen, however, the relative importance of the axes varies according to the type of experience in question. The knowledge axis predominated in his study of the emergence of clinical medicine and of the sciences of life, labor, and language. The power axis commanded priority in the analysis of penal practices.

But the historical periodization with which Foucault was most familiar itself became problematic when he sought to analyze the subject axis in its own integrity.[8] His analysis of discourse on sexuality in the seventeenth to the nineteenth centuries, intended to reveal various modalities of relation to the self, showed the subject axis to be overdetermined by the knowledge and power axes. This hindered his project of studying forms of relation to the self "in and of themselves."[9] The modern period in which the experience of sexuality was constituted shrouded the subject axis because of the knowledge explosion about sexuality in the domains of biology, medicine, psychopathology, sociology, and ethnology. New normative systems, moreover, from the medical, judicial, and educational realms, made it difficult to isolate new forms of relation to the self as discrete elements constituting our modern experience of sexuality.[10] In order to expose these forms of relation to self without the surplus of meaning provided by the entanglement of these relations with complex domains of knowledge and systems of normativity, Foucault moved back in history to periods prior to the formation of sexuality as experience.[11]

There is a third reason for Foucault's turn to antiquity. He recognized subjugation as resulting from the modern form of power which he calls "pastoral,' but he also recognized it as a new interpretation—"a new distribution, a new organization"—of a subjugation rooted much more deeply in our history.[12] Structurally, Foucault's reformulation of his sexuality series harkens back to *Histoire de la folie*.[13] In that early work, as we have seen, Foucault revealed the practical manner in which madness was problematized morally as the condition for its problematization in terms of truth; i.e., madness was practically constituted as a moral problematic and only then would it become a problematic of truth for the discipline of psychiatry. In his reformulation of the sexuality series, Foucault wants to reveal a similar structure in the constitution of sexuality as a truth problematic; only upon the basis of having been practically constituted as morally problematic would sexuality achieve problematization in terms of truth.

Genealogy, as history of the present, begins with a question posed in the present.[14] What, then, is the contemporary concern that motivated a genealogy of the desiring subject? In our time subjectivity, sexuality, and truth intertwine in a mysterious fashion. Sexuality, in fact, is viewed as the "seismograph" of the truth

of our subjectivity. "Why," Foucault asks, "is there such a fundamental connection among sexuality, subjectivity, and the truth
obligation?"[15] The ways in which psychology, our modern anthropology, our science of the subject, intertwines with modern net-
works of power and knowledge has been of central interest to Foucault from the very beginning. Now, by exploring the genealogy of
the desiring subject, Foucault prepares a genealogy of psychology's
psychoanalytic branch.[16] Foucault's genealogy of the desiring subject results from his recognition of "A will to knowledge which is so
imperious, and in which we are so enveloped, that we not only
seek the truth of sex, but seek, through it, the truth about ourselves. We expect it to tell us about ourselves. From Gerson to
Freud, an entire logic of sex has been constructed, a logic which
organizes the science of the subject."[17] After his genealogies of
madness, the clinic, and the prison, Foucault would not assume
that power's essential function is to repress, to censor, and to for-
bid; instead, he would seek the ways in which power binds together sexuality, subjectivity, and truth in a positive fashion.[18]

In the same way that, in *Surveiller et punir*, Foucault avoided
explicit political and penal theory and, instead, analyzed concrete
disciplinary practices, so here he is not concerned with the history
of ideas about desire, concupiscence, libido, etc. The task, instead,
is genealogy—"to analyze the practices by which individuals were
led to focus their attention on themselves, to decipher, recognize,
and acknowledge themselves as subjects of desire, bringing into
play between themselves and themselves a certain relationship
that allows them to discover, in desire, the truth of their being, be
it natural or fallen."[19] How were individuals led to practice a
"hermeneutics of desire" upon themselves? By what means were
we led to see ourselves as subjects of desire such that we could
come to experience ourselves as subjects of sexuality?

Foucault's turn to the Greeks and Romans results from his
desire to defamiliarize the taken-for-granted notion of sexuality in
which he expressed an interest as early as *Histoire de la folie* and
which he promised to study in his inaugural lecture. His turn to the
Greeks and Romans enables him to step back from this too familiar
notion and "to analyze the theoretical and practical context in
which it made its appearance and with which it is still associated."[20] Such a critical analysis reveals the conditions of the emergence of sexuality as experience; it analyzes the experience of sexuality as the correlative of the three genealogical axes. A
genealogical critique of sexuality entails treating it as "an experience which conjoins a field of study (*connaissance*) (with its own

concepts, theories, diverse disciplines), a collection of rules (which differentiate the permissible from the forbidden, natural from monstrous, normal from pathological, what is decent from what is not, etc.), a mode of relation between the individual and himself (which enables him to recognize himself as a sexual subject amid others)."[21] *L'usage des plaisirs*, then, is a work of critique; that is, it intends to study "that quite recent and banal notion of 'sexuality,'"[22] but it does so by examining its historical conditions of existence.

In his third essay in *On the Genealogy of Morals* Nietzsche examines the ascetic ideal, the notion that a life of self-denial is best for human beings. The three great slogans of the ascetic ideal are "poverty, humility, chastity."[23] The ascetic ideal is manifest, according to Nietzsche, in six different types, and his analysis focuses on three of these: artists, philosophers, and priests. Nietzsche's genealogy of the ascetic ideal provides an illuminating context for appreciating Foucault's genealogy of the desiring subject because it draws our attention to various modes of self-formation, types of relationships that people have been invited or incited to establish with themselves in history.

A. Nietzsche's Genealogy of the Ascetic Ideal

The asceticism of the artist, of Goethe for example, can be a healthy self-discipline that transcends any antithesis between chastity and sensuality. And if the antithesis does reign the healthy are not broken by it; instead they regard "their unstable equilibrium between 'animal and angel'" as "one *more* stimulus to life."[24] The healthy disciplined will manifest in art is in fact "much more fundamentally opposed to the ascetic ideal than is science." Between art and the ascetic ideal is a "genuine antagonism."[25] The artist, however, Wagner for example, is capable of corruption—indeed is ripe for corruption, "for nothing is more easily corrupted than an artist."[26] Nietzsche accuses artists because "they do not stand independently enough in the world and *against* the world for their changing valuations to deserve attention *in themselves*! They have at all times been valets of some morality, philosophy, or religion...."[27] A moralization undergirds even the activity of the artist.

The philosopher's asceticism, like that of the artist, takes two forms. "As long as there are philosophers on earth," according to Nietzsche, "and wherever there have been philosophers (from India to England, to take the antithetical poles of philosophical endowment), there unquestionably exists a peculiar philosophers' irritation at and rancor against sensuality.... There also exists a peculiar philosophers' prejudice and affection in favor of the whole ascetic ideal."[28] But the philosopher's negative judgment against sensuality is not necessarily moralistic—"what has this kind of man to do with virtues!"[29] The philosopher's asceticism can be more a matter of self-affirmation than self-denial, seeing in the asceticism the optimum conditions for intellectual flourishing. Asceticism tames distractions and allows more precise focusing on the philosophical enterprise. The philosopher's asceticism is motivated by self-interest—philosophical self-actualization, self-affirmation, "prudentially motivated self-control"[30]—and is devoid of moralism. Moreover, according to Nietzsche, the philosophical drive must appear immoral: "Draw up a list of the various propensities and virtues of the philosopher—his bent to doubt, his bent to deny, his bent to suspend judgment (his 'ephetic' bent), his bent to analyze, his bent to investigate, seek, dare, his bent to compare and balance, his will to neutrality and objectivity, his will to every *'sine ira et studio'*: is it not clear that for the longest time all of them contravened the basic demands of morality and conscience...?"[31]

Because of this moral corruption inherent in the philosophical stance philosophers were forced to conceal their activity behind a religious veneer. Despised and mistrusted, philosophers were compelled to make themselves feared by appearing as ascetic priests. They castigated and tortured themselves:

the philosophic spirit always had to use as a mask and a cocoon the *previously established* types of the contemplative man—priest, sorcerer, soothsayer, and in any case a religious type—in order to be able to *exist at all: the ascetic ideal* for a long time served the philosopher as a form in which to appear, as a precondition of existence—he had to *represent* it so as to be able to be a philosopher; he had to *believe* in it in order to be able to represent it. The peculiar, withdrawn attitude of the philosopher, world-denying, hostile to life, suspicious of the senses, freed from sensuality, which has been maintained down to the most modern times and has become virtually the *philosopher's pose par excellence*—it is above all a result of the emergency conditions under which philosophy arose and survived at all; for the longest time philosophy would not have been *possible at all* on earth without ascetic wraps and cloak, without an ascetic self-misunderstanding. To put it vividly: the *ascetic priest* provided until the most modern times the repulsive and gloomy caterpillar form in which alone the philosopher could live and creep about.[32]

In order to survive the world's hostility philosophers disguised themselves as ascetic priests.

When healthy philosophical asceticism transforms itself into the ascetism of the priest, asceticism is moralized, and this moralization brings two related changes onto the scene. First, the priest engages in asceticism for its own sake. While the self-affirming philosopher practiced self-discipline in order to avoid distraction and to hone concentration, self-denying priestly asceticism is an end in itself. Secondly, priestly asceticism takes on the spirit of reactive *ressentiment*; that is, the priest wins his self-esteem by condemning others—"You are evil; I am the opposite of you; therefore I am good." As a result the ascetic priest, who identifies goodness with himself and good behavior with his own behavior, wills his asceticism to be universal and condemns all who fail to partake in his ascetical practices; "he *demands* that one go along with him; where he can he compells acceptance of *his* evaluation of existence."[33] While the self-affirming philosopher disciplined himself but remained indifferent to others' sensuality, the ascetic priest condemns all sensuality.

What troubles Nietzsche about the rise of the ascetic priest is the priest's "monstrous" evaluation of human life and the priest's prevalence throughout history and in every culture. The ascetic priest, first, judges human life to be a bridge to another life. He juxtaposes human life "(along with what pertains to it: 'nature,' 'world,' the whole sphere of becoming and transitoriness) with a quite different mode of existence which it opposes and excludes, *unless* it turn against itself, *deny itself*: in that case, the case of the ascetic life, life counts as a bridge to that other mode of existence."[34] While the philosopher practiced self-discipline to enhance his life in the present, the ascetic priest denies our present life, renounces it for the sake of a future, otherworldly life. From Nietzsche's perspective the notion of an ascetic life is self contradictory for the ascetic priest is a "life-inimical species."[35] In spite of the ascetic priest's contradictory character, secondly, Nietzsche invites us to appreciate his universality: "consider how regularly and universally the ascetic priest appears in almost every age; he belongs to no one race; he prospers everywhere; he emerges from every class of society."[36] How do we explain the persistence of this odd character?

The ascetic priest in spite of all appearances to the contrary, according to Nietzsche, must have been life affirming; "this ascetic priest, this apparent enemy of life, this *denier*—precisely he is among the greatest *conserving* and yes-creating forces of life." When the human condition and life itself is degenerating, according to Nietzsche, the human instinct for self-preservation gives rise to the ascetic ideal. As we have seen in his discussion of artists and philosophers, Nietzsche does not believe that suffering, especially the suffering that results from ascetical practices, is intrinsically evil, especially when this suffering has the purpose of enhancing the work of the artist or philosopher. Suffering is most abhorrent precisely when it lacks any reason or purpose, and "every sufferer instinctively seeks a cause for his suffering."[37] The ascetic priest regularly arises and thrives in history because he provides this cause. "'I suffer: someone must be to blame for it'— thus thinks every sickly sheep. But his shepherd, the ascetic priest, tells him: 'Quite so, my sheep! someone must be to blame for it: but you yourself are this someone, you alone are to blame for it—*you alone are to blame for yourself!*'"[38] The ascetic priest manipulates the bad conscience, stimulates the sense of guilt, preaches sin and damnation, and motivates "self-discipline, self-surveillance, and self-overcoming."[39]

Nietzsche's story of the ascetic ideal is certainly interesting in its own right, but what is most important for our purposes and what Foucault draws our attention to are the various kinds of relationships people have been incited to take up with themselves in history. What Foucault sees in Nietzsche and what he wishes to reveal in his own genealogy of the subject is the place of the relationships one establishes with oneself as the central consideration in any ethical system or moral matrix and as, moreover, the way power intervenes most intimately into our lives. Foucault's writings on sexuality form a coherent genealogy of the modern subject. In order to manifest this coherence, however, we must break from the chronology of Foucault's own writings and reorganize his work in accordance with the actual historical sequence.[40] We will thus begin with a discussion of the premodern discourse on sexuality and culminate with the discourse of the moderns.

B. Foucault's Genealogy of the Desiring Subject: The Premodern Experience

In what ways have individuals been called upon to apply techniques to themselves that enable them to recognize themselves as ethical subjects of sexual behavior? These relationships to oneself consist of four dimensions that typically structure moral experience: the ethical substance, the modes of subjection, the forms of elaboration of the self, and the moral teleology.[41] While sexual practices and interdictions concerning sexual conduct remain relatively constant from epoch to epoch, according to Foucault, these four dimensions that structure moral experience are quite fluid.[42]

The ethical substance refers to that aspect of oneself or one's behavior that is at issue, that is relevant for ethical judgment. In our own time, for example, one might argue that feelings provide the ethical substance; for a Kantian, it is intentions; for the Christian, Foucault suggests with some hesitation, it is desires. A study of the ethical substance provides an ontology of moral experience. The mode of subjection, the second dimension that structures ethical experience, denotes "the way in which people are invited or incited to recognize their moral obligations."[43] Divine law, natural law, rationality, aesthetic concerns, for example, have all functioned as modes of subjection in various moralities. An analysis of the mode of subjection offers a deontology of moral experience. The forms of elaboration of the self, thirdly, refers to the activities one employs to form oneself, the ascetical practices one uses "either to moderate our acts, to decipher what we are, or to eradicate our desires, or to use our sexual desire in order to obtain certain aims...."[44] An analysis of the forms of elaboration of the self offers an ascetics of moral experience. The telos, finally, designates the goal of ethical practices; it refers to the type of being one attempts to become by employing the forms of elaboration of the self. Is the asceticism geared to make us "pure, or immortal, or free, or masters of ourselves, and so on"?[45] An analysis of these four dimensions of moral experience would reveal the "field of problematization" that the moral discourse of a given period would have in common and which made such discourse possible. By means of such a study, one would be able "to determine what structured the moral experience of sexual pleasure—its ontology, its deontology, its ascetics, its teleology."[46]

1. The Ethical Substance: Ontology

By comparing the Greek experience of aphrodisia with the Christian experience of the flesh, Foucault clearly delineates the singularity of the Greek ethical substance. Aphrodisia is a vague notion; the Greeks did not manifest much concern for rendering a precise definition, nor "for discovering the insidious presence of a power of undetermined limits and multiple masks beneath what appeared inoffensive or innocent."[47] Neither classification of behaviors nor decipherment of desire was at issue. This lack of precision, according to Foucault, was due, in fact, precisely to this difference of aphrodisia from Christian flesh or modern sexuality; the Greek notion of aphrodisia "was not oriented in the least toward the search for their profound nature, their canonical forms, or their secret potential."[48] Unlike Christian flesh or modern sexuality, aphrodisia did not evoke suspicion.

A main characteristic of aphrodisia, in contrast to Christian flesh or modern sexuality, is a dynamic relationship among action, desire, and pleasure. While one can distinguish these three elements of aphrodisia, they form a dynamic unity. In fact, the breakdown of this unity of act, desire, and pleasure, according to Foucault, would later characterize Christian flesh and modern sexuality. The Christian devaluation of pleasure and the problematization of desire shattered the unity characteristic of Greek aphrodisia. Thus, the object of Greek moral reflection, the ethical substance, was neither act, desire, nor pleasure, but the dynamics, the interplay of all three, "the desire that leads to the act, the act that is linked to pleasure, and the pleasure that occasions desire."[49]

Two factors are most relevant in Greek moral reflection on the aphrodisia. As a dynamic relationship the aphrodisia give rise to a concern with quantity; i.e., intensity and frequency. The moral evaluation of sexual behavior, even when put in terms of naturalness, focuses not upon natural or unnatural practices, nor upon natural or unnatural objects of desire, but upon quantity—moderation or excess, self-restraint or self-indulgence.[50] The second factor that governs Greek moral reflection on aphrodisia concerns "role" or "polarity." In the Christian tradition the experience of the flesh is common to both men and women.[51] In the modern experience of sexuality we perceive a radical disjunction between male and female sexuality. The Greeks experienced sexual pleasures in terms of two distinct roles and functions. They experienced sexual activity in terms of the role one played—subject or object, agent or patient, active or passive, the performer of the act or the one on whom the act is performed, penetrator or penetrated. The role of agent in this ethic is that of the adult, free man; women, boys, and slaves play the role of patient. The moral issue is that of taking one's appropriate role in sexual activity; an adult, free man who allows himself to play the passive role faces moral censure. Along with the question of quantity, thus, the issue of the role one plays in sexual activity provide the two main variables in Greek moral reflection on the dynamics of the aphrodisia: "For a man, excess and passivity were the two main forms of immorality in the practice of the aphrodisia."[52]

Foucault emphasizes that the questions of quantity and role did not become morally problematic because the Greeks considered sexual activity as bad in itself. They did not. There is no hint of a link between sexual activity and anything analogous to a Christian sense of a primordial Fall. The Greeks appreciated sexual activity as natural and necessary. It did, nonetheless, provide a domain for moral concern, and this precisely because of its naturalness. The pleasure derived from sexual activity is, according to the Greek mind, naturally both inferior and intense. Because both animals and humans derive pleasure in this way, the Greeks characterized it as of a qualitatively inferior order. In order to assure the propagation of the species, moreover, nature associated an extremely intense, while nonetheless inferior, pleasure to sexual activity. These two factors, the inferiority and intensity of sexual pleasures, combine to make sexual activity morally problematic. "It was just this natural acuteness of pleasure, together with the attraction it exerted on desire," according to Foucault, "that caused sexual activity to go beyond the limits that were set by nature when she made the pleasure of the aphrodisia an inferior, subordinate, and conditioned pleasure."[53] Nature established a hierarchy of pleasures, but precisely the natural intensity of these pleasures induces people to disregard the natural hierarchy. Sexual activity, thus, by its very nature called forth a dynamic moral discernment appropriate to the dynamic character of the aphrodisia. In Foucault's words, "In the Christian doctrine of the flesh, the excessive force of pleasure had its principle in the Fall and in the weakness that had marked human nature ever since. For classical Greek thought, this force was potentially excessive by nature, and the moral question was how to confront this force, how to control it and regulate its economy in a suitable way."[54]

The Roman moralist Artemidorus functions as a transitional figure in this genealogy of the ethical substance.[55] Artemidorus' hermeneutic principles in his *The Interpretation of Dreams* stand in stark contrast to Freud's method in his work of the same name. Artemidorus viewed sexuality in relational terms; the important matter offered for interpretation in the dream is the relationship between the dreamer and partner. He interpreted sexual dreams in terms of the partners' social, economic, and political relationships. "For instance," Foucault tells us, "if a person dreams that he has sex with his mother, that means he will succeed as a magistrate, since his mother is obviously the symbol of his city or country."[56] Freud would not be so generous to Little Hans.[57] Artemidorus was interested mainly in the social and economic status of the dreamed-of sex partners, rather than in the nature of the sexual act itself. As for the Greeks, the key sexual issue for the Roman Artemidorus is the problem of penetration. One's sexual role as either penetrator or penetrated served as the key to the interpretation of sexual dreams since these sexual roles mirrored and symbolized social, economic, and political roles. With this dominance by the problem of penetration the Roman dream interpreter was drawn to the problem of the dreamer's relationship to other people.

This is not the case with Augustine, Foucault's paradigm for appreciating the early Christian problematization of sexuality. In Augustine, the problem of erection and the problem of one's relationship with oneself supersedes the Roman concern with penetration and the relationship between oneself and other persons. "The famous gesture of Adam covering his genitals with a fig leaf is," in Augustine's interpretation of the Fall, according to Foucault,

> not due to the simple fact that Adam was ashamed of their presence, but to the fact that his sexual organs were moving by themselves without his consent. Sex in erection is the image of man revolted against God. The arrogance of sex is the punishment and consequence of the arrogance of man. His uncontrolled sex is exactly the same as what he himself has been toward God—a rebel.[58]

This Augustinian concern with erection over penetration, and with one's relationship with oneself over one's relationship with others, "bears witness to the new type of relationship that Christianity established between sex and subjectivity."[59] Augustine refers to the source and principle of erection independent of one's will as "libido," and the Christian's task, his "spiritual struggle," is to decipher the movements of his soul to delineate those whose source is libido. Briefly, the Christian's task for Augustine is "a permanent hermeneutics of oneself."[60]

2. The Mode of Subjection: Deontology

The central question for Greek sexual ethics is "how could one, how must one 'make use' (*chresis*) of this dynamics of pleasure, desire, and acts?"[61] This notion of "use" (*chresis*) denotes the second dimension that structures Greek ethical experience, the mode of subjection. An analysis of the mode of subjection entails such questions as, "How does a man enjoy his pleasure 'as one ought'? To what principles does he refer in order to moderate, limit, regulate that activity? What sort of validity might these principles have that would enable a man to justify his having to obey them? Or, in other words, what is the mode of subjection that is implied in this moral problematization of sexual conduct?"[62] Greek moral reflection on sexual behavior intended less to systematize a code of conduct or set of interdictions than to determine "a style" for the use of pleasures. How great or small a role will one allow sexual activity to play in one's life? How will one conduct oneself in sexual relations? "It was not a question of what was permitted or forbidden among the desires that one felt or the acts that one committed," according to Foucault, "but of prudence, reflection, and calculation in the way one distributed and controlled his acts."[63] It required moral discernment regarding one's needs, the question of timing, and the individual's own status.

Foucault emphasizes how individuated the sexual ethic of Greek antiquity was. No universal codification could suffice in an ethic that gave such prominence, first, to the strategic governance of one's own personal needs. One was required to use one's pleasures strategically with the goal of establishing and maintaining a balance in the dynamic relationship between pleasure and desire. Such self-government constituted more of an art, a practice, a technique—a *"techne,"* a *"savoir-faire"*[64]—than a set of universal rules capable of codification. Nor could universal codification characterize an ethic that, secondly, placed so much stress on timing. Whether concerned with the right time for sexual activity in the span of one's life, the appropriate time of year, or the best time of day, the Greek needed a sensitivity to the art of timing. One's own unique status, finally, was determinative in this sexual ethic. In the ethics of Greek antiquity, according to Foucault, "with the exception of a few precepts that applied to everyone, standards of sexual morality were always tailored to one's way of life, which was itself determined by the status one had inherited and the purposes one had chosen."[65] Greeks generally accepted the notion, for instance, that public figures, especially those who exercised authority, ought freely to bind themselves to more rigorous standards of behavior. Manifestatons of moderation were expected of those who were asked to exercise civic responsibility. In this ethic in which the mode of subjection centers on the use of pleasures, Foucault concludes, "We are a long way from a form of austerity that would tend to govern all individuals in the same way, from the proudest to the most humble, under a universal law whose application alone would be subject to modulation by means of casuistry. On the contrary, here everything was a matter of adjustment, circumstance, and personal position."[66] This ethic engaged the Greek to constitute himself as an ethical subject by individualizing his actions rather than by universalizing the principles governing them.

The moralities of antiquity, essentially a practice of liberty, slowly gave way under Christianity. Norms of behavior certainly held sway in antiquity, but "the will to be a moral subject" had as its end the affirmation of the individual's own freedom and the aesthetic character of one's existence; that is, the personal elaboration of one's individual life took center stage. With Christianity moral experience gradually shifted to focus increasingly upon obedience to a code. Christianity, "with the religion of the text, the idea of the will of God," shifted moral attention to a system of rules to which the Christian must subject himself.[67]

But the Christian code itself is not new. Christianity did not invent the code. The Greeks and Romans fabricated a moral tradition "that is to be found again, transposed, metamorphosed, and profoundly revised in Christianity,"[68] but its fundamental tenets are those of the Greeks and Romans. For example, the notion associated with Christianity that sexual expression should be restricted to procreation originated with the Stoics. In order to integrate itself into the Roman Empire Christianity opted to subscribe to this principle.[69] Christianity accepted this tradition, "reinforced it, and gave to it a much larger and more widespread strength than it had had before," according to Foucault: "But the so-called Christian morality is nothing more than a piece of pagan ethics inserted into Christianity."[70]

3. The Form of Relationship with the Self: Ascetics

Any mode of subjection requires a singular form of relationship with the self, the third dimension that structures ethical experience. The Greek term *Enkrateia* refers to "the dynamics of a domination of oneself by oneself and to the effort that this demands."[71] The real difference between later Christian morality and Greek pagan morality is not, as is often assumed, a matter of the interiority, the focus on intentions and desires, of Christian morality in contrast with the exteriority, the concern with action and consequences, of Greek morality. Instead, Foucault maintains, the difference resides in the forms of relationship with the self. The Greek form of relationship with the self underwent a restructuring in Christian morality; the practices and techniques that undergirded this relationship with the self were transformed.

Enkrateia, the dynamics of a domination of the self by the self, entails an "agonistic relationship."[72] Battle, conquest, and struggle provide the metaphors for capturing the relationship. Because by its nature the aphrodisia tend toward excess, the moderate use of pleasures requires one to engage in battle against their tendencies. Foucault insists, nonetheless, that the agonistic language that expresses *enkrateia* does not connote a rejection of this nature—an attitude closer to that of the Christian. Rather the nature of the aphrodisia tended toward domination over and enslavement of the self. The aphrodisia in itself does not constitute the problem; potential enslavement does.

This agonistic relationship is one in which one is engaged with oneself. One battled not with "a different, ontologically alien power," as the later Christians would. The Greek did not battle "the Other"; he crossed swords with himself.[73] The point of this ascetic relationship with the self was not to eliminate desire nor to diminish the intensity of pleasure; control, instead, was the issue. A definitively subdued opponent, after all, no longer offers a challenge. The Greek who wants "to form oneself as a virtuous and moderate subject in the use he makes of pleasures...has to construct a relationship with the self that is of the 'domination-submission,' 'command-obedience,' 'master-docility' type (and not, as will be the case in Christian spirituality, a relationship of the 'elucidation-renunciation,' 'decipherment-purification' type)."[74]

This Greek form of relationship with the self found models in both domestic and civic life. The governance the moderate man exercised over himself patterned itself on the master's rule over his household. Desires stand in relation to the self as servants relate to the master of the house. The individual wanting to be virtuous, moreover, could find his model in the structure of the city. With its hierarchical order the city provides the paradigm for one intent on governing himself.

The agonistic relationship with the self requires training, exercise, and preparation to withstand the trial. Concrete details about the nature of this training, however, are rarely to be found in texts of Greek antiquity. In contrast to the "training, meditation, tests of thinking, examination of conscience, control of representations" which received such meticulous attention in Christian manuals for the direction of souls, Greek texts reveal few details on ascetical practices. According to Foucault, "this 'ascetics' was not organized or conceived as a corpus of separate practices that would constitute a kind of specific art of the soul, with its techniques, procedures, and prescriptions. It was not distinct from the practice of virtue itself; it was the rehearsal that anticipated that practice."[75] Since the training required to achieve self-governance was inseparable from the training necessary to govern others, whether in one's household or the city, such training was integrated with the general task of constituting oneself as a free person. In later Christian direction of souls, however, the ascetics achieved a certain autonomy: "there was to be a differentiation between the exercises that enabled one to govern oneself and the learning of what was necessary in order to govern others; there was also to be a differentiation between the exercises themselves and the virtue, moderation, and temperance for which they were meant to serve as training."[76] In Christianity, however, the "art of the self" would separate off and achieve a status independent of the ethical conduct that had been its concern.

Because it persists in our own time in the psychoanalytic relationship, the Christian practice of self-examination and confession draws Foucault's special attention. Since desire became the ethical substance for the Christian, the Christian was required to exercise a "permanent hermeneutics of oneself" demanding "very strict truth obligations" of the Christian.[77] Not merely a matter of learning the truth of the moral life, one was required constantly to scrutinize oneself as a desiring subject, and rigorous techniques of self-analysis developed in response to these demands in the monasteries of the fourth and fifth centuries; "Detailed techniques were elaborated for use in seminaries and monasteries, techniques of discursive rendition of daily life, of self-examination, confession, direction of conscience and regulation of the relationship between director and directed."[78] These techniques were not intended to enable the monk to achieve the self-mastery of the Greek philosopher; they were meant to assist the monk in deciphering the source of desire—"all the insinuations of the flesh: thoughts, desires, voluptuous imaginings, delectations, combined movements of the body and the soul."[79] Was Satan seducing and deceiving one through these desires? The techniques piqued the monk's suspicion allowing him to scrutinize and test his desires for their purity. Purity for the monk "consists in discovering the truth in oneself and defeating the illusions in oneself...."[80]

Ecclesiastical surveillance of sexuality focused upon monks and seminarians until the middle of the sixteenth century when it was injected into Christian society as a whole;[81] i.e., this "pedagogy of sexuality" was "subsequently laicised and medicalised."[82] As a result, "Western man has become a confessing animal."[83] "We are in a society of speaking sex."[84]

Among the Greeks of antiquity the relationship between master and disciple did not require such intense self-examination and confession. Discourse in the form of instruction tended to go from the direction of the master to the disciple. Since the disciple's goal was self-mastery and autonomy, no reason arises to give complete power to the master by revealing the minutiae of one's interior life; the master/disciple relationship "does not imply a complete and definitive obedience."[85]

This practice of rigorous self-examination and confession, according to Foucault, seems to have originated with the Stoics around the time of the birth of Christianity, but with the Stoics we are still a long way from Christian hermeneutics of the self.[86] Seneca, for example, at first glance appears to be embarked on the task of Christian self-decipherment when he recommends the beauty of ending each day with a thorough examination of conscience: "What could be more beautiful than to conduct an inquest on one's day? What sleep is better than that which follows this review of one's actions?" But Seneca is not a Christian self-hermeneut; "Seneca is a permanent administrator of himself."[87] The point of Stoic self-examination is neither self-decipherment nor self-punishment; the purpose is "to reactivate the rules."[88] In Stoic examination of conscience, according to Foucault, the issue is not a matter of discovering some deep truth of the subject which the individual has, perhaps, forgotten or overlooked during the day. When the Stoic engages in the examination of conscience he does so, not because he has forgotten some deep truth about himself, but because he has forgotten what he should have done; he has forgotten a code of conduct that needs reactivation. "The recollection of errors committed during the day serves to measure the distance which separates what has been done from what should have been done."[89] Stoic examination of conscience, then, grows consistently from the Stoic commitment to maintain an unwavering attitude in the face of life's vicissitudes.

4. Teleology

The telos, the fourth dimension that structures ethical experience, was for the Greeks the achievement of the state of being referred to as sophrosyne. Usually translated as "moderation," sophrosyne connotes a type of freedom. The Greeks struggled with sexual desire, not to maintain innocence or purity as Christians would, but "because they wanted to be free and to be able to remain so."[90] Such freedom entailed the achievement of a mastery over oneself. The dichotomy, familiar to us moderns, between freedom and determinism was not at issue for the Greeks of antiquity; the opposition was freedom or enslavement, "the enslavement of the self by oneself."[91]

But this freedom ought not be understood merely negatively, as the absence of slavery; it involves a positive power that one exercises over oneself and which is bound up with one's power over others. To exercise power over oneself and over others forms a unity. "In fact," Foucault tells us, "the person who, owing to his status, was under the authority of others was not expected to find the principle of his moderation within himself; ...On the other hand, the man who ought to lead others was one who had to be completely in command of himself."[92] The moderation which results from self-mastery represents a key qualification for anyone seeking to exercise authority over others. Foucault calls this mastery "active freedom" and places it in opposition to passivity: "Self-mastery was a way of being a man with respect to oneself; that is, a way of commanding what needed commanding, of coercing what was not capable of self-direction, of imposing principles of reason on what was wanting in reason; in short, it was a way of being active in relation to what was by nature passive and ought to remain so."[93] And this active mastery extended from the personal and sexual through the interpersonal domestic sphere to the realm of the social and political, forming a unity of ethical, sexual, and social "virility."[94] The Greeks associated the active self-mastery required to achieve moderation with masculinity; immoderation signals feminity and passivity with regard to oneself.

This active freedom, self-mastery, this achievement of moderation, entailed a relation to truth. "To rule one's pleasures and to bring them under the authority of the logos," according to Foucault, "formed one and the same enterprise";[95] that is, the achievement of moderation required a type of knowledge. To constitute oneself as an ethical subject and to form oneself as a subject of this knowledge was a single endeavor. Foucault delineates three forms that this relation to logos took: the relation to truth had a structural, instrumental, and an ontological form.

Structurally, first, "moderation implied that the logos be placed in a position of supremacy in the human being and that it be

able to subdue the desires and regulate behavior."⁹⁶ The structure of
the soul itself suggests a hierarchy with reason governing passions
and desires. Instrumentally, second, practical reason must discern
the particulars of one's situation to determine appropriate conduct.
Practical reason must be put into gear in order for the individual to
adjudicate, as Aristotle puts it, "the things he ought, as he ought,
and when he ought."⁹⁷ The third form of relation to the logos Foucault calls "the ontological recognition of the self by the self."⁹⁸ The
sensitive soul recognizes that the dynamism of its desires respond,
not to the immediate beautiful object, but to the memory of Beauty
itself. The soul's relation to truth, through recollection, undergirds
Eros, and that relation enables the soul to restrain its immediate
physical desires. Keeping in clear view the soul's relation to truth
makes possible the achievement of moderation.

This relation to truth did not constitute a Christian
hermeneutics of desire or self-decipherment. Instead, the Greek
relation to truth led to an "aesthetics of existence"—"a way of life
whose moral value did not depend either on one's being in conformity with a code of behavior, or on an effort of purification, but on
certain formal principles in the use of pleasures, in the way one
distributed them, in the limits one observed, in the hierarchy one
respected."⁹⁹ To craft one's life such that it mirrors the ontological
order provides the task for a Greek aesthetics of existence.

C. The Genealogy of the Subject: The Modern Experience

Sixteenth-century treatises on the "art of government" represent a
dovetailing of a revival of Stoicism and the Christian pastoral centered on "the ritualisation of the problem of how to conduct oneself."¹⁰⁰ This concern for the art of government, moreover, resides
at the intersection of two processes: the shattering of feudalism
and the formation of the administered colonial states, and on the
other hand, the Reformation and Counter-Reformation raise the
question of how the individual is to be governed in order to attain
eternal salvation.¹⁰¹

Machiavelli's *The Prince* provoked a stream of anti-Machi-
avellian literature, and this flurry of minor texts indicates the
reformulation of the problematic of government. Typically, those
writing in opposition to Machiavelli focus upon the transcendence
and externality of the Prince in relation to his territory and
emphasize, in contrast, the immanence of the activity of governing
when one speaks of the governing of "a household, souls, children,

a province, a convent, a religious order, or a family."[102] The anti-Machiavellians tend to emphasize the continuity of these forms of government with one another and with the prince's government of his territory. This assertion of the continuity of the art of state government with the "oeconomy" of the family and which affirms the same principles of good government for both, is at this point in the sixteenth century beginning to be referred to as "police."[103] "The art of government as it appears in all this literature," according to Foucault,

> is essentially concerned with answering the question of how to introduce oeconomy, that is the correct manner of managing individuals, goods and wealth within the family (which a good father is expected to do in relation to his wife, children and servants) and of making it thrive—how to introduce this meticulous attention of the father toward his family, into the management of the State.[104]

Not merely a sixteenth-century phenomenon, however, this interest in government as economic management persists into the eighteenth century. In his essay on political economy Rousseau formulates the problem in terms of introducing the wise government of the family into the art of state government, establishing "a form of surveillance, of control which is as watchful as that of the head of a family over his household and his goods."[105]

With the development of the notion of economy into our modern sense of the term, the art of government focused upon the problem of population. The rise of population statistics supplanted the family as the model of good government, but the family remains a privileged element internal to population, "the privileged instrument for the government of the population."[106]

In the present, and with Foucault we must always keep in mind that our concern is the history of the present,[107] the Oedipal triangle of father-mother-son is the dominant metaphor for understanding the family and is, according to Foucault, the psychoanalyst's key instrument for governing individuals: the story of Oedipus, then, is not

> a truth of nature but an instrument of limitation and compulsion that psychoanalysts, since Freud, utilize in order to calculate desire and to make it enter into a familial structure which our society defined at a determined moment. In other words, Oedipus, following Deleuze and Guattari, is not the

secret content of our unconscious, but the form of compulsion which psychoanalysis wants to impose on our desire and our unconscious in the cure. Oedipus is an instrument of power, a certain type of medical and psychoanalytic power which is exercised over desire and the unconscious.[108]

In a discussion following the lectures in which he made these comments, Foucault responded to the claim that the Oedipal triangle manifests a fundamental structure of human existence: "I will respond in absolutely Deleuzian terms: it is absolutely not a fundamental structure of human existence but a certain type of constraint, a relation of power which society, the family, political power establishes over individuals."[109] This is not a distortion of the psychiatric establishment's role; from its very beginning psychiatry's "true vocation," "its climate," "its horizon of birth," "its fundamental project," has been to be "a permanent function of social order."[110] Rooted in early Christian confessional practices, psychoanalysis is our modern theory and practice, moreover, which continues to fortify the priority of the subject established in Western thought since Descartes.[111]

"*Le sexe, raison de tout.*"[112] The logic of sex has become the key to the question of who we are. Sex is, beneath the appearances, that which reveals us to ourselves, and discourse on sex is motivated by the desire to have this secret knowledge revealed. How else to account for the fact that modern men and women "would purchase so dearly the bi-weekly right to laboriously formulate the truth of their desire, and to wait patiently for the benefits of the interpretation?"[113] An immense strategy for producing truth was constructed around sex. Beyond its function as pleasure producing, beyond a matter of right and wrong, licit and illicit, sex was constituted as a problem of truth and falsehood: "we demand that sex speak the truth..., and we demand that it tell us our truth, or rather, the deeply buried truth of that truth about ourselves which we think we possess in our immediate consciousness...."[114] Two ideas intersect in our time, according to Foucault, "that we must not deceive ourselves concerning our sex, and that our sex harbors what is most true in ourselves." It is here "that psychoanalysis has rooted its cultural vigor."[115]

This apparatus for the production of truth, according to Foucault, results from a historical transition whereby traditional confessional practices came to be constituted in scientific terms.[116] The confessional inducement to speak of sex, first, was clinically codified in the interrogation of personal history, questionnaires, and hypnosis. Sex was postulated as causally related to innumerable human ills, secondly, justifying the subjection of sex to interrogation. Thirdly, sex was understood as characterized by latency; the true nature of one's sexuality was viewed as a surreptitious phenomenon whose truth had to be teased out by laborious confessional practices. The truth of sex, fourthly, was not a one-sided matter of an uninformed patient speaking its truth; the full truth of sex required authoritative interpretation. Finally, "sex appeared as an extremely unstable pathological field.... Spoken in time, to the proper party, and by the person who was both the bearer of it and the one responsible for it, the truth healed."[117] Psychoanalysis developed from the institutionalized confessional procedures of the time of the Inquisition and effected a "medicalisation of sexuality..., as though it were an area of particular pathological fragility in human existence."[118] Sex, in short, came to be medically managed.

The analysis of power's functioning in the history of sexuality series is highly reminiscent of *Surveiller et punir*. The transition from a system of penal practices with public floggings and executions to hidden penal practices involved an interiorization of discipline. Similarly, sex came to be something not simply condemned or repressed; rather, sex was managed, regulated, inserted into systems, "not something one simply judged; it was a thing one administered."[119] As in *Surveiller et punir*, power, as it functions in the classification of sexuality, does not react negatively; it has its effect by normalizing human behavior. A norm is established according to which various forms of sexuality are distinguished and regulated. "Such a power has to qualify, measure, appraise, and hierarchize, rather than display itself in its murderous splendor," according to Foucault; "it does not have to draw the line that separates the enemies of the sovereign from his obedient subjects; it effects distributions around the norm."[120] The totally administered society, the normalized society of internalized discipline which Foucault revealed in *Surveiller et punir*, again manifests itself in this history of sexuality.

"A normalizing society is the historical outcome of a technology of power centered on life."[121] In *Les mots et les choses* Foucault revealed that "life" was constituted relatively recently. He showed that the transformation from the classical to the modern episteme was a matter of the "decline of representation." Realities came to be seen as systems of internal relations performing a function rather than as constituted by isolated elements classified according to identity and difference. Temporality was introduced into the interior of things. The positivities of labor, language, and life were constituted, and they function in the modern age as quasi-transcendentals. The conditions for the existence of modern biology emerged, and this new "life" could not be immune from power.

> Western man was gradually learning what it meant to be a living species in a living world, to have a body, conditions of existence, probabilities of life, an individual and collective welfare, forces that could be modified, and a space in which they could be distributed in an optimal manner. For the first time in history, no doubt, biological existence was reflected in political existence.[122]

Living beings, rather than legal subjects, became power's object, and its domain of influence had to extend to the level of life itself.

D. Genealogy as Self-Critical Enlightenment

Foucault himself is responsible for some misunderstandings and facile dismissals of his work. Much has been made of a few of Foucault's comments, especially in interviews, which might allow some readers to take his genealogical histories less than seriously. "I am well aware that I have never written anything but fictions," Foucault declared in 1977.[123] In the same year he ended a lengthy interview—in which he argued forcefully and expressed definite opinions—with a parenthetical comment: "What I have said here is not 'what I think', but often rather what I wonder whether one couldn't think."[124] And in 1980, "In a sense I know very well that what I say is not true.... I know very well that what I have done from a historical point of view is singleminded, exaggerated.... What I am trying to do is provoke an interference between our reality and the knowledge of our past history. If I succeed, this will have real effects in our present history. My hope is my books become true after they have been written—not before."[125] Is it any wonder, then, that astute commentators such as Allan Megill and Larry Shiner, for example, would point to "parodic" dimensions of Foucault's writings?[126] Doesn't Foucault himself speak of "the parodic and farcical use" of history?[127]

But such comments from Foucault are the source of grave misunderstandings, and they draw attention to what is perhaps the most serious contrast between Foucault's and Nietzsche's genealogies. In his *The Uses and Disadvantages of History for Life*, Nietzsche argues that the human task is to cultivate our capacity to forget actively for the sake of enhancing life. Could not Foucault be construed as calling for the same kind of active amnesia when he writes of constructing a "counter-memory"?[128] I do not believe so. Rather, Foucault reads Nietzsche's *Uses and Disadvantages of History for Life* as a description of the social amnesia already accomplished by traditional humanistic historiography.[129] For Foucault, too much active forgetting and covering over of discourse has already taken place. This traditional historiography, and not history *tout court*, is the object of his parody. In response, his desire to construct a counter-memory is intended to make memory function precisely as memory has always been supposed to function; as David Carroll puts it, "to recover what has been forgotten, to restore what has been lost, to perpetuate the presence or being of words and things."[130] Or, with the Czech novelist, Milan Kundera, the human struggle against power is "the struggle of memory against forgetting."[131]

Michel Foucault was notorious for his refusal to allow himself to be situated in a tradition. He repeatedly lashed out at "certain half-witted 'commentators' who persist in labeling me a 'structuralist.'"[132] "I have never been a Freudian, I have never been a Marxist and I have never been a structuralist," he told an interviewer a year before his death.[133] A cheer erupted from the overflow crowd at Berkeley when Foucault announced, "once and for all, that I am not a structuralist, and I confess with the appropriate chagrin that I am not an analytic philosopher: Nobody is perfect."[134] In a 1983 lecture, however, he did indicate a willingness to situate his own work in a tradition that extends "from Hegel to the Frankfurt School by way of Nietzsche and Max Weber."[135]

While claiming that Foucault's work is "arguably the prime instance of neo-Nietzscheanism in contemporary Western thought," J. G. Merquior maintains that Foucault's "systematic disparagement of the Enlightenment" unmistakably marks his departure from Nietzsche.[136] While Nietzsche "paid homage" to the Enlightenment's critical spirit, according to Merquior, Foucault turned out to be "a fierce foe of the Enlightenment."[137] But Merquior accuses Foucault of taking a counter-Enlightenment position while assuming we can take for granted an answer to the question Foucault, following Kant, found it necessary to ask: What is Enlightenment?[138] And what is that critical spirit to which Nietzsche paid homage? By prejudging this issue Merquior begs the question that Foucault sees as "essential to contemporary philosophy."[139]

Because Kant identifies the Enlightenment as the time for humanity to employ its own reason, the Enlightenment calls forth the critique of reason; that is, Enlightenment requires an analysis of "the conditions under which the use of reason is legitimate in order to determine what can be known, what must be done, and what may be hoped." According to Foucault, then, "the Enlightenment is the age of critique."[140] Moreover, Foucault maintains, Kant's text on Enlightenment ought to be thought of in relation to his writings on history because "for the first time rational thought was put in question not only as to its nature, its foundation, its powers and its rights, but also as to its history and its geography; as to its immediate past and the conditions of its exercise, as to its time, its place, and its actuality."[141] For the first time, "with Kant's text on *Enlightenment* one sees philosophy," in Foucault's words, "problematizing its own discursive actuality."[142] In this way Foucault situates the question, what is Enlightenment?, at the juncture of critique and reflection on history. Thus, in his reflection on Kant's text, Foucault is trying to reveal that, contra Merquior, a philosophical reflection which "simultaneously problematizes our relation to the present, our historical mode of being, and the constitution of the self as an autonomous subject"—a clear and obvious description of Foucault's own genealogical project—"is rooted in the Enlightenment."[143] To remain faithfully rooted in the Enlightenment, then, is less a matter of doctrinal fidelity than it is a matter of sustaining an attitude, a "philosophical ethos," as Foucault would have it, which entails "a permanent critique of our historical era."[144] Enlightenment thus connotes an attitude or an ethos, rather than a doctrinal heritage; as Foucault proclaimed in his 1983 lecture course,

> Let us leave to their piety those who wish us to preserve alive and intact the heritage of *Enlightenment*. Such piety is doubtless the most touching of treasons. It is not the legacy of *Enlightenment* which it is our business to conserve, but rather the very question of this event and its meaning, the question of the historicity of the thought of the universal, which ought to be kept present and retained in mind as that which has to be thought.[145]

Rather than making Kant's anthropological turn to the question, what is man?, Foucault seeks to sustain the ethos of Enlightenment by adopting his Nietzschean genealogical approach.

By interpreting the Enlightenment in terms of a philosophical ethos rather than in terms of doctrines, Foucault is able to avoid confusing Enlightenment with the doctrines associated with humanism. Humanism is a set of themes always entangled with value judgments; it provides a vision of the human essence with which men and women are expected to conform, thus offering a universal criterion for moral judgment. These humanistic themes, however, have been so diverse in history that humanism fails to provide such a universal, or even a coherent, object for philosophical reflection: Christianity, the critique of Christianity, science, anti-science, Marxism, existentialism, personalism, National Socialism, and Stalinism have each worn the label "humanism" for a time. Foucault, in contrast, "has given no surrogate," as Ian Hacking ironically phrased it, "for whatever it is that springs eternal in the human breast."[146] In opposition to the set of themes or doctrines associated with humanism, Foucault proposes "the principle of a critique and a permanent creation of ourselves in our autonomy,...a principle that is at the heart of the historical consciousness that the Enlightenment has of itself."[147] What is at stake, then, between Foucault and some of his critics turns less on the commitment to realize Enlightenment than on the understanding of critique and the nature of the autonomy to be achieved.[148]

From *Histoire de la folie* to *Histoire de la sexualité* Foucault has concentrated upon and transformed our manner of conceiving three central concepts of the Western philosophical tradition: truth, power, and the subject. He has shown truth to be "a thing of this world,"[149] intimately enmeshed with relations of power, produced, sustained, and managed by tactics and strategies of power. Foucault's Nietzschean genealogy effects a transformation of contemporary political philosophy by revealing the subtle and apparently innocuous manner in which power functions in our time. Indeed, Foucault's genealogy of modern subjectivity unmasks a new mode of power's functioning that coincides with the sixteenth-century rise of the state[150] and is the underside of the late eighteenth-century constitutional reforms.[151] Those reforms "cut off the head of the king," and Foucault has shown that that same beheading must be accomplished in political theory if it is to be adequate to its task of revealing how power actually functions in modern societies.[152] Foucault's Nietzscheanism facilitates this transformation of contemporary political philosophy. His commitment to genealogical critique allows him to lay bare the multiple relations of forces at the origins of our cherished values, inherited concepts and categories, of the entities we experience, and even ourselves, our individuality, our subjectivity.

If "critique" signifies the analysis of the conditions of our existence, if it reveals the a prioris—whether transcendental or historical—of our thought, discourse, and action, if "critique" unmasks power's surreptitious operations in our lives, if it exposes the systematic distortions of our communicative attempts to reach understanding, then Foucault's project is critique and commitment to Enlightenment.

Abbreviations

ET   English translation

Foucault's writings:
AS	*L'archéologie du savoir*
HF	*Histoire de la folie à l'âge classique*
LMC	*Les mots et les choses*
NC	*Naissance de la clinique*
"NFM"	"Nietzsche, Freud, Marx"
"NGH"	"Nietzsche, l'généalogie, l'histoire"
OD	*L'ordre du discours*
MM&Per	*Maladie mentale et personnalité*
MM&Psych	*Maladie mentale et psychologie*
SP	*Surveiller et punir*
SS	*Le souci de soi*
UP	*L'usage des plaisirs*
VS	*La volonté de savoir*

Nietzsche's writings:
BGE	*Beyond Good and Evil*
BT	*The Birth of Tragedy*
GS	*The Gay Science*
GM	*On the Genealogy of Morals*
TI	*Twilight of the Idols*
TSZ	*Thus Spoke Zarathustra*
UM2	*The Uses and Disadvantages of History for Life* (the second of the *Untimely Meditations*)
WP	*The Will to Power*

Notes

Chapter 1

1. "On the Genealogy of Ethics" in Hubert Dreyfus and Paul Rabinow, *Michel Foucault: Beyond Structuralism and Hermeneutics*, Second Edition (Chicago: University of Chicago Press, 1983), 237.

2. Dreyfus and Rabinow, *Michel Foucault: Beyond Structuralism and Hermeneutics*. My shift of emphasis from that of Dreyfus and Rabinow certainly is not intended to demean their work. Whether genealogy is to be read as a new method (Dreyfus and Rabinow) or as anti-method (Shiner), both works agree and effectively show that it allows Nietzsche and Foucault to distance themselves from "traditional humanistic historiography." Larry Shiner, "Reading Foucault: Anti-Method and the Genealogy of Power-Knowledge" in *History and Theory* 21 (1982).

3. See "An Interview by Stephen Riggins" in *Ethos* I, 2 (Autumn, 1983), 5.

4. "Structuralism and Post-Structuralism" in *Telos* 55 (Spring, 1983), 199.

5. Foucault confirmed this point in his original Preface to Volume 2 of *The History of Sexuality*, printed in Paul Rabinow's *The Foucault Reader* (New York: Pantheon, 1984), 336.

6. "Un dibattito Foucault-Preti" in *Bimestre* 22–23 (1972), 2.

7. "Un dibattito Foucault-Preti," 2.

8. I have tried to use inclusive language whenever possible. It will become clear that "man" is a technical term for Foucault that cannot be replaced by a more inclusive word.

9. *LMC*, 398 (English translation (ET), 387).

10. "Corso del 7 gennaio 1976" in Alessandro Fontana and Pasquale Pasquino (eds.), *Microfisica del Potere* (Torino: Einaudi, 1977),169. English translation by Kate Soper in Colin Gordon (ed.), *Power/Knowledge* (New York: Pantheon, 1980), 84.

11. *Maladie mentale et personnalité* (Paris: Presses Universitaires de France, 1954), 75. When a cited passage from this work remains unchanged in Foucault's radically revised 1962 edition, *Maladie mentale et psychologie*, I use Alan Sheridan's translation (New York: Harper and Row, 1976). Hereafter cited as *MM&Per* and *MM&Psych* respectively. ET, 63.

12. *Folie et déraison: Histoire de la folie à l'âge classique* (Paris: Plon, 1961), v. Except for references to the original Preface, I use the later edition: *Histoire de la folie à l'âge classique* (Paris: Gallimard, 1972), hereafter cited as *HF*. Richard Howard's English translation, *Madness and Civilization* (New York: Vintage Books, 1965) is of a dramatically abridged version. I employ it when available.

13. As Peter Dews suggests, "the intellectual groundplan of *Madness and Civilization* is provided by Nietzsche's *The Birth of Tragedy*." *Logics of Disintegration: Post-Structuralist Thought and the Claims of Critical Theory* (New York: Verso, 1987), 181. Michel Serres claims that *HF* is to the classical age what Nietzsche's *BT* was to ancient Greek culture. *Hermes I: La Communication* (Paris: Les Éditions de Minuit, 1968), 178.

14. "Intervista a Michel Foucault" in *Microfisica del Potere*, 12–13. English translation by Colin Gordon in *Power/Knowledge*, 118–19.

15. In his last writings he forges a distinction between "the political technology of individuals," which he studied throughout the 1960s and 1970s, and "technologies of the self," the concern of his final writings on sexuality. Cf. "The Political Technology of Individuals" in Luther H. Martin, Huck Gutman, and Patrick H. Hutton (eds.), *Technologies of the Self* (Amherst: University of Massachusetts Press, 1988),146.

16. *LMC*, 275 (ET, 263).

17. *LMC*, 327 (ET, 317).

18. Quoted in François Ewald, "Anatomie et corps politiques" in *Critique* 31 (1975), 1228.

19. Foucault most directly affirmed his Nietzscheanism in the last interview he granted, on May 29, 1984, a month before his death. "Le retour de la morale" in *Les Nouvelles* 2937 (June 28–July 5, 1984), 40. English translation by Thomas Levin and Isabelle Lorenz as "Final Interview" in *Raritan* 5, 1 (Summer, 1985), 9.

20. Alan Sheridan, *Michel Foucault: The Will to Truth* (London: Tavistock Publications, 1980), 120.

21. Sheridan, *Michel Foucault: The Will to Truth*, 115.

22. Ewald, "Anatomie et corps politiques," 1237.

23. Sheridan, *Michel Foucault: The Will to Truth*, 218.

24. J. G. Merquior, *Foucault* (Berkeley: University of California Press, 1985), 73. David Pace distinguishes Foucault's work from mainline structuralism on the basis of his use of Nietzsche, as well as Marx, Bachelard, and Bataille, rather than Saussure. "Structuralism in History and the Social Sciences" in *American Quarterly* 30 (1978).

25. Merquior, *Foucault*, 142.

26. Merquior, *Foucault*, 143–46.

27. Merquior, *Foucault*, 99–100.

28. Scott Lash, "Genealogy and the Body: Foucault/Deleuze/Nietzsche" in *Theory, Culture, and Society* 2, 2 (1984), 3.

29. Lash, "Genealogy and the Body," 14.

30. Richard Rorty, "Foucault and Epistemology" in David Couzens Hoy (ed.), *Foucault: A Critical Reader* (New York: Basil Blackwell, 1986), 45.

31. Rorty, "Foucault and Epistemology," 47.

32. Rorty, "Foucault and Epistemology," 46.

33. Rorty, "Foucault and Epistemology," 47.

34. Thomas E. Wartenberg, "Foucault's Archaeological Method: A Response to Hacking and Rorty" in *The Philosophical Forum* 15, 4 (Summer, 1984), 352.

35. Ewald, "Anatomie et corps politiques," 1235. Merquior, *Foucault*, 101. Cf. Thomas R. Flynn, "Foucault and the Politics of Postmodernity" in *Noûs* 23 (1989), 196–97. "Foucault's marching in demonstrations against penal injustices, his presence at a protest in favor of Vietnamese 'boat people' and the like are precisely the *parrhesiastic acts* that require no warrant except the perceived danger to commonly valued human freedom-autonomy in concrete circumstances.... Foucault neither offers nor seeks foundations beyond the presumed commitment of his audience to freedom-autonomy."

36. Ewald, "Anatomie et corps politiques," 1230.

37. Rorty, "Foucault and Epistemology," 47.

38. Wartenberg, "Foucault's Archaeological Method," 355.

39. Pamela Major-Poetzl, *Michel Foucault's Archaeology of Western Culture: Toward a New Science of History* (Chapel Hill: University of North Carolina Press, 1983), 12 and 32.

40. Of course, in a sense, as Foucault points out, "we are all neo-Kantians." Cf. "Une histoire restée muette" in *La Quinzaine Littéraire* 8 (July 1, 1966), 3–4.

41. Gilles Deleuze, *Foucault* (Paris: Les Éditions de Minuit, 1986), 67.

42. Deleuze, *Foucault*, 70.

43. Deleuze, *Foucault*, 81.

44. Deleuze, *Foucault*, 78. Allan Megill, among others, concurs in this assessment and relates Foucault's understanding of power especially with Nietzsche's "On Truth and Lie." Cf. Allan Megill, *Prophets of Extremity* (Berkeley: University of California Press, 1985), 191–92, 240–52, and Major-Poetzl, *Michel Foucault's Archaeology of Western Culture*, 32.

45. Deleuze, *Nietzsche and Philosophy* (New York: Columbia University Press, 1983), especially chap. 2.

46. Deleuze, *Foucault*, 98.

47. Deleuze, *Foucault*, 36.

48. Deleuze, *Foucault*, 78.

49. François Ewald suggests that part 3, chapter 1 of *Surveiller et Punir*, "Docile Bodies," could be read as "the response, in terms of power, to the Transcendental Aesthetic of the *Critique of Pure Reason*." I propose that Foucault's rethinking of the Transcendental Aesthetic begins as early as *Histoire de la folie*. Ewald, "Anatomie et corps politiques,"1261.

50. Deleuze, *Foucault*, 98.

51. John Rajchman, "Ethics after Foucault" in *Social Text* 13/14 (Winter/Spring, 1986), 166–67.

52. Charles Taylor, "Foucault on Freedom and Truth" in *Foucault: A Critical Reader*.

53. Taylor, "Foucault on Freedom and Truth," 93.

54. John Rajchman, *Michel Foucault: The Freedom of Philosophy* (New York: Columbia University Press, 1985), 121.

55. Rajchman, *Michel Foucault: The Freedom of Philosophy*, 58.

56. Rajchman, *Michel Foucault: The Freedom of Philosophy*, 77.

57. Rajchman, *Michel Foucault: The Freedom of Philosophy*, 79.

58. Rajchman, *Michel Foucault: The Freedom of Philosophy*, 78.

59. Foucault has no quarrel with Habermas on fundamentals. He agrees that we risk "lapsing into irrationality" if we abandon the project inaugurated by Kant. The question Foucault asks, however, differs from that of Habermas: "I think the central issue of philosophy and critical thought since the eighteenth century has been, still is, and will, I hope, remain the question, What is this Reason that we use? What are its historical effects? What are its limits, and what are its dangers? How can we exist as rational beings, fortunately committed to practicing a rationality that is unfortunately crisscrossed by intrinsic dangers?" "Michel Foucault: An Interview by Stephen Riggins" in *Ethos* 1, 2 (Autumn, 1983), reprinted as "An Ethics of Pleasure" in *Foucault Live* (Semiotext(e) Foreign Agents Series, 1989), 268. The interview was conducted in English.

60. Barry Smart, *Foucault, Marxism, and Critique* (London: Routledge and Kegan Paul, 1983), 135. Cf. Mark Poster, *Foucault, Marxism, and History* (Cambridge: Polity Press, 1984).

61. Gisela J. Hinkle, "Foucault's Power/Knowledge and American Sociological Theorizing" in *Human Studies* 10, 1 (1986).

62. Foucault's affinities with the thought of Heidegger are brought out by Dreyfus and Rabinow in *Michel Foucault: Beyond Structuralism and Hermeneutics* and by Ijsseling in "Foucault with Heidegger" in *Man and World* 19 (1986). To my mind, the best discussion of the affinities and differences between Foucault and Derrida is Edward Said's "Criticism Between Culture and System" in *The World, the Text, and the Critic* (Cambridge: Harvard University Press, 1983).

63. Allan Megill, *Prophets of Extremity: Nietzsche, Heidegger, Foucault, Derrida* (Berkeley: University of California Press, 1985), 2.

64. Megill, *Prophets of Extremity*, 11.

65. Nietzsche, *BT*, "Attempt at a Self-criticism."

66. Megill, *Prophets of Extremity*, 208.

67. Megill, *Prophets of Extremity*, 341. Megill is quoting Richard Rorty, *Philosophy and the Mirror of Nature* (Princeton University Press, 1979), 360.

68. David Carroll, "Disruptive Discourse and Critical Power: The Conditions of Archaeology and Genealogy" in *Humanities in Society* 5, 3–4 (1982), 181. Reprinted as chapter 5 of Carroll's *Paraesthetics: Foucault, Lyotard, Derrida* (London: Methuen, 1987). I will discuss this dimension of Foucault's Nietzscheanism in chapter 3.

69. Edward Said, "An Ethics of Language" in *Diacritics* 4, 2 (Summer, 1974), 36.

70. *LMC*, 312–13. (ET, 299–300).

71. Angèle Kremer-Marietti, *Michel Foucault: Archéologie et Généalogie* (Librairie Générale Française, 1985), 37. Originally published in 1974, the 1985 edition represents a drastic revision.

72. Axel Honneth, "Foucault et Adorno" in *Critique* XLIL, no. 471–72 (1986), 804.

73. Guy Laforest, "Regards généalogiques sur la modernité: Michel Foucault et la philosophie politique" in *Canadian Journal of Political Science*, 18, 1 (March, 1985), 77–78.

74. Allan Megill, "Foucault, Structuralism, and the Ends of History" in *Journal of Modern History*, 51 (1979), 478ff.

75. Richard Rorty, "Beyond Nietzsche and Marx" in *London Review of Books*, Feb. 19, 1981. Foucault was in Tunisia at the time.

76. Dreyfus and Rabinow, *Michel Foucault: Beyond Structuralism and Hermeneutics*, 104.

77. Gisela Hinkle, "Foucault's Power/Knowledge and American Sociological Theorizing" in *Human Studies* 10 (1986), 39–40. Although Hinkle dates the works according to the appearance of English translations, the periodization remains odd: 1972 and 1970 are early, 1979, 1965, and 1980 are late.

78. Pierre Macherey, "Aux sources de 'L'histoire de la folie'" in *Critique* XLIL, 471–72 (1986).

79. Jean-Paul Margot, "Herméneutique et fiction chez M. Foucault" in *Dialogue* 23 (1984), 643.

Chapter 2

1. Cf. Foucault's 1957 analysis and evaluation of his own discipline. "La recherche scientifique et la psychologie" in Jean-Edouard Morère (ed.), *Des chercheurs francais s'interrogent* (Paris: Presses Universitaires de France, 1957).

2. *MM&Per*, 2. Foucault's early Marxism is especially evident in his employment of Pavlov in *MM&Per* to develop a materialist psychology. In a 1968 interview he claims to have once been a member of the French Communist Party. Cf. "Foucault répond à Sartre," in *La Quinzaine littéraire* 46 (March 1–15, 1968), 21.

3. Cf. Pierre Macherey's excellent comparison of these two works. "Aux sources de 'l'Histoire de la folie'" in *Critique* XLIL, 471–72.

4. For a more extensive discussion of phenomenological psychology, see Foucault's lengthy "Introduction" to Ludwig Binswanger, *Le rêve et l'existence* (Paris: Desclée de Brouwer, 1954). English translation by Forrest Williams, "Dream, Imagination, and Existence," in *Review of Existential Psychology and Psychiatry* 19, 1 (1984–85).

5. *MM&Per*, 71.

6. *MM&Per*, 75.

7. Cf. *MM&Per*, 89–90. "In reality, it is only in history that the conditions of the possibility of psychological structures can be discovered...."

8. *HF*, v.

9. The crucial Socratic maxims for Nietzsche are: "To be beautiful everything must be intelligible," and "Virtue is knowledge; man sins only from ignorance; he who is virtuous is happy." *BT*, especially sections 12 and 14.

10. *HF*, v.

11. In a 1969 essay Foucault summarizes what he wanted to accomplish in *HF* in terms of how unreason, which had been characterized by "social, ethical and religious divisions," came to be "medicalized." "Médecins, juges et sorciers au XVIIe siècle" in *Médecine de France* 200 (1969). In 1962 he referred to a "medicalization" of "para-religious experience." "Les déviations religieuses et le savoir médical" in Jacques LeGoff, *Hérésies et société dans l'Europe pré-industrielle 11e–18e siècles* (Paris: Mouton, 1968), 24.

12. Although he does not use the term "genealogy" at this point in time, by 1976 he refers to *Histoire de la folie* as "a genealogy of psychiatry." See "Questions à Michel Foucault sur la géographie" in *Hérodote* 1 (1976), (ET in *Power/Knowledge*, 64). At the time of *HF*'s publication Foucault expressed his interest in terms of an "interrogation on the very origins of madness." "La folie n'existe que dans une société" in *Le Monde* 5135 (July 22, 1961), 9.

13. *MM&Psych*, 80 (ET, 67).

14. *HF*, 21 (ET, 10).

15. *HF*, 22 (ET, 11).

16. *HF*, 60-61 (ET, 40).

17. *HF*, 66-67 (ET, 45). Note the Kantian expression "form of sensibility." We will see shortly how Foucault rethinks the issues which con-

cerned Kant in the Transcendental Aesthetic. In this passage it is already clear that the forms of sensibility are radically historical in Foucault's rethinking. At the time of *HF*'s publication, Foucault claimed that madness "does not exist outside of the forms of sensibility which isolate it...." "La folie n'existe que dans une société" in *Le Monde* 5135 (July 22, 1961), 9.

18. *HF*, 70.

19. *HF*, 70.

20. *HF*, 74.

21. *HF*, 75 (ET, 47).

22. *HF*, 79 (ET, 51).

23. *HF*, 82 (ET, 55).

24. *HF*, 85 (ET, 58).

25. *HF*, 96.

26. *HF*, 100.

27. *HF*, 104

28. *HF*, 108.

29. *HF*, 106.

30. *HF*, 504–505 (ET, 247).

31. *HF*, 512 (ET, 257).

32. *HF*, 524 (ET, 270).

33. *HF*, 554 (ET, 285).

34. *HF*, 554 (ET, 285).

35. *HF*, 530 (ET, 278).

36. *LMC*, 317 (ET, 306).

37. "Préface à la transgression" in *Critique* 195–96 (August-September, 1963), 756. English translation by Donald F. Bouchard and Sherry Simon in Donald F. Bouchard (ed.), *Language, Counter-Memory, Practice* (Ithaca: Cornell University Press, 1977), 35.

38. *TSZ*, I, 7 and 4.

39. *GM*, I, 13.

40. "Médecins, juges et sorciers au XVIIe siècle" in *Médecine de France* 200 (1969), 121.

41. Cf. "Médecins, juges et sorciers au XVIIe siècle," especially 128.

42. *NC*, vi-vii (ET, x–xi).

43. *NC*, x (ET, xiv).

44. *NC*, xii (ET, xv–xvi). Cf. Mark Cousins and Athar Hussain, *Michel Foucault* (New York: St. Martin's Press, 1984), 7–8, 15.

45. Dreyfus and Rabinow, *Michel Foucault: Beyond Structuralism and Hermeneutics*,15.

46. *NC*, 196 (ET, 191).

47. "...man became a 'psychologizable species' only when his relation to madness made a psychology possible, that is to say, when his relation to madness was defined by the external dimension of exclusion and punishment and by the internal dimension of moral assignation and guilt. In situating madness in relation to these two fundamental axes, early nineteenth-century man made it possible to *grasp* madness and thus to initiate a general psychology.

"This experience of Unreason in which, up to the eighteenth century, Western man encountered the night of his truth and its absolute challenge was to become, and still remains for us, the mode of access to the natural truth of man." *MM&Psych*, 88 (ET, 73–74). Later, "the external dimension of exclusion and punishment" will be explicitly formulated as the power axis, "the internal dimension of moral assignation and guilt" as the subject axis, and the truth axis is evident in the last sentence.

48. "Intervista a Michel Foucault" in Alessandro Fontana and Pasquale Pasquino (eds.) *Microfisica del Potere* (Torino: Giulio Einaudi, 1977), 9–10 (ET, 115). The interview was conducted in 1976.

49. "Space, Knowledge, and Power" in Paul Rabinow (ed.), *The Foucault Reader* (New York: Pantheon, 1984), 252.

50. In 1977 Foucault confirmed this insight into the relationship between space and power: "A whole history remains to be written of *spaces*—which would at the same time be the history of *powers* (both these terms in the plural)...." "L'Oeil du pouvoir" in Jeremy Bentham, *Le Panoptique* (Paris: Pierre Belfond, 1977), 12 (ET in *Power/Knowledge*, 149).

51. *HF*, 56.

52. *HF*, 75 (ET, 46). On Foucault's understanding of "police" see Pasquale Pasquino, "Theatrum Politicum," *I&C*, 4 (Autumn, 1978).

53. *HF*, 61 (ET, 40): "Police, in the precise sense that the classical epoch gave to it—that is, the totality of measures which make work possible and necessary for all those who could not live without it...."

54. *HF*, 60-61 (ET, 40).

55. *HF*, 89-90 (ET, 63).

56. *HF*, 94.

57. *HF*, 418 (ET, 224).

58. *HF*, 421 (ET, 227).

59. *HF*, 439–40.

60. *HF*, 502 (ET, 244).

61. *HF*, 505 (ET, 247).

62. *HF*, 506 (ET, 248).

63. *HF*, 507 (ET, 250).

64. *HF*, 516 (ET, 260). Foucault is quoting Scipion Pinel's account.

65. *HF*, 518–19 (ET, 264).

66. *HF*, 519 (ET, 265).

67. *HF*, 520 (ET, 266).

68. *HF*, 520–21 (ET, 266).

69. *HF*, 521 (ET, 267).

70. *HF*, 27 (ET, 16).

71. *HF*, 35 (ET, 26).

72. *HF*, 72.

73. *HF*, 73.

74. *HF*, 99.

75. *HF*, 112.

76. *HF*, 116.

77. *HF*, 116.

78. Since Foucault maintains that our medical perception of madness is linked to the juridical consciousness of the eighteenth century, we will look more closely at the juridical in the context of the truth axis. At present we will concentrate upon the practical consciousness of madness in the houses of confinement.

79. *HF*, 151.

80. *HF*, 151–52.

81. *HF*, 469.

82. *HF*, 346 (ET, 182).

83. Cf. Jacques Derrida, "Cogito and the History of Madness" in *Writing and Difference* (Chicago: University of Chicago Press, 1978).

84. *HF*, 157.

85. It is worth taking note of a Nietzschean admonition at this point: "To explain how a philosopher's most remote metaphysical assertions have actually been arrived at, it is always well (and wise) to ask oneself first: what morality does this (does *he*—) aim at?" *BGE*, 6.

86. *HF*, 504 (ET, 246).

87. *HF*, 28 (ET, 18).

88. *HF*, 35 (ET, 26).

89. *HF*, 144.

90. *HF*, 146.

91. *HF*, 201.

92. *HF*, 201–202.

93. *HF*, 203.

94. *HF*, 204.

95. *HF*, 207.

96. *HF*, 216.

97. *HF*, 216.

98. *HF*, part 2, chap. 2.

99. *HF*, 256 (ET, 100–101).

100. *HF*, 291–92 (ET, 130).

101. *HF*, 296 (ET, 135).

102. *HF*, 377–78 (ET, 205).

103. *HF*, 507 (ET, 250).

104. *LMC*, 316 (ET, 305).

105. *NC*, xv (ET, xix). Sheridan Smith's translation usually follows the 1973 edition, but in this case he employs the 1963 version. For the 1973 edition Foucault excised the word "structural" to describe his study in an attempt to escape the structuralist label that had been imposed on him.

106. *NC*, x (ET, xiv).

107. *NC*, v (ET, ix).

108. *NC*, 200–201 (ET, 197).

109. *NC*, 12 (ET, 14).

110. Foucault directed an extended study of tertiary spatialization of disease in 1976 which appeared as *Généalogie des équipements de normalisation: les équipements sanitaires* (Fontenay-sous-Bois: Centre d'études, de recherches et de formation institutionnelles [CERFI], 1976). We will discuss this text in chapter 5.

111. *NC*, 30 (ET, 31).

112. "L'extension sociale de la norme," *Politique hebdo*, 212 (March, 1976), 15.

113. *NC*, 15 (ET, 16).

114. *NC*, 16 (ET, 17).

115. *NC*, 17 (ET, 18).

116. *NC*, 19 (ET, 19).

117. *NC*, 19 (ET, 20).

118. *NC*, 22 (ET, 23).

119. *NC*, 23 (ET, 24).

120. *NC*, 24 (ET, 25).

121. *NC*, 26 (ET, 26). Foucault is quoting Lebrun's *Traité théorique sur les maladies épidémiques* (Paris, 1772), 126.

122. *NC*, 27 (ET, 27).

123. *NC*, 30-31 (ET, 31). Translation slightly modified. Minor quibbling perhaps, but *surveillance* seems too important a word in Foucault's vocabulary to render it "supervision" with Sheridan.

124. *NC*, 31-32 (ET, 31–32).

125. *NC*, 32 (ET, 32).

126. Foucault quotes Lanthenas' *Of the Influence of Liberty on Health* of 1792 and captures the political vision of the physician operative in both myths: "Who, then, should denounce tyrants to mankind if not the doctors, who make man their sole study, and who, each day, in the homes of poor and rich, among ordinary citizens and among the highest in the land, in cottage and mansion, contemplate the human miseries that have no other origin but tyranny and slavery?" *NC*, 34 (ET, 33).

127. *NC*, 37 (ET, 38).

128. *NC*, 34 (ET, 34).

129. *NC*, 35 (ET, 34).

130. *NC*, 90 (ET, 91).

131. *NC*, 96 (ET, 96).

132. *NC*, 91 (ET, 91–92).

133. *NC*, 91 (ET, 92).

134. *NC*, 93 (ET, 94).

135. *NC*, 94-95 (ET, 95).

136. *NC*, 109 (ET, 109).

137. *NC*, 112 (ET, 112).

138. *NC*, 114 (ET, 114).

139. *NC*, 116 (ET, 115).

140. Foucault employs the image of the "speaking eye" to capture the essence of clinical experience. *NC*, 115 (ET, 115).

141. *NC*, 199 (ET, 195).

142. *NC*, 199 (ET, 195).

143. *NC*, 200 (ET, 196).

144. *BT*, 12.

145. *NC*, 176 (ET, 172).

146. *NC*, 126 (ET, 125).

147. *NC*, 126 (ET, 125).

148. By 1801, the issue seemed obvious to Bichat: "for twenty years, from morning to night, you have taken notes at patients' bedsides on affections of the heart, the lungs, and the gastric viscera, and all is confusion for you in the symptoms which, refusing to yield up their meaning, offer you a succession of incoherent phenomena. Open up a few corpses: you will dissipate at once the darkness that observation alone could not dissipate." *NC*, 149 (ET, 146).

149. *NC*, 97 (ET, 97).

150. *NC*, 149 (ET, 146).

151. *NC*, 161 (ET, 158).

152. *NC*, 158 (ET, 155).

153. *NC*, 162 (ET, 159).

154. *NC*, 166 (ET, 162).

155. *NC*, 169 (ET, 164).

156. *NC*, x (ET, xiv).

157. "Introduction" to *Rousseau: Juge de Jean Jacques: Dialogues* (Paris: Librarie Armand Colin, 1962), xxiv.

158. *MM&Per*, 2.

159. *MM&Psy*, 2.

160. Compare *MM&Per*, 2 with *MM&Psy*, 2. In a 1965 interview he claims to be less interested in psychology as a science than as a cultural form. "Philosophie et psychologie" in *Dossiers pédagogiques de la radio-télévision scolaire* 10 (February 15–27, 1965), 61.

161. Compare *MM&Per*, 16 with *MM&Psy*, 16.

162. Compare *MM&Per*, 16 with *MM&Psy*, 16

163. Compare *MM&Per*, 17 with *MM&Psy*, 17.

164. *HF*, iv. Foucault discusses what he wanted to do in *HF* in terms of examining the limits a culture establishes for itself in "Débat sur la poésie," *Tel Quel* 17 (Spring, 1964), especially 75. The discussion took place in September 1963.

165. *HF*, iii.

166. Foucault mentions three other experiences residing at our cultural frontiers which would need to be investigated in order to complete the project: the experience of the East, of the dream, and of sexuality. What is most fascinating about these three is that, having been in some way rejected by Western rationality, each is pursued by modern man as the locale of his primitive truth. *HF*, iv.

167. Alan Sheridan, *Michel Foucault: The Will to Truth* (London: Tavistock Publications, 1980), 15.

168. *HF*, v.

169. *HF*, v.

170. *HF*, iii.

171. *HF*, vi.

Chapter 3

1. *Les mots et les choses* should be appreciated as a continuation of Foucault's project in his previous works. Concerned with the same historical periodization as *Histoire de la folie* and *Naissance de la clinique*, it can be viewed as the *Gestalt* of *Histoire de la folie*. As Foucault once put it, "*Histoire de la folie* is the history of difference, *Les mots et les choses* the history of resemblance, of the same, of identity." Language's tendency to include rather than exclude is the concern of *Les mots et les choses*. "Entretien avec Michel Foucault" in Raymond Bellour, *Le lire des autres* (Paris: Éditions de l'Herne, 1971), 137. The interview was conducted in 1966.

2. *Raymond Roussel* (Paris: Gallimard, 1963). English translation by Charles Ruas, *Death and the Labyrinth: The World of Raymond Roussel* (New York: Doubleday, 1986).

3. *LMC*, 398 (ET, 387).

4. James W. Bernauer, *Michel Foucault's Force of Flight: Toward an Ethics for Thought* (Atlantic Highlands, N.J.: Humanities Press International, 1990), 64.

5. Hayden White, "Foucault Decoded: Notes from Underground" in *History and Theory* 12 (1973), 29.

6. In a 1963 essay, Foucault claims, "in terms of ontology, ...to think and to speak are *the same thing*." "Guetter le jour qui vient" in *La Nouvelle Revue Francaise*, 130 (October, 1963), 716.

7. *LMC*, 311 (ET, 298).

8. Bernauer, *Michel Foucault's Force of Flight*, chap. 3. See also Michel Serres, *Hermes I: La Communication* (Paris: Les Éditions de Minuit, 1968), 189.

9. *LMC*, 89 (ET, 75).

10. *LMC*, 77 (ET, 63).

11. Michael Shapiro, *Language and Political Understanding: The Politics of Discursive Practices* (New Haven: Yale University Press, 1981), 141.

12. Carl Hempel, *Philosophy of Natural Science* (Englewood Cliffs, N.J.: Prentice-Hall, Inc., 1966), 48. Hempel argues against Sizi's position that the "facts it adduces...are irrelevant." Foucault's position is that in the context of Renaissance thought governed by the epistemic network of resemblance, these facts are precisely the relevant ones.

13. *L'ordre du discours* (Paris: Gallimard, 1971), 37. English translation by Rupert Swyer in *The Archaeology of Knowledge*, 224, slightly

modified. Swyer renders "*police*" as "policy." To translate "*police*" directly as "police" sustains the relationship between truth and power that Foucault wants to convey. Cf. "Intervista a Michel Foucault" in Fontana and Pasquino, *Microfisica del potere*, 26–27 (ET, 132): "by truth I do not mean 'the ensemble of truths which are to be discovered and accepted,' but rather 'the ensemble of rules according to which the true and the false are separated and specific effects of power attached to the true'...."

14. This seems to be the description of the episteme Foucault ultimately favored. In 1977 he retrospectively defined the episteme as "the strategic deployment which permits of separating out from among all the statements which are possible those that will be acceptable within, I won't say a scientific theory, but a field of scientificity, and which it is possible to say are true or false." "Le jeu de Michel Foucault," in *Ornicar?* (July 10, 1977), 65. English translation by Kate Soper in Colin Gordon (ed.), *Power/Knowledge*, slightly modified; for Foucault's term, "*dispositif*," I prefer Bernauer's "deployment" with its military connotations to Colin Gordon's "apparatus." Cf. James Bernauer, *The Thinking of History in the Archaeology of Michel Foucault* (Ann Arbor: University Microfilms International, 1981), 393ff.

15. "Foucault répond à Sartre" in *La Quinzaine Littéraire*, 46 (March 1–15, 1968), 21.

16. *The Order of Things*, Foreword to the English Edition of *LMC* (1970), xi.

17. *The Order of Things*, Foreword to the English Edition of *LMC* (1970), xi.

18. Charles Taylor, "Foucault on Freedom and Truth" in David Couzens Hoy (editor), *Foucault: A Critical Reader* (Oxford: Basil Blackwell, 1986), 69.

19. H. C. Erik Midelfort, "Madness and Civilization in Early Modern Europe: A Reappraisal of Michel Foucault" in *After the Reformation: Essays in Honor of H. H. Hexster*, edited by Barbara C. Malament (University of Pennsylvania Press, 1980), 249.

20. David Carroll, "Disruptive Discourse and Critical Power: The Conditions of Archaeology and Geneaology" in *Humanities in Society* 5, 3–4 (Summer/Fall, 1982), 176. Reprinted in Carroll, *Paraesthetics: Foucault, Lyotard, Derrida* (New York: Methuen, 1987). Foucault affirms that the reason/unreason problem which interested him in *HF* is now found "at the interior of language." "Débat sur la poésie" in *Tel Quel* 17 (Spring, 1964), 75.

21. "Préface á la transgression" in *Critique* 195–96 (August–September, 1963), 761. English translation by Donald F. Bouchard and Sherry Simon in *Language, Counter-Memory, Practice* (Ithaca, Cornell

University Press, 1977), 42. "Deuxième entretien avec Michel Foucault" in Raymond Bellour, *Le livre des autres* (Paris: Editions de l'Herne, 1971), 198. "Theatrum Philosophicum" in *Critique* 282 (1970), 885 (ET in *Language, Counter-Memory, Practice*, 165). See also "Structuralism and Post-Structuralism" in *Telos* 55 (Spring, 1983), 199; and "An Interview by Stephen Riggins" in *Ethos* I, 2 (Autumn, 1983), 5.

22. *HF*, 26-27 (ET, 15-16).

23. "Le langage à l'infini" in *Tel Quel* 15 (Autumn, 1963), 52 (ET in *Language, Counter-Memory, Practice*, 66). This claim is clarified somewhat in Foucault's response to George Steiner's review of *The Order of Things*. See "Monstrosities in Criticism" in *Diacritics* 1, 1 (Fall, 1971), 60.

24. "Qu'est-ce qu'un auteur?" in *Bulletin de la société francaise de philosophie* 64 (1969), 78 (ET in *Language, Counter-Memory, Practice*, 117).

25. *HF*, 530 (ET, 278).

26. Jürgen Habermas, "The French Path to Postmodernity: Bataille between Eroticism and General Economics" in *New German Critique* 33 (Fall, 1984), 80, my emphasis. Reprinted in *The Philosophical Discourse of Modernity: Twelve Lectures* (Cambridge: The MIT Press, 1987), Lecture 8.

27. Michel Beaujour, "Eros and Nonsense: Georges Bataille" in *Modern French Criticism: From Proust and Valéry to Structuralism*, edited by John K. Simon (Chicago: University of Chicago Press, 1972), 149

28. "Préface à la transgression," 752 (ET, 30).

29. Georges Bataille, *La Littérature et le mal* in *Oeuvres complètes*, Volume 9 (Paris: Gallimard, 1979), 184.

30. "Préface à la transgression," 751 (ET, 29).

31. "Préface à la transgression," 753–54 (ET, 32). A year after he wrote this essay on Bataille, he wrote a new appendix to the second French edition of *Histoire de la folie*, and in a rather obscure passage, a disconcerting passage, he briefly discusses this transgressive language. He delineates four forms of socially excluded language, and the fourth is the language of transgression: "it consists of submitting a *parole* apparently conforming with the acknowledged code, to another code the key to which is given in the *parole* itself, so that the *parole* is doubled within its own bounds: it says what it says, but it adds a silent, extra element which in a muted way enounces what it says and the code according to which it is said. This is not a ciphered language, but a structurally esoteric one. That is to say, that it does not communicate a forbidden meaning while hiding it; from the start it establishes itself in an essential dark fold of the *parole*. A dark fold which hollows the *parole* from inside and perhaps *ad infinitum*. It little matters then what is said in such a language and the

meanings which are produced through it. What really matters is that obscure and central liberation of the *parole* at its very core, that uncontrollable run towards a focus forever deprived of light, which is at first unacceptable for any culture. It is not in its meaning, not in its verbal matter, but in its playing that such a *parole* is a transgression."

32. "Le 'non' du père," *Critique* 178 (March, 1962), 208. English translation in *Language, Counter-Memory, Practice*, 85.

33. This issue will be taken up again in greater detail in section 3 of the present chapter, "The Birth and Death of Man."

34. "La pensée du dehors" in *Critique* 229 (1966), 528.

35. "Préface à la transgression," 761 (ET, 43) and 758 (ET, 38).

36. "Le langage à l'infini," 45. (ET, 55).

37. "Préface à la transgression," 760–61 (ET, 41–42, translation slightly modified).

38. "Préface à la transgression," 762 (ET, 44).

39. *Histoire de la sexualité 2: L'usage des plaisirs* (Paris: Gallimard, 1984), 14–15. English translation by Robert Hurley, *The Use of Pleasures* (New York: Pantheon, 1985), 8–9.

40. *LMC*, 90 (ET, 75).

41. *LMC*, 139 (ET, 127–28).

42. *LMC*, 144 (ET, 132). Foucault's comparison of the work of Aldrovandi (*Monstrorum historia*, 1647) and that of Jonston (*Historia naturalis de quadripedidus*, 1657) clarifies his assertion that the tendency to view language as representation overlooks the density of discourse itself that always prohibits certain dimensions of experience from being expressed. What essentially separates Aldrovandi and Jonston is not their abilities in observation; Aldrovandi was at least Jonston's equal. The difference resides in the fact that so much observed by Aldrovandi is missing in Jonston. Legends and accounts of the ancients, for example, are pushed to the side of the field of visibility constituted by representation.

43. *LMC*, 277 (ET, 265).

44. *LMC*, 288 (ET, 275).

45. See, for example, Charles Gide and Charles Rist, *A History of Economic Doctrines*, translated by R. Richards (Boston: D. C. Heath and Co., 1948), first published in France in 1909 and reprinted numerous times, it has throughout this century been the standard French history of economic thought. "Notwithstanding the originality and vigour displayed by the Physiocrats, they can only be regarded as the heralds of the new

science. Adam Smith, it is now unanimously agreed, is its true founder."
(p. 68).

46. *LMC*, 177 (ET, 166).

47. *LMC*, 180 (ET, 169).

48. *LMC*, 186–87 (ET, 175).

49. *LMC*, 192 (ET, 180).

50. *LMC*, 235 (ET, 222–23). Cantillon, Quesnay, and Condillac likewise employed the concept of labor in their economic thought, and like
them Smith used the concept as a measure of exchange value: "Labour,
therefore, is the real measure of the exchangeable value of all commodi-
ties." Foucault is quoting Smith's *Inquiry into the Nature and Causes of
the Wealth of Nations.* The passage can be found in the first paragraph of
chapter 5 of any unabridged edition. See, for example, The Modern
Library edition, 30.

51. *LMC*, 237 (ET, 224).

52. *LMC*, 237 (ET, 225).

53. *LMC*, 266 (ET, 253).

54. *LMC*, 268 (ET, 255–56).

55. *LMC*, 68-70 (ET, 54–56).

56. *LMC*, 70 (ET, 56).

57. *LMC*, 93 (ET, 79).

58. *LMC*, 96 (ET, 82).

59. *LMC*, 97 (ET, 83). The entire sentence is emphasized in Foucault's text. Cousins and Hussain provide an illuminating reading of *LMC*
as interpretation of the Port-Royal Grammar. See Cousins and Hussain,
Michel Foucault (New York: St. Martin's Press, 1984), chap. 2.

60. *LMC*, 131 (ET, 115).

61. *LMC*, 248 (ET, 235, translation slightly modified).

62. *LMC*, 293 (ET, 280).

63. *LMC*, 294 (ET, 282), *"pour s'épaissir et recevoir une pesanteur
propre."*

64. *LMC*, 308 (ET, 295).

65. *LMC*, 320 (ET, 309).

66. *LMC*, 329 (ET, 318).

67. *LMC*, 321 (ET, 310).

68. *LMC*, 329 (ET, 318).

69. *LMC*, 329 (ET, 318).

70. *LMC*, 323 (ET, 312), "*souverain soumis, spectateur regardé.*"

71. "Jean Hyppolite (1907–1968)" in *Revue de métaphysique et de morale* 74, 2 (April–June, 1969), 132.

72. "Philosophie et psychologie" in *Dossiers pédagogiques de la radio-télévision scolaire*, 10 (February 15–27, 1965), 65.

73. *LMC*, 327 (ET, 317).

74. *LMC*, 352 (ET, 341).

75. *LMC*, 338 (ET, 327). "…in Hegelian phenomenology, it was the *An sich* as opposed to the *Für sich*; for Schopenhauer it was the *Unbewusste*; for Marx it was alienated man; in Husserl's analysis it was the implicit, the inactual, the sedimented, the non-effected—in every case, the inexhaustible double that presents itself to reflection as the blurred projection of what man is in his truth, but that also plays the role of a preliminary ground upon which man must collect himself and recall himself in order to attain his truth."

76. Hubert Dreyfus and Paul Rabinow, *Michel Foucault: Beyond Structuralism and Hermeneutics* Second Edition (Chicago: University of Chicago Press, 1983), 31.

77. *LMC*, 352 (ET, 341), "*dédoubler le dogmatisme.*"

78. *LMC*, 256 (ET, 243, translation slightly modified: I render "*critique*" as "critique" rather than "criticism").

79. *LMC*, 275 (ET, 263).

80. "Foucault répond à Sartre," 20.

81. *LMC*, 353 (ET, 342).

82. *LMC*, 353–54 (ET, 342–43). Translation slightly modified. While the standard translation is fine and, perhaps, flows more smoothly, I want to bring out the fact that throughout the passage Foucault employs the verb *veulent* which carries overtones of a "will to knowledge" undergirding anthropological thought.

83. "Entretien avec Michel Foucault" in Raymond Bellour, *Le livre des autres* (Paris: Éditions de l'Herne, 1971), 143.

84. *LMC*, 316 (ET, 305).

85. Stéphane Mallarmé, "Crise de vers" in *Oeuvres complètes* (Paris:

Gallimard, 1945), 367. *Selected Prose Poems, Essays, and Letters*, translated by Bradford Cook (Baltimore: Johns Hopkins University Press, 1956).

86. Stéphane Mallarmé, "Crise de vers," 366.

87. *LMC*, 316–17 (ET, 305).

88. *LMC*, 317 (ET, 306).

89. *LMC*, 318 (ET, 307).

90. "Qu'est-ce qu'un auteur?" 77 and 95 (ET,115 and 138).

91. *LMC*, 388 (ET, 376).

92. *LMC*, 389 (ET, 378).

93. *LMC*, 393 (ET, 381).

94. *LMC*, 391 (ET, 379).

95. *LMC*, 386 (ET, 374).

96. Foucault has characterized his own work as an internal ethnology of our culture and of our rationality. See "Deuxième entretien avec Michel Foucault," 205 and "Conversazione con Michel Foucault" in Paolo Caruso, *Conversazione con Levi-Strauss, Foucault, Lacan* (Milano: U. Mursia and Co., 1969), 103.

97. *LMC*, 389–90 (ET, 378).

98. *LMC*, 390 (ET, 378).

99. *LMC*, 391. "Défaire" has quotation marks in Foucault's text. The word connotes "to undo" or "to unmake" as well as "to defeat."

100. *LMC*, 392–93 (ET, 381).

Chapter 4

1. *TSZ*, 1, 15. All references to Nietzsche's writings are to section or aphorism number.

2. *GS*, 301.

3. *BGE*, 3.

4. *BGE*, 3.

5. *BGE*, 9.

6. *BGE*, 9.

7. *BGE*, 22.

8. *WP*, 409.

9. *BGE*, 212.

10. *GM*, Preface, 7.

11. *GM*, P, 4.

12. *GM*, P, 4.

13. *GM*, P, 7.

14. *GM*, 1, 1.

15. *GM*, 1, 2.

16. *BGE*, 199. See also 201, 202.

17. *TSZ*, 142.

18. *GM*, 1, 10.

19. *GM*, 2, 12.

20. *GM*, 2, 12.

21. *GM*, 2, 12.

22. *GM*, 2, 12.

23. Gilles Deleuze, *Nietzsche and Philosophy*, translated by Hugh Tomlinson (New York: Columbia University Press, 1983), 119.

24. *GM*, 1, 13.

25. *GM*, 1, 13.

26. *WP*, 548.

27. *WP*, 550.

28. *TI*, "Four Great Errors, 3.

29. *WP*, 485.

30. *WP*, 551.

31. *TI*, "Four Great Errors," 5.

32. *GM*, 1, 13.

33. *WP*, 480.

34. *WP*, 480.

35. *WP*, 481.

36. Friedrich Nietzsche, *Daybreak*. Translated by R. J. Hollingdale (Cambridge: Cambridge University Press, 1982), 2.

37. *Daybreak*, 3.

38. Speech of June 4, 1794, quoted in *Daybreak*.

39. *Daybreak*, 3.

40. *GM*, P, 5.

41. *GM*, P, 5.

42. *GM*, P, 3.

43. *GM*, P, 3.

44. *GM*, P, 3.

45. *WP*, 254. See also *GS*, 345.

46. *GM*, P, 6.

47. *GM*, P, 6.

48. *GM*, P, 6.

49. *UM2*, 59.

50. *UM2*, 60.

51. *UM2*, 62.

52. *GM*, 1, 10.

53. *UM2*, 62.

54. *UM2*, 63.

55. *UM2*, 67.

56. *UM2*, 68.

57. *UM2*, 69.

58. *UM2*, 70.

59. *UM2*, 71.

60. *UM2*, 71.

61. *UM2*, 72.

62. *UM2*, 72.

63. *UM2*, 72.

64. *UM2*, 73.

65. *UM2*, 73.

66. *UM2*, 74.

67. *UM2*, 74.

68. *UM2*, 75.

69. *UM2*, 75.

70. *UM2*, 76.

71. Allan Megill, *Prophets of Extremity: Nietzsche, Heidegger, Foucault, Derrida* (Berkeley: University of California Press, 1985), 227–32.

72. Gilles Deleuze, *Foucault* (Paris: Les Éditions de Minuit, 1986), 27.

73. Alan Sheridan, *Michel Foucault: The Will to Truth* (New York: Tavistock Publications, 1980), 89.

74. Sheridan, *Michel Foucault: The Will to Truth*, 116. To support his claim that a radical rupture took place in Foucault's thought in the early to mid-seventies, Sheridan mentions that Foucault never again uses the term "archaeology." After the publication of Sheridan's book, however, Foucault continued to refer to his work as "archaeology." Cf., for example, "What is Enlightenment?" in Paul Rabinow (ed.), *The Foucault Reader* (New York: Pantheon, 1984) and *Histoire de la sexualité 2: L'usage des plaisirs* (Paris: Gallimard, 1984).

75. Barry Smart, *Michel Foucault* (New York: Tavistock Publications, 1985), 42 and 47.

76. Jeffrey Minson, *Genealogies of Morals* (New York: St. Martin's Press, 1985), 115.

77. Francois Russo, "L'archéologie du savoir de Michel Foucault" in *Archives de Philosophie* 36 (1973), 72.

78. James W. Bernauer, *Michel Foucault's Force of Flight: Toward an Ethics for Thought* (Atlantic Highlands, N.J.: Humanities Press International, 1990), 91.

79. Hubert Dreyfus and Paul Rabinow, *Michel Foucault: Beyond Structuralism and Hermeneutics* Second Edition (Chicago: University of Chicago Press, 1983), xxv.

80. Deleuze sees this issue clearly. In *L'archéologie du savoir*, according to Deleuze, Foucault is sketching his conception of political philosophy. Cf. Deleuze, *Foucault*, 19.

81. "Deuxième entretien avec Michel Foucault" (the interview took place in June of 1967) in Raymond Bellour, *Le livre des autres* (Paris: Éditions de l'Herne, 1971), 195.

82. "Pouvoir et corps" in *Quel corps?* 2 (1975), 34 (ET, 61).

83. *AS*, 274 (ET, 210–11).

84. Karlis Racevskis, *Michel Foucault and the Subversion of Intellect* (Ithaca: Cornell University Press, 1983), 77.

85. Charles C. Lemert and Garth Gillan, *Michel Foucault: Social Theory and Transgression* (New York: Columbia University Press, 1982), 48–49.

86. "On the Genealogy of Ethics: An Overview of Work in Progress," in Dreyfus and Rabinow, *Michel Foucault: Beyond Structuralism and Hermeneutics*, 237.

87. Arnold Davidson sets the issue straight: "Archaeology attempts to isolate the level of discursive practices and formulate the rules of production and transformation for these practices. Genealogy, on the other hand, concentrates on the forces and relations of power connected to discursive practices; it does not insist on a separation of rules for production of discourse and relations of power. But genealogy does not so much displace archaeology as widen the kind of analysis to be pursued. It is a question, as Foucault put it in his last writings, of different axes whose 'relative importance...is not always the same for all forms of experience." Arnold I. Davidson, "Archaeology, Genealogy, Ethics" in *Foucault: A Critical Reader*, edited by David Couzens Hoy (Oxford: Basil Blackwell, 1986), 227.

88. Smart, *Michel Foucault*, 47-48, my emphasis.

89. Smart, *Michel Foucault*, 48. Smart is quoting from Foucault's "Two Lectures" in Colin Gordon (ed.), *Power/Knowledge* (New York: Pantheon, 1980), 85.

90. "Est-il donc important de penser?" in *Libération* (May 30–31, 1981), 21. English translation by Thomas Keenan. "Is it really important to think?" in *Philosophy and Social Criticism* 9, 1 (Spring, 1982), 33.

91. Seyla Benhabib calls this type of analysis "defetishizing" critique: "a procedure of analysis whereby the given is shown to be not a natural fact but a socially and historically constituted, and thus changeable, reality." *Critique, Norm, and Utopia: A Study of the Foundations of Critical Theory* (New York: Columbia University Press, 1986), 47.

92. "The Culture of the Self," a lecture by and discussion with Foucault at Berkeley in the spring of 1983. I attended these sessions. Comments on the relationship between archaeology and genealogy were made during the discussion session. A tape recording is available from the Language Laboratory at the University of California at Berkeley.

93. "The Culture of the Self." Martin Jay's follow-up question came in the form of a statement: "Just to make sure that your answer was understood, you never stopped doing archaeology." Foucault: "No, no, no,...no, no, I never stopped doing archaeology. I never stopped doing genealogy. Genealogy defines the target and the finality of the work and archaeology indicates the field with which I deal in order to make a genealogy."

94. "Nietzsche, l'généalogie, l'histoire" in *Hommage à Jean Hyppolite* (Paris: Presses Universitaires de France, 1971). English translation by Donald F. Bouchard and Sherry Simon in Donald F. Bouchard (ed.), *Language, Counter-Memory, Practice* (Ithaca: Cornell University Press, 1977).

95. "Deuxième entretien avec Michel Foucault," 206.

96. *AS* contains no reference to *MM&Per*. The man he sought in that early work now appears to him as "an invention of recent date" due to "be erased, like a face drawn in sand at the edge of the sea." *LMC*, 398 (ET, 387). Nor does *AS* refer to Foucault's 1954 flirtation with phenomenology, his lengthy introduction to the French translation of Ludwig Binswanger's Heidegger-influenced *Daseinanalyse*, entitled *Le rêve et l'existence* (Paris: Desclée de Brouwer, 1954). English translation by Forrest Williams. "Dream, Imagination, and Existence" in *Review of Existential Psychology and Psychiatry*, 19, 1 (1984–85). He now sees phenomenology as bound up with man as the empirico-transcendental double. Cf. *LMC*, 332 (ET, 321).

97. Roger Paden, "Locating Foucault—Archaeology vs. Structuralism" in *Philosophy and Social Criticism*, 11, 2 (Winter, 1986), 31.

98. *AS*, 25 (ET, 15).

99. *AS*, 26 (ET, 16).

100. *OD*, 10–11 (ET, 216).

101. *OD*, 71 (ET, 234). "Ainsi doivent alterner, prendre appui les unes sur les autres et se compléter les descriptions critiques et les descriptions généalogiques."

102. *OD*, 71 (ET, 234).

103. *OD*, 62 (ET, 232).

104. *OD*, 71-72 (ET, 234).

105. "NGH," 145 (ET, 139).

106. "Corso del 7 gennaio 1976" and "Corso del 14 gennaio 1976" in Alessandro Fontana and Pasquale Pasquino (eds.), *Microfisica del Potere* (Torino: Einaudi, 1977), 168. English translation by Kate Soper in *Power/Knowledge*, 83.

107. In Michelle Perrot (ed.), *L'impossible prison* (Paris: Seuil, 1980), 44. English translation by Alan Bass in Kenneth Baynes, James Bohman, and Thomas McCarthy (eds.), *After Philosophy: End or Transformation* (Cambridge: MIT Press, 1987), 104.

108. *L'impossible prison*, 44 (ET, 104), "La démultiplication causale."

109. "NGH," 153 (ET, 147).

110. "NGH," 150 (ET, 144).

111. "Un Dibattito Foucault-Preti," in *Bimestre* 22-23 (September–December, 1972), 2.

112. *GM*, P, 3.

113. "NGH," 148 (ET, 142).

114. "NGH," 148 (ET, 142).

115. "NGH," 148 (ET, 142).

116. "NGH," 150–51 (ET, 144–45).

117. *La Verdad y las Formas Jurídicas* (Barcelona: Gedisa, 1980), 20. This is a Spanish translation by Enrique Lynch. The original title is *A verdade e as formas jurídicas* (Pontificia Universidade Católica do Rio de Janeiro, 1978). I have not been able to locate the original.

118. *GS*, Book 3, 151.

119. *GS*, Book 5, 353.

120. Nietzsche often uses *Herkunft* when his analysis is related to race, as Foucault signals in a footnote, as in *The Gay Science* where his genealogy of sin sees its rootedness in Jewish feeling rather than Greek, as in *Beyond Good and Evil* where he relates modern weakness with the mixing of races, or as in *On the Genealogy of Morals* where his discussion of the etymology of *esthlos* includes racial comparisons. *GS*, 135; *BGE*, 200; *GM*, I,5.

121. "NGH," 151–52 (ET, 145–46).

122. "NGH," 152 (ET, 146).

123. "NGH," 152 (ET, 146). Translation ever so slightly modified. To translate "vaut critique" as "has value as a critique" takes the edge off the word "critique" as a technical term.

124. We follow Foucault here. He cites the text as "*Crépuscule*, Raisons de la philosophie." Nietzsche's title reads "Die "Vernuft" in der Philosophie."

125. Nietzsche, *Twilight of the Idols,* translated by R. J. Hollingdale (New York: Penguin Books, 1968) "'Reason' in Philosophy," I. All references in this paragraph are to this chapter of *Twilight.* I follow Hollingdale's translation.

126. Nietzsche, "'Reason' in Philosophy," I.

127. Nietzsche, "'Reason' in Philosophy," 5.

128. *LMC,* 327 (ET, 317).

129. "NGH," 154 (ET, 148).

130. "NGH," 163 (ET, 156).

131. "NGH," 155 (ET, 148).

132. "NGH," 156–57 (ET, 150). For each clause in this passage Foucault cites a text from Nietzsche: *BGE,* 260 and *GM,* II, 12; *The Wanderer and his Shadow,* 9: *GS,* 111.

133. "NGH," 156 (ET, 150).

134. Dreyfus and Rabinow, *Michel Foucault: Beyond Structuralism and Hermeneutics,* 109.

135. "Qu'est-ce qu'un auteur?" in *Bulletin de la société Francaise de philosophie* 64 (1969), 95. English translation in *Language, Counter-Memory, Practice,* 138.

136. "NGH," 159 (ET, 152).

137. "NGH," 165 (ET, 158).

138. In a 1978 roundtable discussion Foucault put the matter in an interesting fashion: "The history of the 'objectification' of those elements that historians consider as objectively given (if I dare put it thus: of the objectification of objectivities), this is the sort of circle I want to try and investigate." *L'impossible prison,* 55 (ET, 116).

139. "NGH," 167 (ET, 160).

140. "Theatrum Philosophicum" in *Critique* 282 (November, 1970), 887. English translation in *Language, Counter-Memory, Practice,* 168.

141. "NGH," 159 (ET, 153).

142. "NGH," 160 (ET, 154).

143. *AS,* 172–73 (ET, 131).

144. *AS,* 38–39 (ET, 27).

145. "Monstrosities in Criticism" in *Diacritics* 1, 1 (Fall, 1971), 60.

146. "Michel Foucault explique son dernier livre" in *Magazine Littéraire* 28 (April–May, 1969), 23.

147. This is not to suggest that Nietzsche limited his analyses to philology. He attributed many of the philosophers' errors to grammar. Cf. for example, *Twilight of the Idols*, "'Reason' in Philosophy," 5.

148. *AS*, part 3, chap. 1.

149. John Searle, *Speech Acts: An Essay in the Philosophy of Language* (Cambridge University Press, 1969), 26.

150. *AS*, 120 (ET, 91).

151. Tracy B. Strong, *Friedrich Nietzsche and the Politics of Transfiguration* (Berkeley: University of California Press, 1975), 13 and 17.

152. "Entretien avec Michel Foucault" in *Le livre des autres*, 139. *Sous-sol* also carries the connotation of "substratum" or "basement."

153. *AS*, 57 (ET, 41).

154. *AS*, 65 (ET, 47–48).

155. "NFM," 189. Cf. Gary Gutting's interesting analysis of this essay in *Michel Foucault's Archaeology of Scientific Reason* (New York: Cambridge University Press, 1989), 273ff.

156. "NFM," 190.

157. David Couzens Hoy, "Philosophy as Rigorous Philology? Nietzsche and Poststructuralism" in *Fragments: Incompletion and Discontinuity* (New York: New York Literary Forum, 1981), 176.

158. Foucault's reading of Nietzsche, thus, is closer to Sarah Kofman's than to Heidegger's. According to Kofman, "The value of evaluations cannot be referred to a truth of being or to an essence of being because, on the contrary, the essence and the 'truth' are constituted by the interpretations which take hold of being." Sarah Kofman, "Généalogie, Interprétation, Texte," which appears as an appendix to her *Nietzsche et la métaphore* (Paris: Payot, 1972), 179. This essay, which originally appeared in *Critique* (April, 1970), is a critical review of Jean Granier's *Le problème de la vérité dans la philosophie de Nietzsche* which Kofman judges overly influenced by the Heideggerian appropriation of Nietzsche.

159. *AS*, 126 (ET, 95–96).

160. "NFM," 191.

161. Searle, *Speech Acts*, 42–50. Cf. also P. F. Strawson, "Intention and Convention in Speech Acts" in John Searle, *The Philosophy of Language* (Oxford University Press, 1971), 23–38.

162. By citing the enunciative function, Foucault flags the point at which archaeology and genealogy dovetail; he signals the basis for his famous notion of "Power/Knowledge." The archaeologist is quite aware of the fact that discourse is embedded in an associated domain of institution-

al and other non-discursive conditions. *L'archéologie du savoir* simply attempts to respect the integrity of the truth axis; only then is it ready to open onto this embeddedness in non-discursive practices in the genealogy of the power axis.

163. *AS*, 76–77 (ET, 57). *Les mots et les choses* revealed that natural history, for example, did not simply involve a redefinition of concepts. Natural history "was a set of rules for arranging statements in series, an obligatory set of schemata of dependence, of order, and of successions, in which the recurrent elements that may have value as concepts were distributed," and these rules of formation of concepts cry out for analysis.

164. *AS*, 133 (ET, 101).

165. *AS*, 138 (ET, 105).

166. Jürgen Habermas, "What is Universal Pragmatics?" in *Communication and the Evolution of Society*, translated by Thomas McCarthy (Boston: Beacon Press, 1979), 38.

167. "Corso del 14 gennaio 1976," 179–80 (ET, 93).

168. *AS*, 234 (ET, 179).

169. *AS*, 167 (ET, 127).

170. "Deuxième entretien avec Michel Foucault," 201. Cf. for example, Noam Chomsky, *Aspects of the Theory of Syntax* (Cambridge: MIT Press, 1965) and *Reflections on Language* (New York: Random House, 1975).

171. "Deuxiéme entretien avec Michel Foucault," 201.

172. "Corso del 7 gennaio 1976," 165. Since the French text of this lecture has not appeared, the closest thing we have to an original version is the Italian translation by Alessandro Fontana and Pasquale Pasquino in *Microfisica del Potere* (ET, 80). The Italian reads "efficacia delle critiche discontinue, particolari e locali." Since my interpretation places a heavy burden on the word "critique," I render "critiche" as "critique" rather than Colin Gordon's "criticism."

173. "Corso del 7 gennaio 1976," 165 (ET, 80).

174. "Corso del 7 gennaio 1976," 165–66 (ET, 81).

175. "Corso del 7 gennaio 1976," 166 (ET, 81).

176. "Corso del 7 gennaio 1976," 166 (ET, 81).

177. "Corso del 7 gennaio 1976," 167–68 (ET, 82).

178. "Corso del 7 gennaio 1976," 167 (ET, 82).

179. *SP*, 35 (ET, 31).

180. "Entretien avec Michel Foucault" in *Le livre des autres*, 139.

181. John K. Simon, "A Conversation with Michel Foucault" in *Partisan Review*, 38, 2 (1971), 192.

182. "Conversazione con Michel Foucault" in Paolo Caruso, *Conversazione con Levi-Strauss, Foucault, Lacan* (Milano: U. Mursia and Co., 1969), 103.

183. "Conversazione con Michel Foucault," 103.

184. "Conversazione con Michel Foucault," 116.

185. "Non au sexe roi" (ET, 156).

186. "NGH," 163 (ET, 156–57). "Elle a à être la science des remèdes.... de trouver le meilleur antidote."

187. Cf. Benhabib, *Critique, Norm, and Utopia: A Study of the Foundations of Critical Theory*, 61. "Critical philosophy is a philosophy of the present, but one which conceives of the present as a radical future."

188. *LMC*, 311 (ET, 298).

189. Martin Heidegger, "The Age of the World Picture" in *The Question Concerning Technology and Other Essays*, translated by William Lovitt (New York: Harper and Row, 1977), 153.

190. "Intervista a Michel Foucault" in *Microfisica del Potere*, 8 (ET, 144).

191. "Sur la sellette" in *Les nouvelles littéraires* 2477 (March 17, 1975), 3. English translation by Renée Morel in *History of the Present* 1 (February, 1985), 2.

192. "Entretien sur la prison: le livre et sa méthode" in *Magazine Littéraire*, 101 (June, 1975), 32 (ET in *Power/Knowledge*, 49).

193. *GM2*, 12.

194. David Couzens Hoy, "Nietzsche, Hume, and the Genealogical Method" in Yirmiyahu Yovel (editor), *Nietzsche as Affirmative Thinker* (The Netherlands: Martinus Nijhoff, 1986), 21.

Chapter 5

1. "Entretien sur la prison: le livre et sa méthode" in *Magazine Littéraire* 101 (June, 1975), 33. English translation in Colin Gordon (ed.), *Power/Knowledge* (New York: Pantheon, 1980), 53.

2. "Les intellectuels et le pouvoir," in *L'Arc* 49 (1972) 6. English translation by Donald F. Bouchard and Sherry Simon in Donald F.

Bouchard (ed.), *Language, Counter-Memory, Practice* (Ithaca: Cornell University Press, 1977), 210.

3. "Pouvoir et corps" in *Quel corps?* 2 (1975) 33 (ET, 61).

4. "Les rapports de pouvoir passent à l'intérieur des corps" in *Quinzaine Littéraire* 247 (January, 1977), 5. English translation by Leo Marshall in *Power/Knowledge,* 187.

5. *L'impossible prison,* 41 (ET, 102). Translation slightly modified—"reprendre le thème de la généalogie de la morale."

6. *L'impossible prison,* 42 (ET, 102-103). Translation modified—"le lieu d'enchaînement de ce qu'on dit et de ce qu'on fait, des règles qu'on s'impose et des raisons qu'on se donne, des projets et des évidences."

7. *L'Impossible prison,* 43 (ET, 103).

8. Cited as a "personal communication" in Hubert Dreyfus and Paul Rabinow, *Michel Foucault: Beyond Structuralism and Hermeneutics,* Second Edition (Chicago: University of Chicago Press, 1983), 187.

9. *L'Impossible prison,* 53 (ET, 113).

10. "Entretien sur la prison," 27 (ET, 38).

11. "Questions à Michel Foucault sur la géographie" in *Hérodote* 1 (1976), 85. English translation by Colin Gordon in *Power/Knowledge,* 77.

12. *SP,* 27. (ET, 23).

13. *SP,* 34 (ET, 29–30).

14. *LMC,* 359 (ET, 348).

15. "The Political Technology of Individuals," in *Technologies of the Self: A Seminar with Michel Foucault,* edited by Luther H. Martin, Huck Gutman, and Patrick H. Hutton (Amherst: University of Massachusetts Press, 1988),146.

16. "Corso del 14 gennaio 1976," in Alessandro Fontana and Pasquale Pasquino (eds.), *Microfiscia del Potere* (Torino: Einaudi, 1977), 184–85. English translation by Kate Soper in *Power/Knowledge,* 98.

17. "Michel Foucault on Attica" in *Telos* 19 (1974),155. The interview was conducted in 1972.

18. "Michel Foucault on Attica," 156.

19. *La Verdad y las Formas Jurídicas* (Barcelona: Gedisa, 1980), 127–28. Notice how in 1973 he overcompensates for his earlier emphasis, in *Histoire de la folie,* upon power's capacity to exclude: "The factory does not exclude individuals, it binds them to a production apparatus. The

school does not exclude individuals, even when it locks them up, it binds them to an apparatus for the transmission of knowledge. The psychiatric hospital does not exclude individuals, it binds them to an apparatus of correction and normalization. And the same occurs with the reformatory and the prison."

20. *La Verdad y las Formas Jurídicas,* 137.

21. Frank Lentricchia, "Reading Foucault (Punishment, Labor, Resistance)" in *Raritan* I, 4 (Spring, 1982), 7.

22. *GM*, 2, 1.

23. *GM*, 2, 1.

24. *GM*, 2, 1.

25. *GM*, 2, 1.

26. *GM*, 2, 2.

27. *Daybreak,* 9.

28. *GM*, 2, 2.

29. *GM*, 2, 3.

30. *GM*, 2, 3.

31. *GM*, 2, 3.

32. *GM*, 2, 4.

33. *GM*, 2, 4.

34. *GM*, 2, 5.

35. *GM*, 2, 5.

36. *GM*, 2, 6.

37. *GM*, 2, 8.

38. *GM*, 2, 13.

39. *GM*, 2, 13.

40. *GM*, 2, 13.

41. *GM*, 2, 13.

42. *GM*, 2, 14.

43. *GM*, 2, 16.

44. *GM*, 2, 16.

220 *Notes*

45. *GM*, 2, 16.

46. *GM*, 2, 17.

47. Emile Durkheim, "The Evolution of Punishment" in Steven Lukes and Andrew Scull (eds.), *Durkheim and the Law* (New York: St. Martin's Press, 1983), 102–32.

48. "Entretien sur la prison." *Magazine littéraire* 101 (June, 1975), 28. English translation in Colin Gordon (ed.), *Power/Knowledge* (New York: Pantheon, 1980), 39.

49. "Questions à Michel Foucault sur la géographie" in *Hérodote* 1 (1976), 81. English translation in Colin Gordon (ed.), *Power/Knowledge*, 73–74.

50. *SP*, 28 (ET, 23).

51. *SP*, 28 (ET, 23).

52. *SP*, 28 (ET, 23).

53. *SP*, 22 (ET, 17).

54. *SP*, 22-23 (ET, 17).

55. *SP*, 24 (ET, 19).

56. *SP*, 23 (ET, 18).

57. *SP*, 52 (ET, 48).

58. *SP*, 53 (ET, 49–50).

59. *SP*, 59 (ET, 55).

60. *SP*, 61 (ET, 57).

61. *SP*, 64 (ET, 60–61).

62. *SP*, 90 (ET, 87).

63. *SP*, 80 (ET, 77–78), translation modified. Sheridan renders "les mécanismes de pouvoir qui encadrent l'existence des individus" as "the mechanisms of power that frame the everyday lives of individuals." I think Foucault is making a stronger claim in his historical ontology.

64. *SP*, 95–96 (ET, 93).

65. *SP*, 97 (ET, 94).

66. *SP*, 111 (ET, 109).

67. *SP*, 112 (ET, 110).

68. *SP*, 76 (ET, 74).

69. *SP*, 76 (ET, 74).

70. *SP*, 102 (ET, 100).

71. *SP*, 101 (ET, 98).

72. *SP*, 102 (ET, 99).

73. "Intervista a Michel Foucault" in *Microfisica del Potere*, 18–19. English translation by Colin Gordon in *Power/Knowledge*, 124–25.

74. *SP*, 131–32 (ET, 128–29).

75. *SP*, 172 (ET, 170).

76. *SP*, 215 (ET, 214).

77. "Entretien sur la prison," 28 (ET, 40).

78. *SP*, 143 (ET, 141).

79. "Questions à Michel Foucault sur la géographie," 77 (ET, 69).

80. "L'oeil du pouvoir," the preface to Jeremy Bentham, *Le Panoptique* (Paris: Pierre Belfond, 1977),12. English translation by Colin Gordon in Colin Gordon (ed.), *Power/Knowledge* (New York: Pantheon, 1980), 149.

81. *SP*, 145 (ET, 143).

82. "L'oeil du pouvoir," (ET, 153).

83. *SP*, 174 (ET, 172).

84. "L'oeil du pouvoir," (ET, 154).

85. *La Verdad y las Formas Jurídicas*, 98.

86. *La Verdad y las Formas Jurídicas*, 119–20.

87. *La Verdad y las Formas Jurídicas*, 118.

88. *SP*, 202 (ET, 200).

89. "L'oeil du pouvoir," 19 (ET, 155).

90. "Entretien avec Michel Foucault" in *Pro-Justicia* 3–4 (October, 1973), 7.

91. "L'extension sociale de la norme" in *Politique hebdo* 212 (March, 1976), 213.

92. *Généalogie des équipements de normalisation: les équipements sanitaires* (Fontenoy-sous-Bois: CERFI, 1976), 14.

93. *Généalogie des équipements de normalisation*, 19.

94. *Généalogie des équipements de normalisation*, 23.

95. *Généalogie des équipements de normalisation*, 53.

96. *Généalogie des équipements de normalisation*, 66.

97. *SP*, 153–54 (ET, 152).

98. "Entretien sur la prison," 28 (ET, 39).

99. *La Verdad y las Formas Jurídicas*, 133.

100. *Généalogie des équipements de normalisation*, 27–28.

101. *SP*, 181 (ET, 178).

102. *SP*, 185 (ET, 182).

103. *SP*, 183 (ET, 181).

104. *SP*, 185–86 (ET, 183).

105. *SP*, 187 (ET, 184).

106. *SP*, 192 (ET, 190).

107. *SP*, 196 (ET, 194).

108. *Généalogie des équipements de normalisation*, 35.

109. *Moi, Pierre Rivière, ayant égorgé ma mère, ma soeur et mon frère...* (Paris: Gallimard, 1973), 73. English translation by Frank Jellinek in *I, Pierre Riviere, having slaughtered my mother, my sister, and my brother* (New York: Pantheon, 1973), 54–55.

110. "Entretien avec Michel Foucault" in *Cahiers du cinéma* 271 (November, 1976), 52.

111. "Entretien sur la prison," 32 (ET, 49).

112. "L'evolution de la notion d' 'individu dangereux' dans la psychiatrie legale" in *Déviance et Société* 5, 4 (1981), 404. The essay originally appeared in English translation as "About the Concept of the "Dangerous Individual" in 19th-Century Legal Psychiatry, *International Journal of Law and Psychiatry* 1 (1978), 2.

113. "L'evolution de la notion d' 'individu dangereux' dans la psychiatrie legale," 404 (ET, 2).

114. "L'evolution de la notion d' 'individu dangereux' dans la psychiatrie legale," 404 (ET, 2).

115. *La Verdad y las Formas Jurídicas*, 97.

116. "L'evolution de la notion d' 'individu dangereux' dans la psychiatrie legale," 404 (ET, 2).

Chapter 6

1. Cf. *Histoire de la sexualité 1, La volonté de savoir* (Paris: Galli-mard, 1976). Hereafter cited as *VS*. Part 4, Sections 3 and 4. Apparently Foucault attempted to complete the project outlined in Volume One and "very nearly died of boredom writing those books." "Une esthétique de l'existence" in *Le monde aujoùrd'hui* (July, 1984). English translation in Lawrence D. Kritzman (ed.), *Michel Foucault: Politics, Philosophy, Cul-ture* (New York: Routledge, 1988).

2. *Histoire de la sexualité 2: L'usage des plaisirs* (Paris: Gallimard, 1984). Hereafter cited as *UP*. Because of Foucault's untimely death days after the publication of the second and third volumes, and in accordance with his wish, Volume Four on the Church Fathers should never appear. Sufficient material is available in lecture and interview form to allow us to reconstruct the general outlines of Foucault's analysis of the Christian experience.

3. "Sexual Choice, Sexual Act," an interview with James O'Higgins in *Salmagundi*, 58-59 (Fall 1982/Winter 1983), 10. Reprinted in *Politics, Philosophy, Culture*, 287.

4. *UP*, 10 (ET, 4).

5. Foucault explicitly affirms the continuity of his history of sexuali-ty project with Nietzschean genealogy. When asked whether his sexuality series amounts to "a new genealogy of morals," Foucault replied, "Not withstanding the solemnity of the title and the grandiose mark that Niet-zsche has left on it, I'd say yes." "Un esthétique de l'existence" (ET, 48).

6. *UP*, 11 (ET, 5).

7. "Original Preface" in Paul Rabinow (ed.), *The Foucault Reader* (New York: Pantheon, 1984), 336.

8. In his last interview Foucault expressed regret that his previous books had focused upon the power and truth axes at the expense of the subject axis. "Le retour de la morale" in *Les Nouvelles* 2937 (June 28–July 5, 1984), 38. English translation by Thomas Levin and Isabelle Lorenz in *Raritan* (Summer 1985). Reprinted in *Politics, Philosophy, Culture*, 243.

9. "Original Preface," 339.

10. "Original Preface," 339.

11. As Foucault put it in a 1984 interview, "instead of studying sex-uality on the borders of knowledge and power, I have tried to go further back, to find out how, for the subject himself, the experience of his sexuali-ty as desire had been constituted." "Une esthétique de l'existence" (ET, 48).

12. "The Subject and Power," Afterword in Dreyfus and Rabinow, 214.

13. In spite of the apparent rupture in the body of his work occasioned by his turn to Greek antiquity, Foucault emphasizes the continuity of this project with his previous writings. "I don't think there is a great difference between these books and the earlier ones." "Une esthétique de l'existence." ET, 48. "In this respect, these books are very similar to the ones I wrote on madness and penal history." "Le souci de la vérité" in *Magazine Littéraire*, 207 (May, 1984), 18. English translation in *Politics, Philosophy, Culture*, 257.

14. "Le souci de la vérité," 21. ET, 262.

15. "Sexuality and Solitude" in David Rieff (ed.), *Humanities in Review I* (New York: Cambridge University Press, 1982), 11.

16. We must take seriously Bernauer's admonition: "The failure to recognize the confrontation with Freud that is taking place in Foucault's last works has often prevented commentators from appreciating his intentions and organization in these writings, most especially with regard to their central history of the man of desire." James W. Bernauer, *Michel Foucault's Force of Flight* (Atlantic Highlands, N.J.: Humanities Press International, 1990), 167. "The history of the deployment of sexuality, as it has evolved since the classical age," according to Foucault, "can serve as an archaeology of psychoanalysis." VS, 172 (ET, 130).

17. "L'Occident et la vérité du sexe" in *Le Monde* 9885 (Nov. 5, 1976), 24. English translation by Lawrence Winters in *Substance* 20 (1978), 6. Gerson, a fifteenth-century educator and mystic, wrote the first treatise on sin, according to Foucault. VS, 154 (ET, 117).

18. "L'Occident et la vérité du sexe," 24 (ET, 6).

19. *UP*, 11 (ET, 5).

20. "Original Preface," 333.

21. "Original Preface," 334.

22. *UP*, 9 (ET, 3).

23. *GM* III, 8.

24. *GM* III, 2.

25. *GM* III, 25.

26. *GM* III, 25.

27. *GM* III, 5.

28. *GM* III, 7.

29. *GM* III, 8.

30. Alexander Nehamas, *Nietzsche: Life as Literature* (Cambridge: Harvard University Press, 1985), 116.

31. *GM* III, 9.

32. *GM* III, 10.

33. *GM* III, 11.

34. *GM* III, 11.

35. *GM* III, 11.

36. *GM* III, 11.

37. *GM* III, 15.

38. *GM* III, 15.

39. *GM* III, 16.

40. We may be free about chronology, it seems, since the order in which these works appeared is the opposite of the order in which they were written. Cf. "Le retour de la morale," 37 (ET, 242).

41. Cf. *UP*, 39 (ET, 32) and "On the Genealogy of Ethics: An Overview of Work in Progress" in Hubert Dreyfus and Paul Rabinow, *Michel Foucault: Beyond Structuralism and Hermeneutics,* Second Edition (Chicago: University of Chicago Press, 1983),352.

42. For example, "you have nearly the same restrictive, the same prohibition code in the fourth century B.C. and in the moralists and doctors at the beginning of the Empire. But I think that the way they integrate those prohibitions in relation to oneself is completely different." "On the Genealogy of Ethics," 341.

43. "On the Genealogy of Ethics," 353.

44. "On the Genealogy of Ethics," 354.

45. "On the Genealogy of Ethics," 355.

46. *UP*, 45 (ET, 37).

47. *UP*, 47 (ET, 38).

48. *UP*, 48-49 (ET, 39–40).

49. *UP*, 52-53 (ET, 43).

50. For the Greek, "[s]exual activity is represented, perceived as violence, and therefore problematized from the point of view of the difficulty there is in controlling it." "Le Souci de la vérité," 20 (ET, 261).

51. Among the significant transformations that Christianity would bring was the extension of the ethic of the flesh to women as well as men. In Greek antiquity the ethic of self-control was directed only to the person who must master himself and others, not to those whose ethic is one of obedience. Cf. "Le Souci de la vérité," 20 (ET, 261).

52. *UP*, 57 (ET, 47).

53. *UP*, 59 (ET, 49).

54. *UP*, 60 (ET, 50).

55. Cf. Foucault's analysis of Artemidorus' *The Interpretation of Dreams* of the second century C.E. in part I of *Le souci de soi*. Because of his central role in *SS*, and since the fourth volume of the history of sexuality has never appeared, it is easy to over-estimate Artemidorus' importance in his own right for Foucault. Artemidorus' *Interpretation of Dreams* functions in the genealogy as a whole as a paradigm of the Roman period which vividly displays a contrast with the Christian understanding of sexuality (as manifest in Augustine) and the modern (as manifest in Freud). For this reason I refer to him as a transitional figure. Cf. Foucault's important essay, "Sexuality and Solitude."

56. "Sexuality and Solitude," 13. Artemidorus maintained clear objections to sexual relations between mother and son. "But it is noteworthy," according to Foucault, "that he assigns it a predictive value that is often favorable...." *SS*, 35 (ET, 22).

57. Recall that Freud interpreted Hans's horse phobia as resulting from his repressed, erotic longing for his mother which manifested itself in dreams. "Hans really was a little Oedipus who wanted to have his father 'out of the way, to get rid of him,' so that he might be alone with his beautiful mother and sleep with her." Sigmund Freud, "Analysis of a Phobia in a Five-Year-Old Boy in James Strachey (ed.), *The Standard Edition* 10 (London: Hogarth, 1955), 111.

58. "Sexuality and Solitude," 14.

59. "Sexuality and Solitude," 14.

60. "Sexuality and Solitude," 15.

61. *UP*, 62 (ET, 52).

62. *UP*, 63 (ET, 53).

63. *UP*, 63-64 (ET, 53–54).

64. *UP*, 73 (ET, 62).

65. *UP*, 70 (ET, 60).

66. *UP*, 72-73 (ET, 62).

67. "Une esthétique de l'existence" (ET, 49). Part of Foucault's decision to shift his attention to antiquity is because this Christian notion of obedience to a set of rules, in our time, is dead. "And to this absence of morality corresponds, must correspond, the search for an aesthetics of existence."

68. "Le souci de la vérité," 18 (ET, 256).

69. "Les rapports de pouvoir passent à l'intérieur des corps" in *Quinzoine Littéraire* 247 (January, 1977), 6. English translation by Leo Marshall in Colin Gordon (ed.), *Power/Knowledge* (New York: Pantheon, 1980), 197.

70. "Sexuality and Solitude," 12.

71. *UP*, 76 (ET, 65).

72. *UP*, 77 (ET, 65).

73. *UP*, 79 (ET, 68).

74. *UP*, 82 (ET, 70).

75. *UP*, 89 (ET, 77).

76. *UP*, 90 (ET, 77).

77. "Sexuality and Solitude," 15.

78. "Le jeu de Michel Foucault" in *Ornicar?* 10 (July 1977), 68 (ET, 200).

79. *VS*, 28 (ET, 19).

80. "Sexuality and Solitude," 16.

81. "Le jeu de Michel Foucault," 68.

82. "Les rapports de pouvoir passent à l'intérieur des corps," 5 (ET, 186).

83. *VS*, 80 (ET, 59).

84. "L'Occident et la vérité du sexe," 24 (ET, 6).

85. "Truth and Subjectivity." Audiotape (Language Library at the University of California at Berkeley: October 20–21, 1980).

86. "Truth and Subjectivity."

87. "Truth and Subjectivity."

88. "Truth and Subjectivity."

89. "Truth and Subjectivity."

90. *UP*, 91 (ET, 78).

91. *UP*, 92 (ET, 79).

92. *UP*, 93–94 (ET, 80).

93. *UP*, 96 (ET, 82-83).

94. *UP*, 96 (ET, 83).

95. *UP*, 99 (ET, 86).

96. *UP*, 100 (ET, 86).

97. *UP*, 101 (ET, 87).

98. *UP*, 101 (ET, 88).

99. *UP*, 103 (ET, 89).

100. "La governamentalità" in *Aut Aut* 167–68 (September–December, 1978), 12. English translation by Rosi Braidotti, "Governmentality," in *Ideology and Consciousness* 6 (Autumn, 1979), 5.

101. "La governamentalità," 12 (ET, 5–6).

102. "La governamentalità," 16 (ET, 8).

103. By the eighteenth century, sex too became a police matter. *VS*, 35 (ET, 24).

104. "La governamentalità," 17 (ET, 10).

105. "La governamentalità," 17 (ET, 10). Up to the end of the eighteenth century, "[t]he marriage relation was under constant surveillance." *VS*, 52 (ET, 37).

106. "La governamentalità," 17 (ET, 10). Cf. also *VS*, 35 (ET, 25).

107. "Le Souci de la vérité," 21 (ET, 262).

108. *La Verdad y las Formas Jurídicas* (Barcelona: Gedisa, 1980), 37.

109. *La Verdad y las Formas Jurídicas*, 147.

110. "Enfermement, Psychiatrie, Prison" in *Change: La folie encerclée* 32–33 (October, 1977), 77–78. ET, 180–81, modified; "C'est la vraie vocation de la psychiatrie. Et c'est son climat, et c'est son horizon de naissance."

111. *La Verdad y las Formas Jurídicas*, 15. Cf. *VS*, 62 (ET, 45).

112. *VS*, 103.

113. "L'Occident et la vérité du sexe," 24 (ET, 7).

114. *VS*, 93 (ET, 69).

115. "Introduction" to *Herculine Barbin: Being the Recently Discovered Memoirs of a Nineteenth Century French Hermaphrodite*, x.

116. Two distinct orders of scientific knowledge developed in the nineteenth century according to distinct rules of formation: a biology of reproduction and a medicine of sex. *VS*, 73 (ET, 54).

117. *VS*, 90 (ET, 67).

118. "Les rapports de pouvoir passent à l'intérieur des corps," 6 (ET, 191). Cf. also "Le jeu de Michel Foucault," 78 (ET, 211).

119. *VS*, 35 (ET, 24).

120. *VS*, 189–90 (ET, 144).

121. *VS*, 190 (ET, 144).

122. *VS*, 187 (ET, 142).

123. "Les rapports de pouvoir passent à l'intérieur des corps," 6 (ET, 193).

124. "Pouvoirs et stratégies" in *Les Révoltes Logiques* 4 (1977), 97. English translation by Colin Gordon in *Power/Knowledge*, 145.

125. "Conversation with Michel Foucault," *Threepenny Review* I, 1 (Winter/Spring, 1980), 5.

126. Allan Megill, *Prophets of Extremity: Nietzsche, Heidegger, Foucault, Derrida* (Berkeley: University of California Press, 1985), 227ff. Larry Shiner, "Reading Foucault: Anti-Method and the Genealogy of Power/Knowledge" in *History and Theory*, 21 (1982).

127. "NGH," 167 (ET, 160).

128. "NGH," 167 (ET, 160).

129. It is for this reason, according to François Ewald, that Foucault shuns the "great" authors and "great" texts or at least treats them on an equal plain with other documents he has dredged up, those documents which the traditional use of the "greats" has made us forget. "Anatomie et corps politiques," 1230, 1232.

130. David Carroll, "Disruptive Discourse and Critical Power: The Conditions of Archaeology and Genealogy" in *Humanities in Society* 5, 3–4 (Summer/Fall, 1982), 187.

131. Milan Kundera, *The Book of Laughter and Forgetting* (New York: Penguin, 1980).

132. *The Order of Things*, Foreword to the English Edition, xiv.

133. "Structuralism and Post-Structuralism" in *Telos* 55 (Spring, 1983), 198.

134. "Truth and Subjectivity," the Howison Lecture delivered at the University of California at Berkeley, October 20, 1980.

135. "Un cours inédit" in *Magazine littéraire* 207 (May, 1984), 39. English translation by Colin Gordon in *Economy and Society* 15, 1 (February, 1986), 96.

136. J. G. Merquior, *Foucault* (Berkeley: University of California Press, 1985), 143, 145. While I obviously agree with Merquior that Foucault ought to be interpreted as a Nietzschean thinker, I disagree with his tendency to reduce this Nietzscheanism to irrationalism.

137. Merquior, *Foucault*, 101.

138. Kant's essay, "An Answer to the Question: What is Enlightenment?" had such urgency for Foucault that he continually raised it for discussion. To my knowledge, he raised it for the first time in a 1977 interview with Bernard Henri Levy ("Non au sexe roi" in *Le Nouvel Observateur* 644), and he pursued the question the following year in his introduction to the English edition of George Canguilhem's *On the Normal and the Pathological*. In 1979 he raised it again in his review of Jean Daniel's *L'ère des ruptures* (*Le Nouvel Observateur* 754) and again a year later in his "Postface" to *L'Impossible Prison*. In 1982 he raised Kant's essay on Enlightenment in his "Afterword" to Dreyfus and Rabinow and in an interview, "Space, Knowledge, and Power." The following year he discussed the essay in the interview, "Structuralism and Post-Structuralism," and his first lecture of his 1983 course at the Collège de France focused on this essay by Kant (cf. "Un cours inédit" in *Magazine littéraire*, 207, May, 1984). Finally, he suggested Kant's essay as the focus for discussions in Berkeley with Habermas, and in 1984 his own essay, "What is Enlightenment?" appeared.

139. "La vie: l'expérience et la science," 6 (ET, xii).

140. "What is Enlightenment?" in Paul Rabinow (ed.), *The Foucault Reader* (New York: Pantheon, 1984), 38.

141. "La vie: l'expérience et la science," 5 (ET, x), translation slightly modified: the last few lines of the French read "celle de son passé immédiat et de ses conditions d'exercice, celle de son moment, de son lieu, et de son actualité."

142. "Un cours inédit," 35. English translation by Colin Gordon, "Kant on Enlightenment and Revolution" in *Economy and Society* 15 (February, 1986), 89. Translation slightly modified; Colin Gordon renders "sa propre actualité discursive" with the neologism "its own discursive present-ness."

143. "What is Enlightenment?" 42.

144. "What is Enlightenment?" 42. Cf. Thomas R. Flynn, "Foucault and the Politics of Postmodernity" in *Noûs* 23 (1989), 193. "That *any* of the claims of the Enlightenment thinkers should be held beyond questioning, [Foucault] maintains in implicit criticism of Habermas, is contrary to the critical spirit of that great event itself, a violation of its guiding *ethos*."

145. "Un cours inédit," 39 (ET, 95).

146. Ian Hacking, "The Archaeology of Foucault" in David Couzens Hoy (ed.), *Foucault: A Critical Reader* (New York: Basil Blackwell, 1986), 40.

147. "What is Enlightenment?" 44.

148. Cf. David R. Hiley, "Foucault and the Question of Enlightenment," in *Philosophy and Social Criticism*, 11, 1 (Summer, 1985), 74.

149. "Intervista a Michel Foucault" in *Microfisica del Potere*, 25. English translation by colin Gordon in *Power/Knowledge*, 131.

150. Cf. "The Subject and Power" in Dreyfus and Rabinow, *Michel Foucault: Beyond Structuralism and Hermeneutics*, Second Edition (Chicago: University of Chicago Press, 1983), 213. In contrast to those political theories that view the state as a form of power which ignores individuals, Foucault wants "to underline the fact that the state's power...is both an individualizing and a totalizing form of power. Never, I think, in the history of human societies...has there been such a tricky combination in the same political structures of individualization techniques, and of totalization procedures."

151. Cf. "Sur la sellette," an interview conducted by Jean-Louis Ezine, in *Les nouvelles littéraires* 2477(March 17, 1975), 3. English translation by Renée Morel in *History of the Present* 1 (February, 1985), 2. "For a certain bourgeois liberalism to become possible at the level of institutions, it was necessary to have, at the level of what I call 'micro-powers,' a much stricter investment of individuals, it was necessary to organize the grid of bodies and behaviors. Discipline is the underside of democracy." Translation slightly modified. Morel omits the reference to the investment of individuals.

152. "Intervista a Michel Foucault," 15 (ET, 121).

Bibliography

This bibliography consists of six sections. Section A lists the writings of Michel Foucault used in this study. Section B lists Nietzsche's writings used in this study. Section C lists those secondary writings used in this study that directly address the relationship between Foucault and Nietzsche. Section D contains secondary works on Michel Foucault and Section E, secondary works on Nietzsche. Finally, Section F lists miscellaneous writings that proved helpful in the preparation of this study.

For a chronological bibliography of Michel Foucault's writings see James Bernauer and Thomas Keenan, "The Works of Michel Foucault, 1954–1984" in *Philosophy and Social Criticism*, Volume 12, No. 2–3, 1987, reissued as *The Final Foucault* (The MIT Press, 1988). Another helpful bibliography that includes secondary sources is Michael Clark, *Michel Foucault: An Annotated Bibliography* (New York: Garland Publishing, Inc., 1983).

A. The Writings of Michel Foucault

1. Books

L'archéologie du savoir. Paris: Gallimard, 1969. English translation by A. M. Sheridan Smith, *The Archaeology of Knowledge.* New York: Harper Colophon, 1976.

Folie et déraison: Histoire de la folie à l'âge classique. Paris: Plon, 1961. Reissued as *Histoire de la folie à l'âge classique.* Paris: Gallimard, 1978. Except for references to the original 1961 Preface, I use the 1978 edition in the present study. Dramatically abridged English translation by Richard Howard, *Madness and Civilization.* New York: Pantheon, 1965.

Généalogie des équipements de normalisation: les équipements sanitaires. Fontenay-sous-Bois: Centre d'études, de recherches et de formation institutionnelles (CERFI), 1976. A study done under the direction of Michel Foucault.

Histoire de la sexualité I: La volonté de savoir. Paris: Gallimard, 1976. English translation by Robert Hurley, *The History of Sexuality I: An Introduction.* New York: Pantheon, 1978.

Histoire de la sexualité 2: L'usage des plaisirs. Paris: Gallimard, 1984. English translation by Robert Hurley, *The Use of Pleasure.* New York: Pantheon, 1985.

Histoire de la sexualité 3: Le souci de soi. Paris: Gallimard, 1984. English translation by Robert Hurley, *The Care of the Self.* New York: Pantheon, 1986.

Maladie mentale et personnalité. Paris: Presses Universitaires de France, 1954.

Maladie mentale et psychologie. Paris: Presses Universitaires de France, 1962. English translation by Alan Sheridan, *Mental Illness and Psychology.* New York: Harper and Row, 1976.

Moi, Pierre Rivière, ayant égorgé ma mère, ma soeur et mon frère.... Study directed by Michel Foucault. Paris: Gallimard, 1973. English translation by Frank Jellinek. *I, Pierre Riviere, having slaughtered my mother, my sister, and my brother.* New York: Pantheon, 1975.

Les mots et les choses. Paris: Gallimard, 1966. English translation (unidentified), *The Order of Things: An Archaeology of the Human Sciences.* New York: Pantheon, 1971.

Naissance de la clinique: Une archéologie du regard médical. Paris: Presses Universitaires de France, 1963, 1972. English translation by Alan Sheridan Smith, *The Birth of the Clinic: An Archaeology of Medical Perception.* New York: Pantheon, 1973.

L'ordre du discours. Paris: Gallimard, 1971. English translation by Rupert Swyer, "The Discourse on Language" in *The Archaeology of Knowledge.* New York: Harper Colophon, 1976.

Raymond Roussel. Paris: Gallimard, 1963. English translation by Charles Ruas, *Death and the Labyrinth: The World of Raymond Roussel.* New York: Doubleday and Company, 1986.

Surveiller et punir: Naissance de la prison. Paris: Gallimard, 1975. English translation by Alan Sheridan, *Discipline and Punish: The Birth of the Prison.* New York: Pantheon, 1977.

La Verdad y las Formas Jurídicas. Barcelona: Gedisa, 1980. This is a Spanish translation by Enrique Lynch of five lectures delivered in 1973 at the Catholic University of Rio de Janeiro.

2. Essays and Interviews

"A Conversation with Michel Foucault." John K. Simon. *Partisan Review* 38, 2, 1971.

"Conversation with Michel Foucault." *Threepenny Review* I, 1, Winter/Spring, 1980.

"Conversazione con Michel Foucault." In Paolo Caruso, *Conversazione con Levi-Strauss, Foucault, Lacan.* Milano: U. Mursia and Co., 1969.

"Corso del 7 gennaio 1976" and "Corso del 14 gennaio 1976." Alessandro Fontana and Pasquale Pasquino (eds.). *Microfisica del Potere.* Torino: Einaudi, 1977. English translation by Kate Soper in *Power/Knowledge.* Edited by Colin Gordon. New York: Pantheon, 1980.

"Un cours inédit." *Magazine littéraire* 207, May, 1984. English translation by Colin Gordon. "Kant on Enlightenment and Revolution." *Economy and Society* 15, February, 1986.

"The Culture of the Self." Audiotape. Language Laboratory of the University of California at Berkeley. Spring, 1983.

"Débat sur la poésie." *Tel Quel* 17, Spring, 1964.

"Débat sur le roman." *Tel Quel* 17, Spring, 1964.

"Deuxième entretien avec Michel Foucault." In Raymond Bellour, *Le livre des autres.* Paris: Éditions de l'Herne, 1971.

"Les déviations religieuses et le savoir médical." Jacques LeGoff, *Hérésies et société dans l'Europe pré-industrielle lle-18e siècles.* Paris: Mouton, 1968.

"Un dibattito Foucault-Preti." *Bimestre* 22–23, September–December, 1972.

"Distance, aspect, origine." *Critique* 198, November, 1963.

"Enfermement, Psychiatrie, Prison." *Change: La folie encerclée* 32–33, October, 1977.

"Entretien avec Michel Foucault." *Cahiers du cinéma* 271, November, 1976.

"Entretien avec Michel Foucault." In Raymond Bellour, *Le livre des autres.* Paris: Éditions de l'Herne, 1971.

"Entretien avec Michel Foucault." *Pro-Justicia* 3–4, October, 1973.

"Entretien sur la prison: le livre et sa méthode." An interview conducted by J. J. Brochier. *Magazine Littéraire* 101, June, 1975. English translation in *Power/Knowledge.*

"Une esthétique de l'existence." *Le monde aujoùrd'hui* July, 1984. English translation in Lawrence D. Kritzman, editor, *Michel Foucault: Politics, Philosophy, Culture.* New York: Routledge, 1988.

"Est-il donc important de penser?" *Libération* May 30–31, 1981. English translation by Thomas Keenan. "Is it really important to think?" *Philosophy and Social Criticism* 9, 1, Spring, 1982.

"L'evolution de la notion d' 'individu dangereux' dans la psychiatrie legale." *Déviance et Société* 5, 1981. Originally appeared in English. "About the Concept of the 'Dangerous Individual' in 19th-Century Legal Psychiatry." *International Journal of Law and Psychiatry* 1, 1978.

"L'extension sociale de la norme." *Politique hebdo* 212, March, 1976.

"La folie n'existe que dans une société." *Le Monde* 5135, July 22, 1961.

"Foucault répond à Sartre." *La Quinzaine littéraire* 46, March 1–15, 1968.

"On the Genealogy of Ethics: An Overview of Work in Progress." An interview conducted with Hubert Dreyfus and Paul Rabinow in the second edition of their *Michel Foucault: Beyond Structuralism and Hermeneutics*. Chicago: University of Chicago Press, 1983.

"La gouvernamentalità." *Aut Aut* 167–68, September–December, 1978. English translation by Rosi Braidotti. "Governmentality." *Ideology and Consciousness* 6, Autumn, 1979.

"Guetter le jour qui vient." *La Nouvelle Revue Francaise* 130, October, 1963.

"Une histoire restée muette." *La Quinzaine Littéraire* 8, July 1, 1966.

"L'homme, est-il mort: Un entretien avec Michel Foucault." *Arts et loisirs* 38, June 15, 1966.

"Human Nature: Justice versus Power." In *Reflexive Water: The Basic Concerns of Mankind*. Edited by Fons Elder. London: Souvenir Press, 1974.

"Les Intellectuels et le pouvoir." *L'Arc* 49, 1972. English translation by Donald F. Bouchard and Sherry Simon in *Language, Counter-Memory, Practice*. Edited by Donald F. Bouchard. Ithaca: Cornell University Press, 1977.

"An Interview by Stephen Riggins." *Ethos* I, 2, Autumn, 1983.

"Intervista a Michel Foucault." in *Microfisica del Potere*. Edited by Alessandro Fontana and Pasquale Pasquino. English translation by Colin Gordon in *Power/Knowledge*.

"Introduction." In the English translation of *Herculine Barbin, Being the Recently Discovered Memoirs of a Nineteenth Century Hermaphrodite*. Translated by Richard McDougall. New York: Pantheon Books, 1980.

"Introduction." In Ludwig Binswanger, *Le rêve et l'existence*. Paris: Desclée de Brouwer, 1954. English translation by Forrest Williams. "Dream, Imagination, and Existence." *Review of Existential Psychology and Psychiatry* 19, 1, 1984–85.

"Introduction." In *Rousseau: Juge de Jean Jacques: Dialogues*. Paris: Librarie Armand Colin, 1962.

"Jean Hyppolite (1907–1968)." *Revue de métaphysique et de morale* 74, 2, April–June, 1969.

"Le jeu de Michel Foucault." *Ornicar?* July 10, 1977. English translation by Colin Gordon in *Power/Knowledge*.

"Le langage à l'infini." *Tel Quel* 15, Autumn, 1963. English translation in *Language, Counter-Memory, Practice*.

"Le langage de l'espace." *Critique* 203, April, 1964.

"Médecins, juges et sorciers au XVIIe siècle." *Médecine de France* 200, 1969.

"Michel Foucault explique son dernier livre." *Magazine Littéraire* 28, April-May, 1969.

"Michel Foucault on Attica." *Telos* 19, 1974.

"Monstrosities in Criticism." *Diacritics* 1, 1, Fall, 1971.

"Nietzsche, Freud, Marx." *Cahiers de Royaumont 6: Nietzsche*. Paris: Éditions de Minuit, 1967. English translation by Jon Anderson. *Critical Texts* III, 2, Winter, 1986.

"Nietzsche, l'généalogie, l'histoire." *Hommage à Jean Hyppolite*. Paris: Presses Universitaires de France, 1971. English translation in *Language, Counter-Memory, Practice*.

"Non au sexe roi." *Le Nouvel Observateur* 644, March 12, 1977. English translation by David Parent. "Power and Sex: An Interview with Michel Foucault." *Telos* 32, Summer, 1977.

"Le 'non' du père." *Critique* 178, March, 1962. English translation in *Language, Counter-Memory, Practice*.

"L'Occident et la vérité du sexe." *Le Monde* 9885, November 5, 1976. English translation by Lawrence Winters in *Substance* 20, 1978.

"L'Oeil du pouvoir." In Jeremy Bentham, *Le Panoptique*. Paris: Pierre Belfond, 1977. English translation by Colin Gordon in *Power/Knowledge*.

"Omnes et Singulatim: Towards a Criticism of 'Political Reason.'" In *The Tanner Lectures on Human Values II*. Edited by Sterling McMurrin. Salt Lake City: University of Utah Press, 1981.

"La pensée du dehors." *Critique* 229, 1966.

"Philosophie et psychologie." *Dossiers pédagogiques de la radio-télévision scolaire* 10, February 15–27, 1965.

"Polemics, Politics, and Problemizations: An Interview with Michel Foucault." In *The Foucault Reader*. Edited by Paul Rabinow. New York: Pantheon, 1984.

"The Political Technology of Individuals." In *Technologies of the Self: A Seminar with Michel Foucault*. Edited by Luther H. Martin, Hick Gutman, and Patrick H. Hutton. Amherst: University of Massachusetts Press, 1988.

"La poussière et le nuage." In *L'Impossible Prison*. Edited by Michelle Perrot. Paris: Éditions du Seuil, 1980.

"Pouvoir et corps." *Quel corps?* 2, 1975. English translation by Colin Gordon in *Power/Knowledge*.

"Pouvoirs et stratégies." *Les Révoltes Logiques* 4, 1977. English translation by Colin Gordon in *Power/Knowledge*.

"Préface à la transgression." *Critique* 195–96, August–September, 1963. English translation in *Language, Counter-Memory, Practice*.

"Preface to *The History of Sexuality, Volume II*." In *The Foucault Reader*.

"La prose d'Actéon." *La Nouvelle Revue Francaise* 135, March, 1964.

"Qu'est-ce qu'un auteur?" *Bulletin de la société francaise de philosophie* 64, 1969. English translation in *Language, Counter-Memory, Practice*.

"Questions à Michel Foucault sur la géographie." *Hérodote* 1, 1976. English translation by Colin Gordon in *Power/Knowledge*.

"Les rapports de pouvoir passent à l'intérieur des corps." *Quinzaine Littéraire* 247, January 1–15, 1977. English translation by Leo Marshall in *Power/Knowledge*.

"La recherche scientifique et la psychologie." *Des chercheurs francais s'interrogent*. Edited by Jean-Edouard Morère. Paris: Presses Universitaires de France, 1957.

"Réponse à une question." *Esprit* 371, May, 1968. English translation by

Anthony Nazzaro. "History, Discourse, and Discontinuity." *Psychological Man.* Edited by Robert Boyers. New York: Harper and Row, 1975.

"Le retour de la morale." *Les Nouvelles* 2937, June 28–July 5, 1984. English translation by Thomas Levin and Isabelle Lorenz in *Raritan* 5, 1, Summer, 1985.

"Sexual Choice, Sexual Act." An interview with James O'Higgins. *Salmagundi* 58–59, Fall 1982/Winter 1983.

"Sexuality and Solitude." *Humanities in Review* 1. Edited by David Rieff. New York: Cambridge University Press, 1982.

"La situation de Cuvier dans l'histoire de la biologie II." *Revue d'histoire des sciences et de leurs applications* 23, 1, January–March, 1970.

"Le souci de la vérité." *Magazine Littéraire* 207, May, 1984. English translation in *Politics, Philosophy, Culture.*

"Space, Knowledge, and Power." In *The Foucault Reader.*

"Structuralism and Post-Structuralism." *Telos* 55, Spring, 1983.

"The Subject and Power." In Dreyfus and Rabinow, *Michel Foucault: Beyond Structuralism and Hermeneutics.* Chicago: University of Chigaco Press, 1983.

"Sur la sellette." *Les nouvelles littéraires* 2477, March 17, 1975. English translation by Renée Morel. *History of the Present* 1, February, 1985.

"Table ronde du 20 mai 1978." In *L'Impossible Prison.* Edited by Michelle Perrot. Paris: Éditions du Seuil, 1980. English translation by Alan Bass. "Questions of Method." *After Philosophy: End or Transformation?* Edited by Kenneth Baynes, James Bohman, and Thomas McCarthy. Cambridge: The MIT Press, 1987.

"Theatrum Philosophicum." *Critique* 282, November, 1970. English translation in *Language, Counter-Memory, Practice.*

"Truth and Subjectivity." Audiotape. Language Laboratory at the University of California at Berkeley. October 20–21, 1980.

"La vie des hommes infâmes." *Les Cahiers du Chemin* 29, January 15, 1977. English translation by Paul Foss and Meaghan Morris in *Michel Foucault: Power, Truth, Strategy.* Edited by Meaghan Morris and Paul Patton. Sydney: Feral Publications, 1979.

"La vie: l'experience et la science." *Revue de la métaphysique et de morale* 90, 1985.

"What is Enlightenment?" In *The Foucault Reader.*

B. The Writings of Friedrich Nietzsche

Werke in Drei Bänden. Edited by Karl Schlechta. Munich: Carl Hanser Verlag, 1966.

The following English translations were used in this study:

The Antichrist. Translated by Walter Kaufmann. *The Portable Nietzsche.* New York: Viking, 1973. Written 1888, originally published 1895.

Beyond Good and Evil. Translated by R. J. Hollingdale. New York: Penguin Books, 1973. Originally published 1886.

The Birth of Tragedy. Translated by Walter Kaufmann. New York: Vintage, 1967. Originally published 1872.

Daybreak. Translated by R. J. Hollingdale. Cambridge: Cambridge University Press, 1982. Originally published 1881.

Ecce Homo. Translated by Walter Kaufmann. New York: Vintage, 1967. Written 1888, originally published 1908.

The Gay Science. Translated by Walter Kaufmann. New York: Vintage, 1974. Originally published 1882.

On the Genealogy of Morals. Translated by Walter Kaufmann and R. J. Hollingdale. New York: Vintage, 1967. Originally published 1887.

Human, All Too Human. Translated by Marion Faber. Lincoln: University of Nebraska Press, 1984. Originally published 1878.

Thus Spoke Zarathustra. Translated by Walter Kaufmann. *The Portable Nietzsche.* New York: Viking, 1973. Originally published from 1883–92.

Twilight of the Idols. Translated by R. J. Hollingdale. New York: Penguin Books, 1968. Originally published 1889.

The Uses and Disadvantages of History for Life. Translated by R. J. Hollingdale. *Untimely Meditations.* Cambridge University Press, 1983. Originally published 1873.

The Will to Power. Translated by Walter Kaufmann. New York: Vintage, 1968. Written from 1883–88.

C. Secondary Sources on the Nietzsche/Foucault Relationship

Ansell-Pearson, Keith. "The Significance of Michel Foucault's Reading of Nietzsche." *Nietzsche-Studien: Internationales Jahrbuch für die Nietzsche-Forschung* Band 20, 1991.

Arac, Jonathan. "The Function of Foucault at the Present Time." *Humanities in Society,* 3, 1, Winter, 1980.

Bapty, Ian. "Nietzsche, Derrida and Foucault: Re-excavating the Meaning of Archaeology." Edited by Ian Bapty and Tim Yates. *Archaeology after Structuralism.* London: Routledge, 1990.

Bové, Paul. "The End of Humanism: Michel Foucault and the Power of Disciplines." *Humanities in Society* 3, 1, Winter, 1980.

Carroll, David. "Disruptive Discourse and Critical Power: The Conditions of Archaeology and Genealogy." *Humanities in Society* 5, 3–4, Summer/Fall, 1982.

Connolly, William E. *The Terms of Political Discourse.* Princeton University Press, 1983.

Cotesta, Vittorio. *Linguaggio Potere Individuo: Saggio su Michel Foucault.* Dedalo Libri, 1979.

Davidson, Arnold I. "Archaeology, Genealogy, Ethics." *Foucault; A Critical Reader.* Edited by David Couzens Hoy. Oxford: Basil Blackwell, 1986.

Deleuze, Gilles. *Foucault.* Paris: Les Éditions de Minuit, 1986.

de Man, Paul. "Genesis and Genealogy in Nietzsche's *The Birth of Tragedy.*" *Diacritics* Winter, 1972.

Dews, Peter. *Logics of Disintegration: Post-Structuralist Thought and the Claims of Critical Theory.* New York: Verso, 1987.

Dews, Peter. "Power and Subjectivity in Foucault." *New Left Review* 144, March-April, 1984.

Dreyfus, Hubert. "Beyond Hermeneutics: Interpretation in Late Heidegger and Recent Foucault." *Hermeneutics: Questions and Prospects.* Edited by Gary Shapiro and Alan Sica. Amherst: University of Massachusetts Press, 1984.

Dreyfus, Hubert and Rabinow, Paul. *Michel Foucault: Beyond Structuralism and Hermeneutics,* Second Edition. Chicago: University of Chicago Press, 1983.

Ewald, Francois. "Anatomie et corps politiques." *Critique* 31, 1975.

Flynn, Bernard. "Sexuality, Knowledge and Power in the Thought of Michel Foucault." *Philosophy and Social Criticism* 8, 3, Fall, 1981.

Flynn, Bernard Charles. "Foucault and the Body Politic." *Man and World* 20, 1987.

Fraser, Nancy. "Michel Foucault: A 'Young Conservative'?" *Ethics* 96, October 1985.

Guédon, Jean Claude. "Michel Foucault: The Knowledge of Power and the Power of Knowledge." *Bulletin of the History of Medicine* 51, 1977.

Hinkle, Gisela. "Foucault's Power/Knowledge and American Sociological Theorizing." *Human Studies* 10, 1986.

Honneth, Axel. "Foucault et Adorno." *Critique* XLIL, 471–72.

Hoy, David Couzens (ed.). "Introduction." *Foucault: A Critical Reader.* New York: Basil Blackwell, 1986.

Ijsseling, S. "Foucault with Heidegger." *Man and World* 19, 1986.

Ingram, David. "Foucault and the Frankfurt School: A Discourse on Nietzsche, Power and Knowledge." *Praxis International* 6, 3, October, 1986.

Johnson, J. Scott. "Reading Nietzsche and Foucault: A Hermeneutics of Suspicion?" *American Political Science Review,* 85, 2, June, 1991.

Kaufmann, J. N. "Foucault historien et 'historien' du présent." *Dialogue,* XXV, 1986.

Kemp, Peter. "Review Essay" on Dreyfus and Rabinow, *Michel Foucault: Beyond Structuralism and Hermeneutics*

Kremer-Marietti, Angèle. *Michel Foucault: Archéologie et Généalogie.* Librairie Générale Française, 1985.

Laforest, Guy. "Regards généalogiques sur la modernité: Michel Foucault et la philosophie politique." *Canadian Journal of Political Science* XVIII, 1, March, 1985.

Lash, Scott. "Genealogy and the Body: Foucault/Deleuze/Nietzsche." *Theory, Culture, and Society* 2, 2, 1984.

Lemert, Charles and Gillan, Garth. *Michel Foucault: Social Theory and Transgression.* New York: Columbia University Press, 1982.

Lentricchia, Frank. "Reading Foucault (Punishment, Labor, Resistance)." *Raritan* I, 4, Spring, 1982.

Macherey, Pierre. "Aux sources de 'L'histoire de la folie.'" *Critique* XLIL, 471–72.

Major-Poetzl, Pamela. *Michel Foucault's Archaeology of Western Culture.* Chapel Hill: University of North Carolina Press, 1983.

Margot, Jean-Paul. "Herméneutique et fiction chez M. Foucault." *Dialogue* 23, 1984.

Megill, Allan. "Foucault, Structuralism, and the Ends of History." *Journal of Modern History* 51, 1979.

Megill, Allan. *Prophets of Extremity. Nietzsche, Heidegger, Foucault, Derrida.* Berkeley: University of California Press, 1985.

Merquior, J. G. *Foucault.* Berkeley: University of California Press, 1985.

Minson, Jeffrey. "Strategies for Socialists? Foucault's Conception of Power." Mike Gane. *Towards a Critique of Foucault.* Routledge, Kegan Paul, 1986.

Pace, David. "Structuralism in History and the Social Sciences." *American Quarterly* 30, 1978.

Paden, Roger. "Locating Foucault—Archaeology vs. Structuralism." *Philosophy and Social Criticism* 11, 2, Winter, 1986.

Paternek, Margaret A. "Norms and normalization: Michel Foucault's overextended panoptic machine." *Human Studies* 10, 1987.

Pippin, R. "Nietzsche and the Origin of the Idea of Modernism." *Inquiry* 26, 1983.

Pizer, John. "The Use and Abuse of 'Ursprung': On Foucault's Reading of Nietzsche." *Nietzsche-Studien*, Band 19, 1990.

Poster, Mark. *Existential Marxism in Postwar France.* Princeton University Press, 1975.

Racevskis, Karlis. *Michel Foucault and the Subversion of Intellect.* Ithaca: Cornell University Press, 1983.

Rajchman, John. *Michel Foucault: The Freedom of Philosophy.* New York: Columbia University Press, 1985.

Rajchman, John. "Nietzsche, Foucault and the Anarchism of Power." *Semiotext(e)* 3, 1, 1978.

Rorty, Richard. "Beyond Nietzsche and Marx." *London Review of Books*, February 19, 1981.

Rorty, Richard. "Foucault and Epistemology." Edited by David Couzens Hoy. *Foucault: A Critical Reader.* New York: Basil Blackwell, 1986.

Said, Edward. "An Ethics of Language." *Diacritics* 4, 2, Summer, 1974.

Sax, Benjamin C. "Foucault, Nietzsche, History: Two Modes of the Genealogical Method." *History of European Ideas* 11, 1989.

Scott, Charles E. *The Question of Ethics: Nietzsche, Foucault, Heidegger.* Bloomington: Indiana University Press, 1990.

Sheridan, Alan. *Michel Foucault: The Will to Truth.* London: Tavistock Publications, 1980.

Shiner, Larry. "Foucault, Phenomenology and the Question of Origins." *Philosophy Today,* Winter, 1982.

Shiner, Larry. "Reading Foucault: Anti-Method and the Genealogy of Power-Knowledge." *History and Theory* 21, 1982.

Taylor, Charles. "Foucault on Freedom and Truth." *Foucault: A Critical Reader.*

Thiele, Leslie Paul. "The Agony of Politics: The Nietzschean Roots of Foucault's Thought." *American Political Science Review,* 84, 3, September, 1990

Turner, Bryan S. "The Discourse of Diet." *Theory, Culture and Society* 1, 1, Spring, 1982.

Veyne, Paul. "Foucault révolutionne l'histoire." *Comment on écrit l'histoire.* Éditions du Seuil, 1978.

Wartenberg, Thomas E. "Foucault's Archaeological Method: A Response to Hacking and Rorty." *Philosophical Forum,* 15, 4, Summer, 1984.

White, Hayden. "Foucault Decoded: Notes from Underground." *History and Theory,* 12, 1973.

Wolin, Richard. "Foucault's Aesthetic Decisionism." *Telos* 67, Spring, 1986.

D. Secondary Works on Foucault

1. Books

Arac, Jonathan (ed.). *After Foucault: Humanistic Knowledge, Postmodern Challenges.* Rutgers University Press, 1988.

Bernauer, James W. *Michel Foucault's Force of Flight: Toward an Ethics for Thought.* Atlantic Highlands, N.J.: Humanities Press International, 1990.

Bernauer, James W. *The Thinking of History in the Archaeology of Michel Foucault.* Ann Arbor: University Microfilms International, 1981.

Carroll, David. *Paraesthetics: Foucault, Lyotard, Derrida.* New York: Methuen, 1987.

Cotesta, Vittorio. *Linguaggio Potere Individuo: Saggio su Michel Foucault.* Bari: Dedalo Libri, 1979.

Cousins, Mark and Hussain, Athar. *Michel Foucault.* New York: St. Martin's Press, 1984.

Deleuze, Gilles. *Foucault.* Paris: Les Éditions de Minuit, 1986.

Dews, Peter. *Logics of Disintegration: Post-Structuralist Thought and the Claims of Critical Theory.* New York: Verso, 1987.

Dreyfus, Hubert and Rabinow, Paul. *Michel Foucault: Beyond Structuralism and Hermeneutics,* Second Edition. University of Chicago Press, 1983.

Gane, Mike (ed.). *Towards a Critique of Foucault.* New York: Routledge and Kegan Paul, 1986.

Grumley, John E. *History and Totality: Radical Historicism from Hegel to Foucault.* New York: Routledge, 1989.

Guedez, Annie. *Foucault.* Paris: Éditions Universitaires, 1972.

Gutting, Gary. *Michel Foucault's Archaeology of Scientific Reason.* New York: Cambridge University Press, 1989.

Habermas, Jürgen. *The Philosophical Discourse of Modernity: Twelve Lectures.* Cambridge: The MIT Press, 1987.

Hoy, David Couzens (ed.). *Foucault: A Critical Reader.* New York: Basil Blackwell, 1986.

Kremer-Marietti, Angèle. *Michel Foucault: Archéologie et généalogie.* Librairie Générale Française, 1985.

Lemert, Charles C. and Gillan, Garth. *Michel Foucault: Social Theory and Transgression.* New York: Columbia University Press, 1982.

Major-Poetzl, Pamela. *Michel Foucault's Archaeology of Western Culture: Toward a New Science of History.* Chapel Hill: University of North Carolina Press, 1983.

Megill, Allan. *Prophets of Extremity.* Berkeley: University of California Press, 1985.

Merquior, J. G. *Foucault.* Berkeley: University of California Press, 1985.

Minson, Jeffrey. *Genealogies of Morals.* New York: St. Martin's Press, 1985.

Perrot, Michelle (ed.) *L'impossible prison.* Paris: Seuil, 1980.

Poster, Mark. *Foucault, Marxism, and History.* Cambridge: Polity Press, 1984.

Racevskis, Karlis. *Michel Foucault and the Subversion of Intellect.* Ithaca: Cornell University Press, 1983.

Rajchman, John. *Michel Foucault: The Freedom of Philosophy.* New York: Columbia University Press, 1985.

Rassam, Joseph. *Michel Foucault: Las Palabras y Las Cosas.* Madrid: Editorial Magisterio Español, S.A., 1978.

Rella, Franco. *Il mito dell'altro: Lacan, Deleuze, Foucault.* Milano: Feltrinelli, 1978.

Shapiro, Michael J. *Language and Political Understanding: The Politics of Discursive Practices.* New Haven: Yale University Press, 1981.

Sheridan, Alan. *Michel Foucault: The Will to Truth.* London: Tavistock Publications Ltd., 1980.

Sini, Carlo. *Semiotica e filosofia: Segno e linguaggio in Peirce, Nietzsche, Heidegger e Foucault.* Bologna: Il Mulino, 1978.

Smart, Barry. *Foucault, Marxism, and Critique.* London: Routledge and Kegan Paul, 1983.

Smart, Barry. *Michel Foucault.* New York: Tavistock Publications, 1985.

2. Articles

Bernauer, James. "Michel Foucault's Ecstatic Thinking." *Philosophy and Social Criticism*, 12, 2–3, Summer, 1987.

Carroll, David. "Disruptive Discourse and Critical Power: The Conditions of Archaeology and Genealogy." *Humanities in Society*, 5, 1982.

Davidson, Arnold I. "Archaeology, Genealogy, Ethics." In *Foucault: A Critical Reader*.

Dean, Mitchell. "Foucault's Obsession with Western Modernity." *Thesis Eleven* 14, 1986

Derrida, Jacques. "Cogito and the History of Madness." *Writing and Difference*. Chicago: University of Chicago Press, 1978.

Dews, Peter. "Power and Subjectivity in Foucault." *New Left Review* 144, March–April, 1984.

Dreyfus, Hubert. "Beyond Hermeneutics: Interpretation in Late Heidegger and Recent Foucault." Gary Shapiro and Alan Sica (eds.). *Hermeneutics: Questions and Prospects*. Amherst: University of Massachusetts Press, 1984.

Dreyfus, Hubert L. and Rabinow, Paul. "What is Maturity? Habermas and Foucault on 'What is Enlightenment?'" In *Foucault: A Critical Reader*.

Ewald, François. "Anatomie et corps politiques." *Critique* 31, 1975.

Flynn, Bernard. "Sexuality, Knowledge and Power in the Thought of Michel Foucault." *Philosophy and Social Criticism* 8, 3, Fall, 1981.

Flynn, Bernard Charles. "Foucault and the Body Politic." *Man and World* 20, 1987.

Flynn, Bernard Charles. "Michel Foucault and the Husserlian Problematic of a Transcendental Philosophy of History." *Philosophy Today* 22, 1978.

Flynn, Thomas. "Foucault as Parrhesiast: His Last Course at the Collège de France (1984)." *Philosophy and Social Criticism* 12, 2–3, 1987.

Flynn, Thomas R. "Foucault and the Politics of Postmodernity." *Noûs* 23, 1989.

Forrester, John. "Michel Foucault and the History of Psychoanalysis." *History of Science*, 18, 1980.

Fraser, Nancy. "Michel Foucault: A 'Young Conservative'?" *Ethics* 96, October, 1985.

Gillan, Garth. "Foucault's Philosophy." *Philosophy and Social Criticism* 12, 2–3, 1987.

Guédon, Jean Claude. "Michel Foucault: The Knowledge of Power and the Power of Knowledge." *Bulletin of the History of Medicine*, 51, 1977.

Habermas, Jürgen. "Taking Aim at the Heart of the Present." In *Foucault: A Critical Reader*.

Hacking, Ian. "The Archaeology of Foucault." In *Foucault: A Critical Reader*.

Hiley, David R. "Foucault and the Question of Enlightenment." *Philosophy and Social Criticism* 11, 1, Summer, 1985.

Hoy, David Couzens. "Taking History Seriously: Foucault, Gadamer, Habermas." *Union Seminary Quarterly Review* 34, 2, Winter, 1979.

Ijsseling, S. "Foucault with Heidegger." *Man and World* 19, 1986.

Laforest, Guy. "Regards généalogiques sur la modernité: Michel Foucault et la philosophie politique." *Canadian Journal of Political Science*, 18, 1, March, 1985.

Lash, Scott. "Genealogy and the Body: Foucault/Deleuze/Nietzsche." *Theory, Culture, and Society* 2, 2, 1984.

Lash, Scott. "Postmodernity and Desire." *Theory and Society*, 14, 1985.

Lentricchia, Frank. "Reading Foucault (Punishment, Labor Resistance)." *Raritan* 1, 4, Spring, 1982; and 2, 1, Summer, 1982.

Margot, Jean-Paul. "Herméneutique et fiction chez M. Foucault." *Dialogue* 23, 1984.

McCarthy, Thomas. "The Critique of Impure Reason: Foucault and the Frankfurt School." *Political Theory* 18, 1990.

McDonell, Donald. "On Foucault's Philosophical Method." *Canadian Journal of Philosophy* 7, September, 1977.

Megill, Allan. "Foucault, Structuralism, and the Ends of History." *Journal of Modern History*, 51, 1979.

Midelfort, H. C. Erik. "Madness and Civilization in Early Mdoern Europe: A Reappraisal of Michel Foucault." *After the Reformation: Essays in Honor of H. H. Hexster*. Edited by Barbara C. Malament. University of Pennsylvania Press, 1980.

Pace, David. "Structuralism in History and the Social Sciences." *American Quarterly* 30, 1978.

Paden, Roger. "Foucault's Anti-Humanism." *Human Studies* 10,1, 1987.

Paden, Roger. "Locating Foucault—Archaeology vs. Structuralism." *Philosophy and Social Criticism*, 11, 2, 1986.

Pasquino, Pasquale. "Theatrum Politicum." *I&C* 4, Autumn, 1978.

Paternek, Margaret A. "Norms and Normalization: Michel Foucault's Overextended Panoptic Machine." *Human Studies* 10, 1, 1987.

Poster, Mark. "Foucault, Post-Structuralism, and the Mode of Information." Edited by Murray Krieger. *The Aims of Representation*. New York: Columbia University Press, 1987.

Racevskis, Karlis. "Michel Foucault, Rameau's Nephew, and the Question of Identity." *Philosophy and Social Criticism* 12, 2–3, 1987.

Rajchman, John. "Ethics after Foucault." *Social Text* 13/14, Winter/Spring, 1986.

Rorty, Richard. "Beyond Nietzsche and Marx." *London Review of Books*, February 19, 1981.

Rorty, Richard. "Foucault and Epistemology." In *Foucault: A Critical Reader*.

Roth, Michael. "Foucault's History of the Present." *History and Theory* 20, 1981.

Rubenstein, Diane. "Food for Thought: Metonymy in the late Foucault." *Philosophy and Social Criticism* 12, 2–3, 1987.

Russo, Francois. "L'archéologie du savoir de Michel Foucault." *Archives de Philosophie* 36, 1973.

Said, Edward. "An Ethics of Language." *Diacritics* 4, 2, Summer, 1974.

Said, Edward. "Michel Foucault as an Intellectual Imagination." *Boundary* I, 1972.

Said, Edward. "The Problem of Textuality: Two Exemplary Positions." *Critical Inquiry* 4, Summer, 1978.

Schneck, Stephen F. "Michel Foucault on Power/Discourse, Theory and Practice." *Human Studies* 10, 1, 1987.

Schürmann, Reiner. "What Can I Do? in an Archaeological-Genealogical History." *Journal of Philosophy* 82, 10, October, 1985.

Seem, Mark D. "Liberation of Difference: Toward a Theory of Antiliterature." *New Literary History*, 5, 1973.

Shiner, Larry. "Reading Foucault: Anti-Method and the Genealogy of Power-Knowledge." *History and Theory* 21, 1982.

Silverman, Hugh. "Michel Foucault's Nineteenth Century System of Thought and the Anthropological Sleep." *Seminar* 3, 1979.

Taylor, Charles. "Foucault on Freedom and Truth." In *Foucault: A Critical Reader*.

Veyne, Paul. "Foucault révolutionne l'histoire." *Comment on écrit l'histoire: Essai d'épistémologie*. Paris: Seuil, 1978.

Wartenberg, Thomas E. "Foucault's Archaeological Method: A Response to Hacking and Rorty." *The Philosophical Forum* 15, 4, Summer, 1984.

Waterman, Shaun. "Discourse and Domination: Michel Foucault and the Problem of Ideology." Edited by Ian Bapty and Tim Yates. *Archaeology After Structuralism*. London: Routledge, 1990.

Watson, St. "Kant and Foucault: On the Ends of Man." *Tijdschrift voor Filosofie* 47, March, 1985.

White, Hayden. "Foucault Decoded: Notes from Underground." *History and Theory* 12, 1973.

D. Secondary Works on Nietzsche

1. Books

Allison, David (ed.). *The New Nietzsche*. Cambridge: The MIT Press, 1985.

Andler, Charles. *Nietzsche: sa vie et sa pensée, Vol. II*. Paris: Gallimard, 1958.

Bernstein, John Andrew. *Nietzsche's Moral Philosophy*. Cranbury, NJ: Associated University Presses, Inc., 1987.

Bueb, Bernhard. *Nietzsches Kritik der praktischen Vernunft*. Stuttgart: Ernst Klett Verlag, 1970.

Carroll, Louise Ann. *Nietzsche's Concept of Happiness*. Ann Arbor: University Microfilms International, 1983.

Clark, Maudemarie. *Nietzsche's Attack on Morality*. Ann Arbor: University Microfilms International, 1976.

Clark, Maudemarie. *Nietzsche on Truth and Philosophy*. Cambridge University Press, 1990.

Cooper, David E. *Authenticity and Learning: Nietzsche's Educational Philosophy*. London: Routledge and Kegan Paul, 1983.

Danto, Arthur C. *Nietzsche as Philosopher.* New York: The Macmillan Company, 1965.

Deleuze, Gilles. *Nietzsche and Philosophy.* Translated by Hugh Tomlinson. New York: Columbia University Press, 1983. Originally, *Nietzsche et la philosophie.* Presses Universitaires de France, 1962.

Desmond, William. *Desire, Dialectic, and Otherness: An Essay on Origins.* New Haven: Yale University Press, 1987.

Granier, Jean. *Le problème de la vérité dans la philosophie de Nietzsche.* Paris: Éditions du Seuil, 1966.

Houlgate, Stephen. *Hegel, Nietzsche and the Criticism of Metaphysics.* Cambridge University Press, 1986.

Kaufmann, Walter. *Nietzsche: Philosopher, Psychologist, Antichrist.* Princeton University Press, 1950.

Klossowski, Pierre. *Nietzsche et le cercle vicieux.* Paris: Mercure de France, 1969.

Kofman, Sarah. *Nietzsche et la métaphore.* Paris: Payot, 1972.

Love, Nancy S. *Marx, Nietzsche, and Modernity.* New York: Columbia University Press, 1986.

Magnus, Bernd. *Nietzsche's Existential Imperative.* Bloomington: Indiana University Press, 1978.

Munson, Malcolm Edward. *Genealogy and Moral Critique: A Reconstruction and Appraisal of Nietzsche's Genealogy of Morals.* Ann Arbor: University Microfilms International, 1983.

Murin, Charles. *Nietzsche Probleme: Généalogie d'une pensée.* Montreal and Paris: Les Presses de l'Université de Montréal et la Librairie philosophique J. Vrin, 1979.

Nehamas, Alexander. *Nietzsche: Life as Literature.* Cambridge: Harvard University Press, 1985.

Röttges, Heinz. *Nietzsche und die Dialektik der Aufklärung.* Berlin: Walter de Gruyter, 1972.

Schacht, Richard. *Nietzsche.* London: Routledge and Kegan Paul, 1983.

Schrift, Alan D. *Nietzsche and the Question of Interpretation: Between Hermeneutics and Deconstruction.* New York: Routledge, 1990.

Schutte, Ofelia. *Beyond Nihilism: Nietzsche without Masks.* Chicago: University of Chicago Press, 1984.

Silk, M. S. and Stern, J. P. *Nietzsche on Tragedy.* Cambridge University Press, 1981.

Stambaugh, Joan. *The Problem of Time in Nietzsche.* Lewisburg: Bucknell University Press, 1987.

Strong, Tracy B. *Friedrich Nietzsche and the Politics of Transfiguration.* Berkeley: University of California Press, 1975.

Thiele, Leslie Paul. *Friedrich Nietzsche and the Politics of the Soul.* Princeton University Press, 1990.

Warren, Mark. *Nietzsche and Political Thought.* Cambridge: The MIT Press, 1988.

Wilcox, John T. *Truth and Value in Nietzsche.* Washington, D.C.: University Press of America, 1982.

2. Articles

Assoun, Paul-Laurent. "Nietzsche et le Réelisme." In Paul Rée, *L'Origine des sentiments moraux.* Translated by Michel-François Demet. Paris: Presses Universitaires de France, 1982.

Bergoffen, Debra B. "Why a Genealogy of Morals?" *Man and World* 16, 1983.

de Man, Paul. "Genesis and Genealogy in Nietzsche's *The Birth of Tragedy.*" *Diacritics*, Winter, 1972.

Hoy, David Couzens. "Nietzsche, Hume, and the Genealogical Method." *Nietzsche as Affirmative Thinker.* Edited by Yirmiyahu Yovel. The Netherlands: Martinus Nijhoff, 1986.

Hoy, David Couzens. "Philosophy as Rigorous Philology? Nietzsche and Poststructuralism." *Fragments: Incompletion and Discontinuity.* New York: New York Literary Forum, 1981.

Maurer, Reinhart. "Nietzsche und die Kritische Theorie." *Nietzsche-Studien: Internationales Jahrbuch für die Nietzsche-Forschung*, 10/11, 1981/1982.

Pippin, Robert B. "Nietzsche and the Origin of the Idea of Modernism." *Inquiry* 26.

Scharff, Robert. "Nietzsche and the 'Use' of History." *Man and World* VII, 1974.

Shklar, Judith N. "Subversive Genealogies." *Daedalus*, 101, 1, Winter, 1972.

Solomon, Robert C. (ed.). *Nietzsche: A Collection of Critical Essays.* New York: Doubleday Anchor, 1973.

Strong, Tracy B. "Language and Nihilism: Nietzsche's Critique of Epistemology." *Theory and Society*, 3, 1976.

Warren, Mark. "Nietzsche's Concept of Ideology." *Theory and Society*, 13, 1984.

E. Miscellaneous Background Works

Alexander, Franz G. and Selesnick, Sheldon T. *The History of Psychiatry: An Evaluation of Psychiatric Thought and Practice from Prehistoric Times to the Present.* New York: Harper and Row, 1966.

Artemidorus. *The Interpretation of Dreams.* Park Ridge, N.J.: Noyes Press, 1975.

Bataille, Georges. *Erotism: Death and Sensuality.* Translated by Mary Dalwood. San Francisco: City Lights Books, 1986.

Bataille, Georges. *Visions of Excess: Selected Writings, 1927–1939.* Translated by Allan Stoekl, with Carl R. Lovitt and Donald M. Leslie, Jr. Minneapolis: University of Minnesota Press, 1985.

Benhabib, Seyla. *Critique, Norm, and Utopia: A Study of the Foundations of Critical Theory.* New York: Columbia University Press, 1986.

Benjamin, Walter. *Charles Baudelaire: A Lyric Poet in the Era of High Capitalism.* Translated by Harry Zohn. London: Verso Editions, 1983.

Blanchot, Maurice. *L'Entretien infini.* Paris: Gallimard, 1969.

Chomsky, Noam. *Aspects of the Theory of Syntax.* Cambridge: MIT Press, 1965.

Chomsky, Noam. *Reflections on Language.* New York: Random House, 1975.

Connolly, William E. *Politics and Ambiguity.* Madison: University of Wisconsin Press, 1987.

Deleuze, G. and Guattari, F. *Anti-Oedipus: Capitalism and Schizophrenia.* Minneapolis: University of Minnesota Press, 1983.

Durkheim, Emile. *Durkheim and the Law.* Edited by Steven Lukes and Andrew Scull. New York: St. Martin's Press, 1983.

Frege, Gottlob. *Translations from the Philosophical Writings of Gottlob Frege.* Edited by P. Geach and M. Black. New York: Philosophical Library, 1952.

Freud, Sigmund. *The Standard Edition of the Complete Psychological Works of Sigmund Freud.* Edited by James Strachey. London: Hogarth, 1953–1974.

Gallop, Jane. *Intersections: A Reading of Sade with Bataille, Blanchot, and Klossowski.* Lincoln and London: University of Nebraska Press, 1981.

Geuss, Raymond. *The Idea of a Critical Theory: Habermas and the Frankfurt School.* Cambridge University Press, 1981.

Gide, Charles and Rist, Charles, *A History of Economic Doctrines*, translated by R. Richards. Boston: D. C. Heath and Co., 1948.

Habermas, Jürgen. "The French Path to Postmodernity: Bataille between Eroticism and General Economics." *New German Critique* 33 Fall, 1984.

Habermas, Jürgen. *Communication and the Evolution of Society.* Translated by Thomas McCarthy. Boston: Beacon Press, 1979.

Havet, Jacques (ed.). *Main Trends of Research in the Social and Human Sciences*, I, 2. The Hague: Mouton Publishers, 1978.

Heidegger, Martin. *The Question Concerning Technology and Other Essays.* Translated by William Lovitt. New York: Harper and Row, 1977.

Hempel, Carl. *Philosophy of Natural Science.* Englewood Cliffs, N.J.: Prentice-Hall Inc., 1966.

Horkheimer, Max. *Critical Theory: Selected Essays.* Translated by Matthew J. O'Connell and others. New York: Seabury Press, 1972.

Horkheimer, Max and Adorno, Theodor W. *Dialectic of Enlightenment.* Translated by John Cumming. New York: Seabury Press, 1972.

Kundera, Milan. *The Book of Laughter and Forgetting.* New York: Penguin, 1980.

Levin, David Michael. *The Opening of Vision: Nihilism and the Postmodern Situation.* New York: Routledge, 1988.

250   *Bibliography*

MacIntyre, Alasdair. *Three Rival Versions of Moral Enquiry: Encyclopaedia, Genealogy, and Tradition.* University of Notre Dame Press, 1990.

Mallarmé, Stéphane. *Oeuvres complétes.* Paris: Gallimard, 1945.

Mallarmé, Stéphane. *Selected Prose Poems, Essays, and Letters.* Translated by Bradford Cook. Baltimore: Johns Hopkins University Press, 1956.

Poster, Mark. *Existential Marxism in Postwar France: From Sartre to Althusser.* Princeton University Press, 1975.

Putnam, Hilary. *Reason, Truth and History.* Cambridge University Press, 1981.

Redner, Harry. *The Ends of Philosophy: An Essay in the Sociology of Philosophy and Rationality.* Rowman and Allanheld, 1986.

Rorty, Richard. *Philosophy and the Mirror of Nature.* Princeton University Press, 1979.

Roth, Michael S. *Knowing and History: Appropriations of Hegel in Twentieth-Century France.* Ithaca: Cornell University Press, 1988.

Rouse, Joseph. *Knowledge and Power: Toward a Political Philosophy of Science.* Ithaca: Cornell University Press, 1987.

Rusche, Georg and Kirchheimer, Otto. *Punishment and Social Structure.* New York: Russell and Russell, 1968. Originally issued 1939.

Said, Edward. *Beginnings: Intention and Method.* New York: Columbia University Press, 1985.

Said, Edward. *The World, the Text, and the Critic.* Cambridge: Harvard University Press, 1983.

Schürmann, Reiner. "Anti-Humanism. Reflections of the Turn Towards the Post-Modern Epoch." *Man and World* 12, 1979.

Searle, John. *The Philosophy of Language.* Oxford University Press, 1971.

Searle, John. *Speech Acts: An Essay in the Philosophy of Language.* Cambridge University Press, 1969.

Serres, Michel. *Hermes I: La Communication.* Paris: Les Éditions de Minuit, 1968.

Stoekl, Allan. *Politics, Writing, Mutilation: The Cases of Bataille, Blanchot, Roussel, Leiris, and Ponge.* Minneapolis: University of Minnesota Press, 1985.

Weiss, Allen S. "Impossible Sovereignty: Between The Will to Power and The Will to Chance." *October* 36, Spring, 1986.

Index

a priori, concrete and historical, 6, 12, 28–29, 51, 60, 68, 71–72, 79, 82, 105, 114, 119
aesthetic Socratism, 51–52, 62, 126
aestheticism, 15
aesthetics of existence, 175, 227 n 67
Althusser, L., 2
analytics, 122–123
anthropology, 7, 59, 64–65, 70, 74–75, 78, 106, 108, 113–114, 123, 131, 160
aphrodisia, 165–168, 171
archaeology, 6, 57, 60–61, 66, 68–70, 113–119, 121, 139, 210 n 74; and genealogy, 6, 9, 101–106, 113–119, 211 n 87, 215 n 162
Artaud, A., 16, 27, 63
Artemidorus, 167, 226 n 55 and 56
ascetic ideal, 161–164
ascetics. See practices, ascetical
Attica, 131–132
Augustine, 168
Austin, J. L., 118
author, role of, 16, 116
autopsy, 6, 52–54, 149
axes, genealogical. See genealogy

Bachelard, G., 189 n 24
Bacon, F., 71
Bataille, G., 2, 16, 27, 62–65, 189 n 24, 203 n 31

Beajour, M., 64
Beckett, S., 16, 78
Benhabib, S., 211 n 91, 217 n 187
Bentham, J., 149
Bernauer, J., 58, 102, 202 n 14, 224 n 16
Bichat, X.,151
biology, 66–68, 74, 78, 107, 178
Blanchot, M., 2, 62–63, 65
blasphemy, 25
body, 9–10, 126–127, 151–152
Borges, J. L., 62
Bosch, H., 40, 56, 62
Brueghel, P., 62

Calvin, J., 22, 36
Canguilhem, G., 60
Carroll, D., 16, 62, 180
Catholic church, 36
Cervantes, M., 62
Chomsky, N., 119
Christianity, 83, 158, 165, 170, 172, 182
confession. See practices, confessional
counter-memory, 3, 9, 78–79, 180
counter-sciences,7, 78–79
critique, genealogical, 2, 6, 14–15, 17, 60, 78, 81–82, 94–95, 104–107, 114, 120–122, 129, 139, 160–161, 180–183; of

critique *(Continued)*
  reason (Kant), 7–8, 65, 75,
  92–95, 123, 139, 181; of reason
  (Foucault), 107, 110–111; of
  medical rationality, 28–29, 44;
  local, 3, 120–122; diagnostic,
  121–122; defetishizing, 211 n 91
Cuvier, G., 68

Davidson, A., 211 n 87
death, 6, 3€, 45, 52–53, 62, 78, 93;
  of God, 64–65, 76; of man, 76–79
delirium, transcendence of, 43
Deleuze, G., 2, 3, 10, 11–13, 83, 89,
  101, 113, 129, 176–177
Derrida, J., 15, 191 n 62
Descartes, R., 2, 10, 11, 16, 39, 55,
  62, 71, 101, 126, 177
Dews, P., 188 n 13
dialectics, 7, 21, 55, 59, 62, 65, 75,
  78, 126
Diderot, D., 62
discourse, 15, 16, 119, 123
dispositif, 202 n 14
Dreyfus, H., 1, 17, 29, 75, 102, 112,
  122, 187 n 2, 191 n 62
Dürer, A., 62
Durkheim, E., 132, 140

economics, 68–71, 74
Enlightenment, 6, 15, 52, 106, 126,
  179–183, 230 n 138, 231 n 144
Entstehung, 109–110
enunciative function, 117
episteme, 6, 60–61, 66–67, 69, 71
Erasmus, 40, 62, 126
Erfindung, 110
ethical substance, 165
ethnology, 7, 78–79
Euripides, 4, 20, 52, 62, 126
eventalisation, 108
Ewald, F., 9, 11, 190 n 49, 229 n 129

Flaubert, G., 63
Flynn, T., 189 n 35, 231 n 144
forces, relations of, 3, 5, 8, 12, 30,
  66, 73, 112, 118, 124

forgetting, active, 3, 8, 96, 133, 180
formation, rules of, 6–7, 104–105,
  115–119
Frankfurt School, 180
freedom, 15; and truth, 13–14
Freud, S., 116, 160, 167–168, 176,
  180, 224 n 16, 226 n 57

gaze, 7, 27–28, 33–35, 41, 45, 48,
  51, 54, 149–150, 153
Geburt, 109
genealogy, 4, 9–10, 13, 19, 107–114,
  129, 187 n 2; as critique, 8,
  14–15, 17, 28, 58, 94–95,
  104–105, 107–110, 114,
  120–122, 129, 139; and three
  axes, 1, 3–4, 11, 17, 20,29, 45,
  56–59, 103, 125, 137, 158–160,
  195 n 47; English, 82, 86–88,
  132, 135, 139; and archaeology
  (*See* archaeology); Nietzschean,
  81–101, 133–139; and the body,
  9–10, 126–127, 140
general grammar, 71–73, 107
Gillan, G., 103
Goethe, J., 161
Grünewald, M., 62
Guattari, F., 176
Gutting, G., 215 n 155

Habermas, J., 14, 63, 118, 191 n 59,
  230 n 138, 231 n 144
Hacking, I., 182
Hegel, G. W. F., 2, 10, 11, 14, 121,
  126, 149, 180, 206 n 75
Heidegger, M., 3, 15, 17, 58, 77,
  108, 116, 123, 191 n 62, 215 n
  158
Hempel, C., 60, 201 n 12
Herkunft, 109–110
hermeneutics of the desiring subject, 160, 168, 172–173
heterogeneous (Bataille), 63
Hinkle, G., 15, 17, 192 n 77
historical ontology. *See* genealogy
history, effective, 8, 113; monumental, 97–98; antiquarian, 98–100;

critical, 100; of the present, 101, 120–121, 125, 129, 159, 176; traditional, 8
Hölderlin, F., 16, 27, 63, 64
homo psychologicus, 19, 58, 106, 131
homosexuality, 25
Honneth, A., 16
Hôpital Général, 22–23, 30, 56
Hoy, D., 116, 127
human sciences, 7, 58, 60–61, 66, 78, 103–104, 140, 153
humanism, 131, 148, 182
Hume, D., 90, 145
Husserl, E., 108, 206 n 75
Hyppolite, J., 2

ideology, 12, 129, 131
individual, modern, 2–3, 5, 6, 28, 31–32, 36–37, 131–132, 140–142, 146–155; dangerous, 155
individualization, 5, 10, 140, 150–151, 154, 231 n 150; anthropological, 146
interpretation, 116–117

James, W., 122
Jay, M., 105

Kafka, F., 63
Kant, I., 2, 4, 6, 8, 12, 15, 28, 65, 68, 73–75, 92–93, 101, 114, 123, 126, 139, 149, 165, 180–181, 191 n 59, 193 n 17, 230 n 138
Kaufmann, W., 3
Kremer-Marietti, A., 16
Klossowski, P., 62–65
Kofman, S., 215 n 158
Kundera, M., 180

labor, 30, 58, 70, 73–74
Laforest, G., 16
Lamarck, 68
language, 15, 27, 29, 44–45, 50–51, 58–61, 71–74, 77–79, 90, 100, 119, 122–124; and knowledge, 3,

6, 57, 77–78, 104; in the space of death, 7, 61–66; and man, 76
Lash, S., 10
Lemert, C., 103
life, 12–13, 58, 67–68, 73–74, 78, 179; enhancement of, 8, 81, 93, 95–100, 120, 125, 151, 163–164, 180
limit-experiences,54
linguistics, 7, 78–79
literature, 7, 16, 57, 62–64
Luther, M., 22, 36

Machiavelli, 175
Macherey, P., 17
madness, history of, 20; constitution of, 58; problematization in terms of truth, 42–44, 159; moral problematization of, 5, 20–26, 36–37, 42, 56, 63, 159; cosmic/tragic experience of, 40; critical experience of, 40–41; practical experience of, 41; juridical consciousness of, 41
Major-Poetzl, P., 11
Mallarmé, S., 77–78
man, 3, 7, 13, 54, 58, 65, 73–79, 97, 100, 106, 123–124, 134, 140, 145–146, 148, 187 n 8; death of, 73, 76–79; as empirico-transcendental doublet, 74
Margot, J. P., 17
Marx, K., 17, 116, 189 n 24, 206 n 75
Marxism, 2–3, 9, 15, 120, 180, 182, 192 n 2
medicine, 6, 22, 27–28, 38, 41–54, 112, 117–118; medical knowledge and rationality, 5–7, 26–32, 42, 44–45; medicalization of society, 46, 150–152, 178
Megill, A., 15–16, 101, 179, 190 n 44
mental illness, 4, 7, 20
Merquior, J. G., 9–11, 180–181
metaphysics, 11, 101, 112, 116, 123–124

Minson, J., 102
Mirabeau, 96
mode of subjection, 165, 168–170
moralization, 20–26, 38, 55. *See also* madness, moral problematization of

natural history, 66–68, 107
Nerval, G., 27, 63
Nietzsche, F., and genealogy, 1, 5, 8–9, 28–29, 108–113, 132–139; and Mallarmé, 77–78; and critique, 8, 81, 89, 94–95; and Foucault, 2–3, 11, 15–17, 108–127, 180, 188 n 19; and language, 6, 27, 44, 57, 73, 77–78, 90; and tragedy, 7, 20–21; and power, 85, 88, 92, 96
nihilism, 93
normalization, 5, 10, 34, 40, 46, 132, 151, 154, 178

Oedipal triangle, 176–177
origin, 8, 81, 108–110
overman, 2, 13, 27, 65, 76

Pace, D., 189 n 24
Paden, R., 106
panopticon, 149–150
philology, 71–74, 114
philosophy, 181; limits of, 11, 121–122; as diagnosis, 11, 101, 121, 125
physics, 84–85, 126
Pinel, P., 26, 32–35, 40
Platonism, 83, 113
police, 5, 22, 29–31, 35, 48, 176, 195 nn 52 and 53; discursive, 60–61
Poster, M., 15
power, 10, 12, 66, 73, 101, 103, 112, 118, 124, 129, 131, 177–178; and knowledge, 2, 11, 31, 119, 130, 140, 148, 153–154, 160; Leviathan model of, 30; positive functioning of, 5–7, 15, 30–32, 160, 182; plastic (Nietzsche), 96, 120; pastoral, 159; monarchical,

142–143, representational, 143–146; disciplinary, 147–155, 178; axis, 6, 20, 29–35, 45–49
practices, 129, 133, 141–142, 154; discursive and nondiscursive, 3, 12; ascetical, 135, 147, 165, 170–173; confessional, 172–173, 177–178; penal. *See* power
Preti, G., 2, 108
Proust, M., 63
psychiatry, 27–28, 31, 115, 118–119, 125, 155, 159, 177, 193 n 12
psychoanalysis, 7, 78–79, 120, 160, 172, 176–178, 224 n 16
psychology, 4–5, 21, 28, 30, 40, 44, 54, 58, 78, 86, 90, 106, 112, 146, 160; evolutionary, 19; phenomenological, 19; individual, 19, 39; Marxist, 3, 19, 192 n 2

Quakers, 26, 33

Rabinow, P., 1, 17, 29, 75, 102, 112, 122, 187 n 2, 191 n 62
Rajchman, J., 13–14
Rée, P., 82, 86, 109, 139
referential, 115
religion, 31, 33–34, 37, 64, 110, 135, 161–164
representation, 60, 67, 69–72, 75. *See also* practices, representational
resemblance, 60, 67, 69, 71
ressentiment, 89, 139, 163
Ricardo, D., 69–70
Rivière, P., 154
Rorty, R., 10–11, 16
Rousseau, J. J., 176
Russell, B., 77
Russo, F., 102

Sade, Marquis de, 16, 27, 41
Said, E., 16, 191 n 62
Sartre, J.-P., 76
Saussure, F. de, 77, 189 n 24
Schopenhauer, A., 93, 110, 206 n 75

Searle, J., 114, 117–118
Seneca, 173
Serres, M., 58, 188 n 13
sexuality, 24, 62, 64, 157–161; and
    the flesh, 158, 166, 172. *See also*
    medicalization
Shakespeare, W., 62
Shapiro, M., 60
Sheridan, A., 9–10, 101
Shiner, L., 179, 187 n 2
ship of fools, 21
Simon, J., 121
Smart, B., 15, 102, 104
Smith, A., 69–70
sociology, 19, 78
Socrates, 7, 20, 51–52, 113, 126,
    193 n 9
space, 4–5, 7, 12, 29–30, 32–33,
    45–49, 53, 57, 116, 142, 148–152,
    195 n 50; of death. *See* language
spatialization of disease, 45–49, 52,
    198 n 110
statements, 114–119, 122, 126
Stoicism, 84–85, 91, 126, 170, 173,
    175
Strong, T., 115
structuralism, 9, 29, 106, 119, 180,
    189 n 24, 197 n 105
stultifera navis, 21
subject axis, 2, 5, 6, 20, 36–40,
    52–54, 157–160
substratum, 7, 27, 82, 89–90, 101,
    116, 124
surveillance, 34, 48, 142, 147–152,
    164, 172, 176

Taylor, C., 13–14, 61

technologies of the self, 188 n 15
teleology, 31, 55, 108, 112–113, 126,
    136, 165, 173
thing-in-itself, 7, 82, 89
time, 4, 5, 7, 12, 47, 58, 66, 68,
    70–73, 96, 142, 148, 151–152,
    178
totality, 120–122
tragedy, 122; moralization of, 4, 7,
    20–21, 52, 55, 62–65, 126
transcendental aesthetic, 4, 7, 12,
    190 n 49, 193 n 17. *See also*
    space, time
transgression, 7, 16, 59, 62, 64–65,
    203 n 31
truth, production of, 119, 177; axis,
    5–6, 20, 40–44, 49–52, 103–104
Tuke, S., 26, 32–35, 40, 44

unconscious of science, 61
unreason, 24–27, 31–32, 38, 40, 42,
    44
unthought, 75
Ursprung, 8, 109

Van Gogh, V., 41

Wagner, R., 161
Wartenberg, T., 11
wealth, analysis of, 68–71, 107
Weber, M., 180
Whitehead, A. N., 77
will to truth, 126, 160
work, 33–34
writing, and confession, 152–155

Zarathustra, 2, 27, 83, 87